Eugenio Mon....
The Poetry of the Later Years

THE EUROPEAN HUMANITIES
RESEARCH CENTRE

UNIVERSITY OF OXFORD

The European Humanities Research Centre of the University of Oxford organizes a range of academic activities, including conferences and workshops, and publishes scholarly works under its own imprint, LEGENDA. Within Oxford, the EHRC bridges, at the research level, the main humanities faculties: Modern Languages, English, Modern History, Literae Humaniores, Music and Theology. The Centre stimulates interdisciplinary research collaboration throughout these subject areas and provides an Oxford base for advanced researchers in the humanities.

The Centre's publications programme focuses on making available the results of advanced research in medieval and modern languages and related interdisciplinary areas. An Editorial Board, whose members are drawn from across the British university system, covers the principal European languages. Titles include works on French, German, Italian, Portuguese, Russian and Spanish literature. In addition, the EHRC co-publishes with the Society for French Studies, the British Comparative Literature Association and the Modern Humanities Research Association. The Centre also publishes *Oxford German Studies* and *Film Studies*, and has launched a Special Lecture Series under the LEGENDA imprint.

Enquiries about the Centre's publishing activities should be addressed to:
Professor Malcolm Bowie, Director

Further information:
Kareni Bannister, Senior Publications Officer
European Humanities Research Centre
University of Oxford
47 Wellington Square, Oxford OX1 2JF
enquiries@ehrc.ox.ac.uk
www.ehrc.ox.ac.uk

LEGENDA

EUROPEAN HUMANITIES RESEARCH CENTRE

University of Oxford

Eugenio Montale
The Poetry of the Later Years

❖

ÉANNA Ó CEALLACHÁIN

LEGENDA

European Humanities Research Centre
University of Oxford
2001

Published by the
European Humanities Research Centre
of the University of Oxford
47 Wellington Square
Oxford OX1 2JF

LEGENDA is the publications imprint of the
European Humanities Research Centre

ISBN 1 900755 45 9

First published 2001

British Library Cataloguing in Publication Data
A CIP catalogue record for this book is available from the British Library

LEGENDA series designed by Cox Design Partnership, Witney, Oxon
Printed in Great Britain by
Information Press
Eynsham
Oxford OX8 1JJ

Copy-Editor: Dr Jeffrey Dean

CONTENTS

ACKNOWLEDGEMENTS

This book is based on my doctoral thesis, *Figurations of Ideology and the Retreat from History in the Later Poetry of Eugenio Montale*, submitted to the University of Cambridge in 1998.

I am grateful to the National University of Ireland for financial support in the form of a Travelling Studentship, without which it would not have been possible for me to embark initially on research for the thesis. I am also indebted in particular to Professor Piero Calì and Professor Catherine O'Brien for the encouragement and inspiration they provided when I was a student at University College, Cork.

I wish to thank the University of Glasgow and the Italian Cultural Institute for Scotland for their generous financial support for this publication. I am grateful also to Mondadori for permission to quote from the works of Eugenio Montale.

I should like to thank my initial supervisor in Cambridge, Dr Judy Davies, as well as Professor Patrick Boyde, who so efficiently took over the supervision of my work. I am grateful for all the advice and stimulating insight provided. My thanks go also to Diego Zancani, to Kareni Bannister and Graham Nelson at the EHRC and in particular to Jeffrey Dean for his meticulous and erudite copy-editing.

I am most grateful also to my friends and colleagues in Glasgow, especially to Professor Eileen Anne Millar for her support and advice over many years.

Finally, I owe an immeasurable debt of gratitude to my late mother and my father, and to my wife Arabella Infantino for her endless patience, encouragement, and support.

LIST OF ABBREVIATIONS

Poetic texts:

OV   *L'opera in versi*, critical edn., ed. Rosanna Bettarini and Gianfranco Contini (Turin: Einaudi, 1980)

TP   *Tutte le poesie*, ed. Giorgio Zampa, I Meridiani (Milan: Mondadori, 1984)

XI, XII   Xenia I, Xenia II (followed by the number of the individual poem)

Ossi   *Ossi di seppia* (1925)
Occasioni   *Le occasioni* (1939)
Bufera   *La bufera e altro* (1956)
Diario   *Diario del '71 e del '72* (1973)
Quaderno   *Quaderno di quattro anni* (1978)

Prose texts:

PR   *Prose e racconti*, ed. Marco Forti, I Meridiani (Milan: Mondadori, 1995)

SM   *Il secondo mestiere: prose 1920–1979*, ed. Giorgio Zampa, 2 vols., I Meridiani (Milan: Mondadori, 1996)

SMAMS   *Il secondo mestiere: arte, musica, società*, ed. Giorgio Zampa, I Meridiani (Milan: Mondadori, 1996)

INTRODUCTION

It is generally agreed that Montale's poetic work falls into two major periods: the first characterized by the use of intense, emblematic modes, containing hidden or transfigured historical meanings (the first three collections: *Ossi, Occasioni* and *Bufera*); and a later period, from *Satura* onwards, with an ostensibly more open and immediately communicative manner.[1] This book focuses principally on providing a reading of this later poetry, from a perspective that sees the texts and their meanings as inseparable from the historical and, broadly speaking, ideological context in which the poet was writing. Montale's ideological outlook, at times expressed directly in the poems, at times only implicitly, at times apparently not at all, can be seen nevertheless to underpin his work as a whole, especially when this is viewed in its diachronic development. Indeed, the broad division of his work into two periods can itself be seen as a function of the poet's ideological perspectives and his interaction with historical events, as can the decade of poetic silence (approximately 1954–63) separating the two bodies of work.

In examining the later poetic texts this study seeks to cast light on the many ways in which they come to constitute figurations of the poet's changing relationship with contemporary history and culture. 'Figurations' is intended here in the broadest possible sense to include the full range of symbolic, allegorical, structural and linguistic devices employed by Montale at different times: in short, the myriad ways in which poetic texts transpose reality. The critical approach adopted is essentially a pragmatic one, seeking to remain methodologically open and unbound by any one theoretical orthodoxy, while utilizing different critical tools as required. However, I do pay particular attention to certain figurative and structural areas, in which connection I am especially indebted to the very different approaches of two critics: Romano Luperini, who stresses the importance of allegory as a fundamental component of Montale's entire production, and Angelo

Marchese, whose semiological analysis provides a conceptual model to which I refer repeatedly.

Luperini's allegorical reading establishes a useful framework within which to consider the relationship between texts and history in Montale. To some extent echoing earlier work by Jacomuzzi, Luperini sees allegory, or more precisely, 'allegorismo', as the dominant mode in the poet's work. It is a view widely (though not universally) shared by other critics.[2] In the first three books, Luperini argues, there is an alternation between symbolism and 'allegorismo', with the latter coming progressively to the fore. Montale's problematic relationship with the symbolist lyric tradition marks what the critic calls 'un fondamentale e forse decisivo momento di crisi del grande filone dell'orfismo romantico-decadente'. Montale is seen by Luperini as the poet of the crisis and consequent 'disfacimento' of that tradition: in Montale's work, the crises of Western civilization and of the symbolist poetic tradition are seen to coincide, in particular in the passage from *La bufera* to *Satura*, via the years of silence.[3] Montale's use of allegorical devices does not remain constant: there are considerable changes, from the 'allegorie piene' of the 1930s and '40s to the pessimistic 'allegorismo negativo' of certain texts in *Satura*, to a last phase of 'allegoria vuota', in which the text tends to undermine its own messages: poetry denies the very possibility of discourse in a metatextual allegory of meaninglessness.[4]

Montale's choice of allegorical rather than symbolic modes, which emerges and develops over time, is particularly significant because of two key characteristics of allegory in relation to temporal and historical reality. Firstly, as Luperini observes, while 'il simbolo tende a essere simultaneo [...] l'allegoria si colloca nel tempo, si dispone in un continuum, e quindi si scioglie nella successione storica, aspira alla narratività'. The role of narrative structures, large and small, changes as Montale's work moves progressively away from 'allegoria piena', and an awareness of this changing role is an important element in interpreting the poetry in its broader historical context. Secondly, 'il simbolo è individuale e soggettivo, mentre l'allegoria mira a un senso collettivo e sociale [...] (una convenzionalità [...] socialmente stipulata)'.[5] The choice of allegorical modes of expression ties Montale's poetry in its very fabric to a perspective that tends to transcend the merely individual, aspiring to a discourse that communicates in a precise cultural and historical context. In this sense he could not be further from the self-absorbed, wilful obscurity of *ermetismo*, of poetry as 'un giuoco di suggestioni sonore', which he rejected in 'Intenzioni (intervista immaginaria)' (*SMAMS* 1481).[6] As Elio Gioanola observes: 'È probabile che Montale abbia segnato la crisi definitiva, nella storia della nostra lirica, del petrarchismo, cioè della poesia come spettacolo dell'io e fascino narcisistico dei ritmi e dei suoni'. Montale's poetry, rather, is a complex construction of meanings, more properly comparable in its allegorical character to the work of '[il] più alto dei modelli', Dante.[7]

Angelo Marchese's semiological reading of Montale contains an important insight which constitutes a further premiss for significant parts of my analysis in this book. Following Jurij Lotman's structuralist approach to spatial concepts in texts, Marchese outlines a system of 'connotatori spaziali' in *Le occasioni*, spatial indicators that translate the author's 'ideological vision'.[8] Marchese takes up Lotman's 'cultural model' of bipartite space, which involves inner and outer zones (labelled 'IN' and 'ES'), corresponding to culturally defined distinctions between notions such as 'us' and 'them', or culture and barbarism.[9] The frontier that divides a limited inner zone from a limitless outer zone is represented schematically by Lotman as a circle. The model that Marchese goes on to 'verify' in Montale's text is slightly more complex, involving two concentric circles: it consists of an 'interno' (IN), which may take the form of an interior physical setting (representing truth, order, authenticity), surrounded by an immediate, physical exterior world ('ES_I', representing violence, disorder, chaos) separated from IN by a barrier portrayed for example by an image such as that of a window. Outside the circle of 'ES_I', however, and beyond a further 'frontier' may lie 'ES_2' (a non-physical space, the invisible world), which may have more complex connotations, both negative and positive.[10] Marchese convincingly applies this model in his reading of numerous texts from *Occasioni* (for example the *mottetto* 'Ti libero la fronte'): this reading highlights the typically negative connotations of external space (the site of threatening storms, etc.) as 'veicolo [...] del male', as opposed to the largely (though not unequivocally) positive connotations of interior space.[11] The relationship between the *io* and these spaces is closely linked to that between him and various female figures, and their presence or absence in any particular zone at any given time.

While recognizing some persuasive elements in Marchese's reading, Luperini sees this structuralist model ultimately as an 'empty shell', leading to a closed interpretative circle of purely 'internal' signs and references, to the exclusion of historical experience and the poet's 'rapporto dialettico col reale'.[12] Luperini's objections to Marchese's method are not without foundation, especially insofar as the latter's approach tends to minimize the historical dimension. Nevertheless, Marchese's analysis provides a model of spatial and conceptual divisions, dichotomies and barriers, which, I believe, is capable of broader application to Montale's poetry. In particular, this model can be used to underline an important thematic and figurative constant: that of the lyrical persona's isolation (tempered only by the significant but intermittent presence of the female *tu*), his detachment from the changing realities that surround him—realities viewed, almost without exception, in negative terms. In this regard, my analysis calls attention to the emergence of a kind of *personaggio Montale* in the poems. There are varying degrees of ironic distance between the poet and his lyrical (or, increasingly, non-lyrical) persona, who becomes ever more prominent in the later collections. The physical and cultural isolation of this *io* reflects on the one hand the poet's attitude of aristocratic detachment from historical reality, but also highlights ironically the persona's own perceived shortcomings, his status as *topo* rather than *aquila*.[13] Thus, while satire and parody are used at times to express the poet's stance of superior disdain, there are also frequent elements of self-doubt and self-parody, as Montale deprecates a world in which he nevertheless feels personally and culturally implicated. The ambiguous nature of the poet's persona encapsulates the paradox of Montale's simultaneous engagement with and retreat from historical reality.

This book is concerned above all with the poetry itself: throughout, detailed readings of individual texts and groups of poems are deliberately placed at the centre of the interpretative process. From the 'Xenia' poems of the 1960s up to the poignant last poems of 1980, the texts are explored in five chapters, which in part overlap chronologically. The different chapters approach the work from a variety of thematic and interpretative angles: the changing role of the female *tu*; the presence of directly polemical material; self-portraits; the playful use of pseudo-theological motifs; the poetics of memory. A full understanding of the poetic texts cannot, however, be gained in a vacuum. Thus, the rest of this introduction is dedicated to outlining and exploring certain aspects of Montale's ideological development and cultural outlook that have a particular bearing on his later poetry. An awareness of the profound disillusionment experienced by the poet in the decade following the fall of Fascism (as expressed in numerous journalistic and narrative writings) is an especially important prerequisite for any discussion of the new and challenging style of poetry that would emerge, following almost ten years of silence, in *Satura* and the subsequent collections.

Montale's Post-War Disillusionment

Montale's seventieth birthday in 1966 was marked by numerous critical and personal tributes, including special editions of *Letteratura* and *La rassegna della letteratura italiana*.[14] In the latter, Walter Binni wrote of the 'historical' meaning of Montale's poetry, in which many of his peers had found, decades earlier, 'l'espressione di una profonda opposizione al tempo della dittatura e, più profondamente, a tutte le sue radici culturali, letterarie e morali', a body of work that constituted 'la essenziale poetica coscienza drammatica di un lungo arco storico'.[15] This reflects the then-conventional view of Montale as a kind of cultural figurehead for a broad swathe of democratic, anti-Fascist political opinion (a notion that was, in a sense, officially sanctioned a year later by his nomination as life Senator by President Saragat). The roots of this view are traced by Pietro Cataldi back to the 1930s and '40s, when the critical élite of Florentine hermeticism adopted as its own the poetry of *Le occasioni*, a 'use' of the work that, apart from promoting the 'madornale equivoco' of a hermetic Montale, also marked the beginning of his 'official' success, 'l'ecumenismo filomontaliano della nostra cultura', which would remain largely unchallenged up to the 1960s.[16] Indeed, in his 1973 monograph, Marco Forti confirms this image of Montale as an anti-Fascist icon: 'Esiste ormai una sorta di leggenda confermata dai fatti e dai ricordi di tanti, sui giovani, scrittori e non, che andarono nella Seconda Guerra Mondiale con Montale nel tascapane; [...] In quegli anni il nome e l'influenza di Montale si proiettarono al di là dello stretto ambito degli addetti ai lavori, degli stessi intellettuali in senso lato, per divenire simbolo di opposizione a un regime politico più che mai squalificato'.[17] This elevation of the poet to iconic status is reflected in a broad critical consensus (as identified by Franco Croce in 1977), which tends to see Montale's poetry as the product of a long, personal 'resistance' to the dramatic storms of history, a resistance whose climactic moment is reached in the immediate aftermath of the Second World War with the explicitly historical *impegno* of 'La primavera hitleriana' (*Bufera*).[18]

Franco Croce also identifies another critical line, however, which gains currency especially in the light of the later poetry of the 1960s and '70s. This is the view that there is 'una costante sfiducia nella Storia' throughout Montale's poetry, and that the apparent engagement of 'La primavera hitleriana' represents an isolated, exceptional moment. In fact, since the publication of *La bufera e altro*, cracks had begun to appear in the broad front of the interpretation of Montale 'in chiave etica e civile', and these cracks would widen with the growth in the 1960s of a new vein of ideological criticism, represented most notably by Franco Fortini and Umberto Carpi and subsequently by Romano Luperini.[19] It is in Carpi's 1971 book, *Montale dopo il fascismo: dalla 'Bufera' a 'Satura'*, that we find what is still the most comprehensive account of Montale's ideology, considered both in its constant elements and in its diachronic development and interaction with historical reality.[20] Carpi's study was the first serious attempt to define Montale's position in concrete historical terms, rather than on the basis of a more or less nebulous concept of democratic anti-Fascism. Though openly polemical in his Marxist approach (against both the 'reactionary' politics expressed in Montale's writings and what he sees as the ahistorical excesses of contemporary structuralist criticism), Carpi nevertheless gives a balanced and rounded ideological and cultural portrait of Montale, based in large part on a careful diachronic reading of the poet's post-war journalistic writings. What emerges is a profile of an ideologically 'static' Montale, whose liberalism and anti-Fascism are based on 'un concetto di libertà tutto legato all'idoleggiamento di una sana, genuina civiltà occidentale', an élitist, bourgeois liberalism which is the constant basis for his various, apparently shifting, political positions, and his varying degrees of political *impegno*, particularly in the decade from the mid-1940s onwards, the period of Montale's passage 'dall'azionismo resistenziale alla delusione postbellica'.[21]

The poet's attitudes to post-war historical realities developed through a number of distinct phases, as revealed through the unprecedented flood of unequivocal political declarations found in his prose writings. The first phase was one of explicit and at times heady *impegno*, expressed initially on the pages of the Florentine journals *La Nazione del Popolo* and *Il Mondo*. It is no coincidence that this was also the period of Montale's short-lived direct involvement in politics, in the form of his membership of the Partito D'Azione and of the cultural committee of the CLN.[22] Thus in 1944 and 1945 we find him repeatedly nailing his political colours to the mast with a frankness and enthusiasm never equalled before or after. In 'Augurio' (19–20 September 1944) he calls on the intellectual élite (artists and scientists) to abandon any temptations of political agnosticism, and 'servire liberamente quelle insopprimibili forze morali e materiali, econo-miche ed etiche, che dovranno pur fare, prima o poi, del nostro continente un'unione federale di liberi Stati di liberi lavoratori' (*SMAMS* 65). And yet, despite the reference to workers' freedom, Montale's position appears simultaneously to be based as much on old bourgeois liberal certainties as on new political realities. He goes on to warn that the intellectuals' service must be given freely ('servire', he cautions, not 'asservirsi'), as part of 'l'attività universale del singolo', thus placing his exhortation firmly 'nel campo dei valori morali' (*SMAMS* 67). Along with this emphasis on the centrality of the individual as the agent of moral choice goes a sometimes intense distaste for the collective, the masses. Thus in 'L'Italia rinunzia?' (published in May 1945), he mounts a vigorous defence of the political role of the bourgeoisie, and specifically of the 'intelligentsia', against charges of responsibility for the rise of Fascism: 'Venivano dal popolo Gobetti e Rosselli, cioè le figure più italianamente ispirate della lunga vigilia antifascista? Erano composte di borghesi le folle che si recavano in stato di perpetuo delirio coatto, dinanzi allo storico balcone di palazzo Venezia?' (*SMAMS* 41). If there is any hope now for the 'popolo, che da solo non saprebbe guidarsi', he continues, it must lie with 'pochi uomini degni di condurlo'.

His argument seeks undoubtedly to evoke Piero Gobetti's legacy of radical liberalism (Montale shares the widespread attitude of reverence for the anti-Fascist martyr Gobetti, publisher of the first edition of *Ossi* and a kind of secular saint for the *azionisti*).[23] But here and elsewhere, the poet's views also echo the older liberal ideals championed by the philosopher Benedetto Croce. The latter (whose anti-Fascist manifesto Montale signed in 1925) was the outstanding figurehead for a traditional, secular-liberal brand of anti-Fascism throughout the *ventennio*.[24] In his *Storia di Europa nel secolo decimonono* (1932), Croce declared that, despite the grave threats it faced, 'libertà' was an eternal value, a force inherent in history ('la sua virtù opera nelle cose stesse'), and it must eventually reassert itself in a peaceful Europe, where it would give rise to 'una nuova nazionalità', leading to an 'unione europea', and thus freeing the continent from the travails of the old illiberal nationalism.[25] Montale's absolute faith in freedom as expressed in 1944 can be seen to spring at least in part from this same matrix. There are clear parallels between Croce's belief in the 'virtù' of freedom and Montale's faith (here and elsewhere) in 'insopprimibili forze', and between the inevitable outcomes foreseen (and hoped for) by the two writers. Despite differences with Croce over aesthetic and theoretical questions, Montale remains faithful to a Crocean ideal of liberty. The poet's emphasis on individual moral choice recalls the ethical basis of Crocean liberalism, which Montale will later celebrate (in 1962) in terms of its 'incitamento alla responsabilità morale' (*SM* 2540). And Montale's unashamed élitism echoes closely Croce's political faith in the noble few rather than the 'volgo'. In 'La storia come storia della libertà' (1937), Croce declared that freedom persisted 'schietta e robusta e consapevole solo negli animi dei pochi, sebbene essi soli siano poi quelli che storicamente contano, come solo ai pochi parlano i grandi filosofi, i grandi poeti, gli uomini grandi'.[26] Montale, as we have seen, seems in no doubt as to who should really 'count' in Italy in 1945: the 'pochi uomini' of the liberal intelligentsia.

Nevertheless, in 'L'Italia rinunzia?' (as in other articles written around this time) we also find much more radical or egalitarian notes, along with a sense of unequivocal *impegno* on the part of the poet. Thus, while warning of the threat of 'forze reazionarie ancora forti e vive', Montale discusses the immediate political problems of the day, declaring the need for 'un governo che sia veramente un autogoverno popolare di uomini nuovi, non compromessi col fascismo'. His language participates clearly in the discourse of the broader Resistance movement, as he refers for example to the Florentine 'tentativo di un autogoverno da parte dei patrioti locali' or to 'la liberazione del nord avvenuta in tanta parte per merito dei patrioti di lassù' (*SMAMS* 38–42). Here the poet is actively engaged in the political debate as an advocate of the radical liberalism of the Partito D'Azione.

Furthermore, any analysis of political and cultural essays such as these must be complemented by an examination of the numerous narrative pieces written in parallel. Indeed, Luperini, in discussing some of the stories from 1944–6 (in particular those excluded from *Farfalla di Dinard*, probably precisely because of their overtly political nature), characterizes Montale's political position in the initial post–war period as one of 'antifascismo molto pronunciato [...] certo "borghese", ma niente affatto timido o conservatore, e anzi abbastanza avanzato e coraggioso'.[27] The most telling example cited is that of

'I galleggianti' (*Nazione del popolo*, 30 October 1944), in which a perplexed and ultimately indignant narrator contemplates the unedifying spectacle of recycled Fascists brazenly regaining positions of influence in post-liberation Florence. Luperini highlights the radical position assumed by the narrator, who asserts the urgent need for an effective purge of those responsible for Italy's disaster, as well as the right of the people ('il povero pantalone') to control such a purge—and, if necessary, not only 'per vie legali' (*PR* 743). Other pieces from 1945–6 confirm the existence at this time of a very practical aspect to Montale's political outlook, an immediate concern with the task of political renewal. This concern is expressed, for example, in a number of satirical sketches: whether of the politically disoriented Menalco ('Senza partito', January 1945), with his leanings towards a facile *qualunquismo* ('Il guaio è che Menalco vorrebbe entrare nel partito che vincerà', *PR* 641); or of the cravenly opportunistic turncoats overheard in 1943 discussing possible methods of executing Mussolini ('Nel parco', June 1945, *PR* 650–2). But along with the vein of ironic humour that predominates in many of these stories and sketches, there are also moments of serious and heartfelt *impegno*. In 'Sulla porrettana' (1946), the narrator expresses his comprehension for the violently intransigent anti-Fascism of a young man who declares 'Io sono un mutilato nell'Anima, non nel corpo. Mi hanno tolto una parte d'anima' (*PR* 697). It is significant here, however, that Montale, as well as stressing the personal, interior source of such *impegno*, also portrays his own position as already isolated: 'Tutti piegarono la testa [...] Solo io dissi un "comprendo" [...] e davvero mi pareva di comprendere per me e per gli altri'. (This sense of isolation and defeat will be echoed notably in 'L'ombra della magnolia ...' (1947): 'Gli altri arretrano / e piegano', *OV* 252.)

Indeed, the general tone of Montale's writings, both narrative pieces and essays, begins to change significantly during 1946. Hints at a possibly negative outcome to the transformation underway in Italy and in Europe as a whole were in fact present even in some of the more optimistic essays of the previous years. But up until now there was always a clear distinction between the negative and positive terms: between, on the one hand, the immediate past of Fascism and, on the other, the present with its relative freedom and potential for future ethical and political reconstruction. It is this distinction that begins to break down in 1946. 'L'asino di Buridano' for example (March 1946), can be seen as marking a transitional phase, with the still undecided

Menalco caught up in a nightmare election in which the various parties on offer all appear tainted with similar degrees of insincerity and bad faith (*PR* 669–73). By 1947, the year of such stories as 'Padri e figli' and 'Aut-aut', it is clear that Montale's outlook has shifted definitively away from his post-liberation optimism. The setting for these two stories, an imaginary 'Livonia' where ethical and political boundaries are deeply uncertain in the wake of the passing of a dictatorial regime, plainly represents his growing disillusionment with the situation in post-war Italy, in which the political hopes and aspirations of the aftermath of the liberation now appear untenable.

While an ill-defined unease concerning future developments can be discerned in some writings from 1946 and 1947, it is in 1948–9 that the nature of this unease begins to be more sharply delineated and a clearer picture emerges of the forces which threaten Montale's liberal ideals of political and cultural renewal. As the world begins to grapple with the new realities of the East–West divide and the military and political stand-off of the Cold War, the poet now rejects both the Soviet socialist and the Western consumerist models of mass society, engaging in bitter polemics against Stalinist collectivization while also denouncing what he sees as the threatened self-destruction of Western civilization. On the one hand, we find an explicitly anti-communist geopolitical stance in many of the articles written for the *Corriere della sera*, where he was employed as a staff journalist from January 1948 (a case in point is his first assignment, the Gandhi obituary, now in *SM* 730–2).[28] The anti-communist polemic is also given narrative expression, for example in 'Un poeta nazionale' (1948), in which the imaginary 'Livonia' (previously used as an allegorical counterpart of post-war Italy in 'Aut-aut' and 'Padri e figli') now clearly represents Stalin's USSR.[29] Here the satirical attack on those intellectuals and artists willing to subordinate individual integrity to ideological expediency (embodied in the figure of the self-serving and ultimately self-deluding 'official' poet) is placed in the darker overall context of the grim realities of totalitarian repression (see *PR* 529–33).

Elsewhere, however, such views are balanced, particularly in the area of cultural politics, by a deep concern over the direction being taken by Western civilization itself. In 'Amico del popolo' (1949), the narrator, 'un insolito tipo di conservatore', replying to an intense young man who aspires to a social function for art, points to a change in the nature of society and considers its consequences for all art and culture:

E poiché la massa probabilmente prevarrà sul popolo (la democrazia americana ha rubato la parola alla pubblicistica del marxismo e l'ha fatta sua) è verosimile che un'arte di popolo anche in avvenire mancherà di qualsiasi fondamento. Dico una arte, nel vecchio senso umanistico o semplicemente umano; naturalmente avremo espressioni, comunicazioni di massa, mode decorative, letterarie, ecc. Fatti pratici, non arte. L'arte continuerà ad essere opera rara, di isolati; senza popolo, purtroppo. (*PR* 793)

This passage contains several key elements of Montale's view of the crisis now threatening Western culture: his contemptuous reduction of the democratic and socialist political models to the uniformity of 'la massa'; a focus on the consequences of the advent of mass culture for art; and the projected survival of cultural values only in the work of isolated individuals. This points to a crisis within Western civilization that is ultimately far more serious than the external communist threat decried elsewhere.

Montale's two trips to Britain in 1948 were a particularly rich source of material for both his poetic and his prose writings.[30] His admiration for British society, with all its foibles and eccentricities, is based on the conviction that in Britain the liberal traditions of respect for individual freedom and privacy have survived as nowhere else. Individualism is the basis of the nonconformist 'dandismo umanistico' that Montale outlines in 'Paradiso delle donne e degli snob' (1948): it is seen in the gesture with which the individual rebels against the 'crushing force' of external reality; it is the mark of a 'disarmonia', a refusal to be reconciled to the world at large, implying both diffidence and optimism, 'disperazione e fede nel destino individuale dell'uomo' (*PR* 268). This ideal of quirky nonconformism (whose line of descent in Montale can, at least generically, be traced back to a similar 'disarmonia' in poems such as 'Non chiederci la parola' in *Ossi di seppia*), while ostensibly apolitical in its terms, nevertheless does contain ideological overtones, in so far as it clearly rejects any collective solution to the problems of humanity. But we are told in the same article (and in others written at this time) that this individualistic ideal is now threatened by the massive mechanization and regimentation of contemporary society:

qui, più che altrove in Europa, la civiltà dell'uomo meccanico mostra il suo volto pauroso. Guai se qualcosa dovesse spezzarsi in un simile ingranaggio di ruote e di leve; guai se l'uomo, chiamate alla vita le macchine, non riuscisse a mantenersi padrone dei mostri da lui scatenati! Oggi il pericolo non sembra probabile in Inghilterra, ma domani, quando il mondo intero sarà un immenso alveare di ordegni aerei e terrestri, potrà esistere ancora l'uomo della strada, l'uomo umano, l'uomo che è il sale e il pepe di ogni civiltà? (PR 265–6)

This threat is ultimately far more serious than that posed by communism. The latter could clearly be fought as an alien ideology, against which Western, liberal civilization could raise its defences. But the new threat springs from within the very civilization to be defended. It is significantly here in England, 'più che altrove in Europa' (America is a different matter), that the spectre of mechanization shows its dreadful face: the bastion of liberal, human values is at risk from the very machines that are the products of this same civilization. The scenario wherein the free and potentially creative individual may be not merely enslaved, but completely annihilated, is indeed apocalyptic, and in such a scenario, the only defence mechanism foreseen by Montale is that of isolation, through which a tiny intellectual élite can conserve 'alcune dimensioni dell'anima umana' (PR 794).

This notion of an élite of privileged individuals is bound up with the very survival of art, which, as an integral part of the humanistic cultural tradition, is equally under threat from the advent of a dehumanized, mass-oriented society. The threatened extinction of art is given narrative expression in 'Una grande ricchezza' (1948) with its dystopic vision of the future, placed significantly in the Western setting of a grotesquely mechanized Toronto. Here there is plainly an element of satire of avant-garde art, in the playful description of the various artefacts of twenty-second-century 'costruttivismo auto-matico'. The satirical element leads in however to the central opposition between the protagonist's fondly remembered 'piccola casa spaziosa' in a backward, primitive Italy and the uninhabitable urban nightmare of technically advanced but dehumanized Toronto (PR 772–6). A similar vision of a mechanized future, where art is scorned as an expression of mere 'sentimento individuale', was already presented a year earlier in 'Grafologia futura' (PR 721).

These fictional visions of the future give expression to what becomes one of the most insistent themes of Montale's essays throughout the 1950s and '60s: the denunciation (in parallel with the polemic against communism) of Western, industrial, consumerist society, which has betrayed its own liberal cultural ideals, centred on the value of the individual, in favour of a new myth of the masses, served by ever-increasing automation and mass production. From 1948 onwards, with the realization that there is no longer any real hope of a new cultural and political order based on traditional liberalism, Montale writes increasingly from the perspective of the isolated intellectual, aware of his own anachronistic status in a world of speed and mass production. As he acknowledges the fact of the political defeat of his brand of *azionismo*, he sees the only possible remaining *impegno* in the realm of the individual, and especially of artistic expression.[31] But in many cases, it is precisely the artists and intellectuals, those he hoped would be the guardians of his humanistic ideals, who have failed to keep faith, as contemporary art and literature, in emulating the progress of society at large, destroy themselves from within.

A few examples from *Auto da fé* show the persistence of this pedal note of denunciation and illustrate the poet's developing sense of the inauthenticity that surrounds him. In 'Mutazioni' (1949), he laments the decline of three cultural phenomena, 'villeggiatura', the consumption of fine wine, and the reading of novels, all of which flourished in a 'slower' age, and are now compromised by the accelerating pace of 'collective' life (*SMAMS* 87). In the face of this new, frenetic rhythm, Montale speculates on the possible advent of a new, better-equipped breed of humanity, whose nervous system will be quite different to that of our own 'traditional, Copernican, classical' organism (*SMAMS* 90). The ironic tone barely conceals a very real sense of disorientation in a world where humanity itself, as an absolute value, is under threat. This hypothesis of a 'uomo nuovo' returns repeatedly, for example in 'Gente in fuga' (1953), where the new man, 'fleeing from time, responsibilities and history' (*SMAMS* 151–2), is in evidence all around, but the poet still holds out the hope that art may survive in some form: 'non è detto che anche l'arte venga meno sulla faccia della terra. [...] Ma si accentuerà nell'arte futura quel carattere preistorico che già colpisce nelle odierne manifestazioni' (*SMAMS* 152). ('Prehistoric', he explains, in the sense that it is non-figurative, not rationally explicable, lacking the essential human dimension of 'una storia individuale'.) Clearly any remaining hope for the future of art is rather slender.

The question of a 'new' art is treated also in 'Fuga dal tempo' (1958), where again its non-rational character is noted, along with its tendency to become an anonymous product: 'sarà estremamente problematico distinguere tra opera d'arte e oggetto d'uso': art will be concerned with 'divertimento' and 'spettacolo' rather than 'contemplazione' (*SMAMS* 135–6). In 'Le magnifiche sorti' (1959—the Leopardian title is, in itself, an eloquent indicator of the author's attitude to contemporary civilization), Montale again links the imminence of a 'new' man ('non più *sapiens* ma solamente *faber*') with that of a new art, this time in the context of a scathing attack on the 'paroxysm of pseudo-communication' of the mass media. In the face of this, the only hope is that the 'few', those whose eyes remain open, will resist the process of 'massification'. Unfortunately, however, the artists in their ivory towers who should constitute this élite are themselves capitulating and indeed contributing to the world of mass production: 'proprio da queste torri è uscita la teoria che fa dell'opera d'arte un oggetto d'uso che si consuma e si butta via' (*SMAMS* 226–31). The sense of disillusionment with the contemporary artistic and intellectual élite is even more pronounced in 'Odradek' (1959). Here the condemnation of 'la massificazione dell'individuo, il *bourrage* dei cervelli, l'appiattimento del singolo nella massicciata del collettivo' leads to a gloomy hypothesis of complete cultural collapse (which, in retrospect, may seem all too prophetic):

Le comunicazioni di massa sono il fondamento della nuova industria culturale, fatalmente portata ad allargarsi su un piano sempre più basso, raggiunto il quale sarà sempre possibile sperare in nuove bassure, realizzando l'ipotesi di un futuro uomo stereofonico, incapace di una visione analitica del reale, refrattario ad ogni possibilità di sintesi e di sintassi. (*SMAMS* 122–3)

In this scenario, one can no longer distinguish the 'true' intellectual from the 'false', when art and literature (especially those of the avant-garde) have capitulated to the industrial model, and their production is reduced to the uniform level of 'merce' (*SMAMS* 126).

The condemnation of inauthenticity amongst the artistic élite acquires a new, bitterly polemical tone when it addresses the question of deliberate intellectual bad faith, as in 'Il mercato del nulla' (1961):

I più hanno compreso che la rinunzia, la protesta, il grido di chi non si rassegna e vuol morire sulla breccia sono, in se stessi, una eccellente materia di commercio. Sorge così la figura moderna di chi, tutto rifiutando e deplorando, prospera e impingua sulle macerie di un mondo che si suppone essere in disfacimento, ma che in verità gode di un benessere medio che non ha precedenti nella storia. Dimostrando che il linguaggio è una finzione priva di ogni contenuto e che l'uomo è sorto per caso dal nulla e che il nulla è la sua vera vocazione, il filosofo può conquistare cattedre e assurgere a reputazione mondiale. Distruggendo l'ipotesi stessa di ogni possibile arte, un artista di oggi può acquistare larga fama e vivere alle spalle del mondo borghese da lui detestato. (*SMAMS* 267–8)

This, for Montale, is the worst possible form of *trahison des clercs*, involving, as it does, those (the creative artists) in whom his slender hopes for the future resided, and tending thus to devalue the artistic sphere as a whole, in a process of degradation in which he too clearly feels implicated: 'Vendiamo la parte migliore di noi, la nostra autenticità, noi che crediamo di essere anime vere; e i nostri clienti sono la vanità, la moda, il conformismo' (1962: *SMAMS* 187). Just as the threat of 'massificazione', perceived initially in terms of mechanization, industrialization and social and cultural regimentation, sprang from within the very Western civilization that should have championed the cause of individual intellectual and spiritual freedom, so, in parallel, those within that civilization best qualified to defend it against itself, have become insidious agents of the descent into cultural and intellectual conformism. By the 1960s, the sense of immersion in a sea of inauthenticity is overwhelming. In the brief 'Francobolli' pieces, contained in the closing section of *Auto da fé* and almost all written between 1963 and 1965, there is a constant preoccupation with contemporary developments in art and literature, and above all with the need to unmask the hypocrisy and degradation that Montale now sees as the basic condition of so much cultural discourse: 'l'indifferenziato formale, la pentola che bolle e manda a galla legumi e còtiche che appena si riesce a distinguere' ('Tutti in pentola', 1963: *SMAMS* 290). With this, we are already, chronologically and thematically, in the environs of the radical scepticism of *Satura*, where culinary degradation will be employed repeatedly as an image of the poet's historical and ideological disgust. From this point on, Montale's poetry becomes (even more than before) 'referto autentico di una dimora nell'inautentico'.[32]

Montale has come a long way from the enthusiastic political and cultural commitment of the immediate post-war years. The possibility of some form of political realization of his liberal ideals has clearly, since the late 1940s, ceased to exist, leading to a deep sense of disillusionment and isolation for the poet in his continuing attachment to those ideals. Even artistic activity, the ultimate rebellion against all that is collective, commercialized, material or mechanized, has now become problematic. The conviction of the supreme importance of the individual is coloured, in 'La solitudine dell'artista' (1952), by the certainty of his isolation: 'L'uomo in quanto essere individuato, individuo empirico, è fatalmente isolato. La vita sociale è un'addizione, un aggregato, non un'unità di individui' (*SMAMS* 53). This is a certainty that is linked, initially, to a possibility of poetic renewal in the last part of *La bufera e altro*, the short-lived triumph of the new, terrestrial poetic myth of 'la Volpe' in the 'Madrigali privati', the aristocratic isolation of the poetic *io* as 'Dio diviso dagli uomini' (*OV* 264). However, the intellectual dignity and integrity inherent in this artistic isolation cannot entirely mitigate the poet's increasing pessimism, as seen again in 'La solitudine dell'artista':

ma ritengo che anche domani le voci più importanti saranno quelle degli artisti che faranno sentire, attraverso la loro voce isolata, un'eco del fatale isolamento di ognuno di noi. In questo senso, solo gli isolati parlano, solo gli isolati comunicano; gli altri—gli uomini della comunicazione di massa— ripetono, fanno eco, volgarizzano le parole dei poeti, che oggi non sono parole di fede, ma potranno forse tornare ad esserlo un giorno. (*SMAMS* 56)

The absence of 'fede', even within the integrity of the private sphere, lies at the root of Montale's poetic silence from 1954 onwards, but is also an essential key to understanding the more radical poetic renewal which follows in the 1960s and '70s.

Notes to the Introduction

1. There is a large and ever-expanding body of criticism on Montale's work. Detailed readings of the earlier poetry (and, in some cases, of the later work also) can be found in the following monographic studies: Marco Forti, *Eugenio Montale: la poesia, la prosa di fantasia e d'invenzione* (Milan: Mursia, 1973); Angelo Jacomuzzi, *La poesia di Montale: dagli 'Ossi' ai 'Diari'* (Turin: Einaudi, 1978); Mario Martelli, *Eugenio Montale: introduzione e guida allo studio dell'opera montaliana* (Florence: Le Monnier, 1982); Romano Luperini, *Storia di Montale* (Rome: Laterza, 1986); Franco Croce, *Storia della poesia di Eugenio Montale* (Genoa: Costa & Nolan, 1991); Pietro Cataldi, *Montale* (Palermo: Palumbo, 1991). Useful monographs in English include: Ghanshyam Singh, *Eugenio Montale: A Critical Study of his Poetry, Prose and Criticism* (New Haven: Yale University Press, 1973); Guido Almansi and Bruce Merry, *Eugenio Montale: The Private Language of Poetry* (Edinburgh: Edinburgh University Press, 1977); Rebecca West, *Eugenio Montale: Poet on the Edge* (Cambridge: Harvard University Press, 1981); Glauco Cambon, *Eugenio Montale's Poetry: A Dream in Reason's Presence* (Princeton: Princeton University Press, 1982); Claire de C. L. Huffman, *Montale and the Occasions of Poetry* (Princeton: Princeton University Press, 1983); Jared Becker, *Eugenio Montale* (Boston: Twayne, 1986). An invaluable interpretative resource for the English-speaking reader is Jonathan

Galassi's bilingual annotated edition, *Eugenio Montale: Collected Poems 1920–1954* (New York: Farrar, Straus and Giroux, 1998).

2. See Romano Luperini, 'Note sull'allegorismo novecentesco: il caso di Montale', *Paragone (Letteratura)* 39 (1988), 54–76. See also Jacomuzzi, *La poesia di Montale*, especially 69–74; and Tiziana de Rogatis, 'Alle origini del dantismo di Montale', *Montale e il canone poetico del Novecento*, ed. M. A. Grignani and R. Luperini (Rome: Laterza, 1998), 189–201 at 197. An argument against an allegorical reading of Montale can be found in Zygmunt Baranski, 'Dante and Montale: The Threads of Influence', *Dante Comparisons*, ed. E. Haywood and B. Jones (Dublin: Irish Academic Press, 1985), 11–48.

3. Luperini, *Storia di Montale*, 254; 'Note sull'allegorismo', 56–7.

4. 'Note sull'allegorismo', 71–4 (Luperini derives the term 'allegoria vuota' from Lukács). It should be noted, however, that Montale does not go nearly as far as Zanzotto and other contemporaries, who focus much more specifically on deconstructions of language and meaning.

5. Luperini, 'Note sull'allegorismo', 55. Jacomuzzi (*La poesia di Montale*, 80) similarly notes the need for a 'mediazione intellettuale'.

6. See also 'Parliamo dell ermetismo', *SMAMS* 1531–4. The mistaken idea of Montale as a 'hermetic' poet , born out of his proximity to the creative and critical circles of Florentine *ermetismo* in the 1930s, persisted for many decades.

7. Elio Gioanola, Introduction to *La poesia di Eugenio Montale: atti del Convegno Internazionale, Milano 12/13/14 settembre, Genova 15 settembre 1982* (Milan: Librex, 1983), 15.

8. Angelo Marchese, *Visiting angel: interpretazione semiologica della poesia di Montale* (Turin: SEI, 1977), 83.

9. See 'Il metalinguaggio delle descrizioni tipologiche della cultura', Jurij M. Lotman and Boris A. Uspenskij, *Tipologia della cultura*, ed. Remo Faccani and Marzio Marzaduri, trans. Manila Barbato Faccani et al., 2nd edn. (Milan: Bompiani, 1995), 145–81, esp. 155–65.

10. Marchese gives the following diagram (*Visiting angel*, 84):

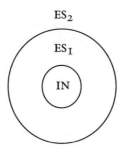

11. Ibid., 121. For further observations on interior/exterior spaces in Montale, see Franco Croce, 'La primavera hitleriana', *Letture montaliane in occasione dell'80° compleanno del Poeta* (Genoa: Bozzi, 1977), 223–53 at 229–31; Vittorio Sereni, 'Il ritorno', ibid., 191–5 at 193; Luperini, *Storia di Montale*, 96; idem, *Montale o l'identità negata* (Naples: Liguori, 1984), 82–3.

12. Luperini, *Montale o l'identità negata*, 79–80.
13. See 'Botta e risposta I', *OV* 278.
14. See *Letteratura*, 79–81 (1966), repr. as *Omaggio a Montale*, ed. Silvio Ramat (Milan: Mondadori, 1966); *La rassegna della letteratura italiana* 70 (1966).
15. Walter Binni, 'Omaggio a Montale', *La rassegna della letteratura italiana* 70 (1966), 227–46 at 229, 233. The recurrence of the term 'omaggio' is an indicator of the overall tone of these tributes.
16. Cataldi, *Montale*, 86–7, 96.
17. Forti, *Eugenio Montale*, 22. See also Geno Pampaloni, 'Con "Le occasioni" dentro lo zaino', *La poesia di Eugenio Montale: atti del Convegno Internazionale tenuto a Genova dal 25 al 28 novembre 1982*, ed. Sergio Campailla and Cesare Federico Goffis (Florence: Le Monnier, 1984), 265–9; also Giulio Nascimbeni's interview with Giorgio Strehler, 'Montale nello zaino di Strehler', *Corriere della sera* (10 Feb. 1996), 25.
18. Croce, 'La primavera hitleriana', 223–5.
19. Cataldi, *Montale*, 137–8.
20. Umberto Carpi, *Montale dopo il fascismo: dalla 'Bufera' a 'Satura'* (Padua: Liviana, 1971).
21. Ibid., 8, 15.
22. Ibid., 21–2. See also Giulio Nascimbeni, *Montale: biografia di un poeta* (Milan: Longanesi, 1986), 104; *Eusebio e Trabucco: carteggio di Eugenio Montale e Gianfranco Contini*, ed. Dante Isella (Milan: Adelphi, 1997), 99–100.
23. On Gobetti's legacy of 'intransigenza morale', see Norberto Bobbio, *Profilo ideologico del novecento italiano* (Turin: Einaudi, 1986), 126–7.
24. See ibid., 141–50; David Ward, *Antifascisms: Cultural Politics in Italy, 1943–46* (London: Associated University Presses, 1996), 43–85. Montale's name appears in a list of signatories of Croce's manifesto published in the Genova paper *Il Lavoro* on 10 May 1925. See *Una dolcezza inquieta: l'universo poetico di Eugenio Montale*, ed. Giuseppe Marcenaro (Milan: Electa, 1996), 47.
25. Benedetto Croce, *Storia di Europa nel secolo decimonono* (Bari: Laterza, 1932), 351–62.
26. Benedetto Croce, *Filosofia, poesia, storia: pagine tratte da tutte le opere*, La letteratura italiana: storia e testi, 75 (Milan: Ricciardi, 1951), 522.
27. Luperini, *Montale o l'identità negata*, 199–200.
28. For further examples, see Carpi, *Montale dopo il fascismo*, 35–8.
29. Forti's statement that this piece alludes to 'l'Italia post-bellica del 1948' (*PR*, p. lv) makes little sense, given the clear references to Soviet-style purges and labour camps.
30. See the entire second section of *Fuori di casa*, now in *PR* 241–78. The first visit, as a guest of the British Council along with Alberto Moravia and Elsa Morante, took place in the spring. The second, in summer, was a strictly journalistic trip, as special correspondent of the *Corriere*. (See Nascimbeni, *Montale: biografia di un poeta*, 113; also 'A cena con Moravia', *PR* 1089.) These trips left their mark in poetry in the 'Flashes e dediche' section of *La bufera e altro*.
31. Carpi, *Montale dopo il fascismo*, 50–61.
32. Franco Fortini, *Ventiquattro voci per un dizionario di lettere* (Milan: Il Saggiatore, 1968), 234.

CHAPTER 1

Mosca and her Predecessors

The dialogue with a female *tu* represents perhaps the most persistent and deeply rooted figurative device employed by Montale. It is, among other things, one of the main vehicles through which he expresses his ideological positions, and the changing identities and attributes of his interlocutors reflect also his changing relationship with historical realities. Before discussing Mosca, the woman who dominates the later poetry, it may be useful to give a brief overview of the roles and functions of the various female figures in the first three collections, in order both to place the figure of Mosca in context and to help exemplify some of the radical thematic and formal changes that characterize the poetry of the later years.

Arletta

The first female figure with an important and enduring role in Montale's poetry was also the last to emerge with a name and clearly-delineated features into the full light of day in both the poetry itself and the critical literature. Arletta, as she is generally known, is the poetic transfiguration of a young girl, Anna degli Uberti, whose family rented the villa beside that of Montale's family in Monterosso for several years around 1920 (see Appendix). In 'Annetta' (1972), the poet makes an expiatory gesture towards her memory:

> Perdona Annetta se dove tu sei
> (non certo tra di noi, i sedicenti
> vivi) poco ti giunge il mio ricordo.
> Le tue apparizioni furono per molti anni
> rare e impreviste, non certo da te volute.
> Anche i luoghi (la rupe dei doganieri,
> la foce del Bisagno dove ti trasformasti in Dafne)
> non avevano senso senza di te.
> [...] (*OV* 490)

Thus Montale finally named explicitly the woman whose presence, though of fundamental importance in many poems, had remained deliberately submerged up till then. The poetic 'luoghi' referred to are unmistakable: the clifftop of 'La casa dei doganieri' (*Occasioni*) and the 'foce' of 'Incontro' (*Ossi*), where she was transformed:

> [...] e farsi mia
> un'altra vita sento, ingombro d'una
> forma che mi fu tolta; e quasi anelli
> alle dita non foglie mi si attorcono
> ma capelli.
>
> Poi più nulla. Oh sommersa!: tu dispari
> qual sei venuta, e nulla so di te.
> [...] (*OV* 97)

From *Le occasioni* to *Satura*, the figure of Arletta is largely eclipsed by those of other *ispiratrici* (notably Clizia), but her enduring (not to say growing) significance begins to be appreciated by critics from the 1970s onwards, in parallel with her explicit re-emergence in new poems. Luciano Rebay, with the help of direct indications on Montale's part, is the first to spell out the extent of the Arletta cycle in *Le occasioni*.[1] The poet underlines the significance of Arletta when he describes her to Cima in 1977 as 'il personaggio più reale e che resiste nel tempo'.[2] Eventually, Grignani extends Arletta's presence right into the heart of *La bufera e altro*, thus bearing out the poet's indication of her 'resistance' throughout his work.[3] So Arletta has assumed, retrospectively, a privileged position in Montale's opus, and indeed this shadowy figure can now be seen to have significant ideological or historical connotations from her earliest appearances.

In 'Incontro', as Jacomuzzi points out, a dense web of Dantesque references and echoes superimposes an 'infernal' moral landscape on the Genoese urban setting and leads to the possibility of an allegorical reading through an embryonic system of 'doppia denotazione'.[4] The 'incontro' of the title can thus also be seen to represent Montale's meeting with Dante's poetry, an encounter between Arletta and Beatrice in which Arletta becomes a 'figura di Beatrice', so that this text highlights Montale's rejection of 'elegy' (the 'tristezza' of the opening line) in favour of 'una conoscenza e una rappresentazione "altra", almeno tendenzialmente allegorica del reale'.[5] This establishes a useful framework for an allegorical reading of this and subsequent collections, so that, beyond the intertextuality of the Dantesque allusions, one can begin to read references to contemporary historical reality, as for example a denunciation of what Cambon calls the 'political and moral atmosphere' of the mid-1920s via such infernal figures as those of the 'incappati di corteo' of 'Incontro'.[6]

Similarly, Arshi Pipa traces a 'hellish atmosphere' through various texts in *Ossi*, and while elements of Pipa's approach are highly questionable (such as his constant search for 'cryptograms' of political opposition), he rightly points out the allegorical function of the relationship with the beloved woman, so that in 'Incontro', for example, 'the poet's ideal of redemptive love is rooted in political reality'.[7] But this poem, coming as it does at the close of the period of *Ossi*, is merely a first inkling of the later centrality of female figures and of their political function. As such it constitutes a prologue to the descent into gathering darkness of *Le occasioni*, as seen in its closing lines:

> [...] Prega per me
> allora ch'io discenda altro cammino
> che una via di città,
> nell'aria persa, innanzi al brulichio
> dei vivi; ch'io ti senta accanto; ch'io
> scenda senza viltà. (*OV* 97)

An atmosphere of deep gloom pervades much of Montale's second collection, written, Cataldi notes, against the background of the consolidation of Fascism and the comprehensive defeat of liberal ideals: 'Al fondo c'è la sconfitta di un'utopia: quella, per intendersi, gobettiana.'[8] The result is a sense of enclosure, suffocation and oppression, in which literature becomes a key value to be preserved. For the Florentine intellectuals grouped around the journals *Solaria* and *Letteratura*, culture and art become the last line of defence, through which ideological opposition can, as Luperini puts it, be sublimated: 'La sublimazione è la risposta che un'intera cultura dà a quel clima di assedio cui alludono molte poesie delle *Occasioni*'. An attachment to a broad European tradition of cultural enlightenment leads to a belief in poetry as a value in itself, to be strenuously defended, and which in turn protects its adepts. In this context Montale's female interlocutor becomes 'l'intermediaria di una religione della cultura e della poesia', a 'religion' that springs from the very concrete historical tragedy of the 1930s.[9]

The need, signalled in the closing lines of 'Incontro', for the *io* to 'feel' Arletta beside him in this tragic atmosphere, is in evidence in several poems in *Occasioni*, most notably 'La casa dei doganieri'. In this poem (dated 1930) the increasingly bleak political outlook has its correlative in troubled meteorological imagery (continuing a vein found already in several texts in *Ossi*):

> Libeccio sferza da anni le vecchie mura
> e il suono del tuo riso non è più lieto:
> la bussola va impazzita all'avventura
> [...] (*OV* 161)

In the 'desolation' of the woman's absence the poetic persona is left in a shadowy, twilight world where meaning is problematic: 'Tu non ricordi la casa di questa / mia sera. Ed io non so chi va e chi resta'. The poem is a memorable early formulation of the insuperable detachment, the 'otherness' of the absent woman ('altro tempo frastorna / la tua memoria'), who is thus seen in opposition to the negative, temporal-historical reality that contains the *io*. It also brings together key elements of Arletta as a 'crepuscular' figure. Thus the twilight setting is laden with associations of loss, absence, regret: 'desolata t'attende dalla sera'; 'ma tu resti sola / né qui respiri nell' oscurità'. The Ligurian coastal landscape, already associated with Arletta in *Ossi*, also contains what is perhaps her most enduring *senhal* (in the somewhat inaccurate sense of this term later famously employed by the poet himself with reference to Clizia[10]), the intermittent light indicating a possible (though uncertain) path to salvation:

> Oh l'orizzonte in fuga, dove s'accende
> rara la luce della petroliera!
> Il varco è qui?

This intermittent gleam of light, in its more usual form of the 'faro', also occurs in 'Vecchi versi', where Arletta's recurrent motifs can also be seen to have historical overtones. Superficially, there is nothing more than the date of composition (1926) and the explicit setting of the Cinque Terre to link this poem to other Arletta texts (although the link is confirmed by Montale's personal statement to Rebay[11]). However, in this 'crepuscolo', her *senhal* shines through: 'il punto atono / del faro che baluginava sulla / roccia del Tino' (*OV* 111). It is this poem, the first in *Le occasioni* proper, that establishes the spatial opposition between interior and exterior that will constitute a fundamental component of some of the collection's most important texts: from this interior scene we can look ahead to those of 'Nuove stanze' or 'Notizie dall'Amiata', where the outside world looms large and threatening.

And here in 'Vecchi versi', through the window (an important recurring element of these spatial representations) comes the macabre intrusion of the moth: 'Era un insetto orribile dal becco / aguzzo [...] / [...] al dosso il teschio / umano' (*OV* 111–12). This sinister intrusion from the exterior world, characterized by the sign of the skull, into the protected realm of home, family and childhood memories (as indicated by the presence of 'mia madre', the nephews' games and the 'volti familiari' of the dead) undoubtedly carries implicit historical resonances. But perhaps more telling is a strictly literary resonance with the crepuscular world of Guido Gozzano. Although Gozzano's 'Le farfalle' (including 'Acherontia Atropos', a poem bearing remarkable coincidental similarities to aspects of 'Vecchi versi') was not published until the 1930s, there is an earlier appearance, in 'La signorina Felicita', of the same sinister moth, including references to the 'segno spaventoso' on its back, and its 'ronzo lamentoso'.[12]

In fact echoes of Gozzano and other *crepuscolari* can be found throughout the Arletta cycle, with its archetypal images of childhood, loss, and above all, premature death.[13] This 'crepuscular' dimension is identified by Becker as a key to the ideological and historical meaning of the poems. For him, the adoption in the 1920s of 'weak' crepuscular motifs (nostalgia for childhood, self-absorption, twilight) must be seen in part as a rejection of D'Annunzian bluster, reflecting the poet's 'antagonism to the triumphant new regime'.[14] This is not to say, however, that Montale subscribes wholeheartedly here to the stance of impotent irony so characteristic of the *crepuscolari*. His distance from their more self-indulgent excesses was clearly signalled in the essay 'Stile e tradizione' (1925), where, while on the one hand rejecting 'superomismo, messianismo e altre bacature', he also lamented the status of poetry as 'una solitaria vergogna individuale' (*SMAMS* 11, 14). So while the literary resonances of the Arletta cycle highlight the isolation of the poetic *io*, his alienation from historical reality and his inability to act in the practical world, these crepuscular resonances are inserted by Montale into an increasingly tragic, Dantesque scenario, rather than one of ironic, Gozzanian isolation.[15]

By the time of 'Eastbourne' (dated '1933 e 1935'), the tragic and historical dimension comes to the fore in a way that tests the boundaries of the Arletta cycle and ultimately demonstrates the limitations of this interlocutor. The coastal setting, despite its geo-graphical dislocation, is in keeping with the girl's previous appearances, as are other *senhals*, such as the 'guizzo' of light reflecting from windows to cliffs, the word 'varco', the gloom of evening ('Si fa tardi'), her 'respiro' (*OV* 170). But the sense of an obscure threat acquires a new urgency here as the characteristic meteorological motif ('Freddo un vento m'investe') is followed by disturbing images of the holiday: wheelchair-bound 'mutilati' (almost certainly war-wounded), the feeling of oppression in the ostensibly festive atmosphere ('La festa / non ha pietà'), culminating in the realization of the ineluctable advance of evil: 'Vince il male [...] La ruota non s'arresta'. The shadowy 'voice' of Arletta is unable to combat this evil, her 'goodness' in the gathering darkness is powerless: 'si dispiega / nel primo buio una bontà senz'armi'. Rebay sees this poem as marking the transition between the Arletta cycle and that of Clizia, and it is certainly true that Arletta comes closer here than anywhere else to becoming a strong figure, a truly redemptive Beatrice.[16] Her emblem of intermittent light acquires a new intensity even at the moment of its defeat by 'il male': 'Anche tu lo sapevi, luce-in-tenebra'. In the darkness, this light gains certainty ('lo sapevi') and an unmistakably religious overtone (with an echo of the Gospel of John).[17] In short, whether or not the figure of Clizia is present in concrete terms in this poem, it is certainly true that in the overall economy of *Le occasioni* (and especially within this fourth section) the failure of the earlier interlocutor here, her appearance and disappearance, prepares the ground for the major texts of the Clizia cycle that follow. In this sense at least, there is a superimposition of the two figures as a new positive allegory of opposition emerges and is given definition and significance against the twilight background of the Arletta cycle.

Gerti, Dora Markus, Liuba

Before considering the Clizia cycle and its historical and ideological implications, brief mention must be made of the enigmatic, tormented figures of Gerti, Dora Markus and Liuba, who appear in the first section of *Le occasioni* (see Appendix). These women are bound together by a common Jewish and Central-European heritage, and their function is distinct from that of Montale's major *ispiratrici*. This is reflected, on one level, in the fact that they maintain their named individuality, rather than assuming a literary *senhal*, such as

Arletta or Clizia. Elio Gioanola sees this as evidence of a lesser degree of assimilation into the 'institutional' paradigm of Montale's *tu*, concluding that these figures (with whom he somewhat arbitrarily bundles Esterina of 'Falsetto') 'non appartengono intimamente al poeta'.[18] Luperini, more convincingly, draws the opposite conclusion from the lesser degree of poetic transfiguration undergone by these figures. Supported by the poet's own declaration ('Queste apparizioni femminili [...] sono la mia voce') he reads Gerti/Dora and Liuba as projections of the poet himself.[19] In this sense they do not become manifestations of the *tu* as the absolute redemptive other, and indeed the 'simbologia stilnovistica' in evidence later in the book is completely absent from this first section. These texts constitute portraits rather than moments of an ideal dialogue: they are examples of what Bonora calls Montale's 'poesia della femminilità' rather than 'poesia d'amore'.[20] Their protagonists appear as prestigious 'extras', who bring, with the exotic flavour of their Central-European names, a more immediate presence of the outside world, a direct human contact with a historical reality that includes, but also transcends, the Italian political tragedy. They are entirely human, earth-bound characters, who, even if acting primarily to reflect images of the poet, also serve to evoke a certain historical atmosphere and landscape. (It may be noted in passing, however, that these troubled, restless figures foreshadow several of the attributes and images later associated with Mosca: the idiosyncratic attachment to totemic objects, the strange mixture of vulnerability and tenacity.)

The texts, 'Carnevale di Gerti' (1928), 'Dora Markus' (1928 and 1939) and 'A Liuba che parte' (1938), introduce and consolidate the sense of impending catastrophe that hangs over the collection as a whole. Dora Markus, enclosed in her 'interno di nivee / maioliche' and clinging to her atavistic 'leggenda' and 'voce', embodies the poet's tenacious holding to a besieged set of cultural values as the only available antidote to the 'fede feroce' of Nazism.[21] While in 'A Liuba che parte' (1938) historical events impinge perhaps more directly than anywhere else in *Occasioni*, although this becomes apparent only with the benefit of the typically laconic note added to later editions: 'Servirà sapere che Liuba — come Dora Markus — era ebrea' (*OV* 899).[22] 'A Liuba' is a masterpiece of lightness and understatement when considered against the background of the historical 'occasion', the enactment of the 1938 racial laws. These are present in the text only in the form of the 'ciechi tempi', an image which in turn

becomes a term of comparison with the 'flutto', another inkling of
the storms to come. But it is precisely the lightness of Liuba's baggage
that ensures her salvation:

> [...]
> La casa che tu rechi
> con te ravvolta, gabbia o cappelliera?,
> sovrasta i ciechi tempi come il flutto
> arca leggera — e basta al tuo riscatto. (OV 123)

Her domestic ark recalls Dora's 'leggenda' and 'destino', but unlike
Dora/Gerti, she at least is able to indicate a fragile, slender possibility
of survival for the culture and values to which she clings. It will
subsequently be the task of Clizia, Montale's Beatrice, to embody
allegorically those values themselves and ultimately to transcend the
boundaries of the poet's besieged interior setting.

Clizia

Le occasioni and the following collection La bufera e altro are largely
dominated by the figure of the woman who will become Clizia,
inspired by the American scholar Irma Brandeis, whom Montale met
in Florence in 1933, and with whom he developed an intense
relationship lasting until 1939 (see Appendix). She is present in only
one text in section I of Occasioni, 'Verso Capua', but she comes to
occupy centre stage in the 'Mottetti', in the longer poems at the close
of the collection, and above all in sections I and V of Bufera, where
she will finally be named as Clizia, after the Ovidean nymph who
loves Apollo and is transformed into a sunflower. Montale later
described the 'Mottetti', the intense, highly charged nucleus of
Occasioni, as 'un romanzetto autobiografico', dominated by the
'assenza–presenza di una donna lontana' (SMAMS 1490). Initially,
they are concerned with the evocation in very human terms of an
obsessive love, dominated by themes of separation and loss: 'Lo sai:
debbo riperderti e non posso'. (The fact that the first three 'mottetti'
may in fact have been inspired by another, earlier relationship has little
bearing on the poetic unity of the group as a whole. Indeed this
diversity of inspiration lends itself to the portrayal of the development
from a human to a transcendent love.) This obsessive relationship takes
its place from the outset in the broader context of Montale's dark,
infernal urban scenarios. Thus the archetypal situation in which the

io, in his interior setting, besieged by a hostile outside world, seeks to establish some contact with the woman, is established from the first 'mottetto':[23]

> [...]
> Un ronzìo lungo viene dall'aperto
> strazia com'unghia ai vetri. Cerco il segno
> smarrito, il pegno solo ch'ebbi in grazia
> da te.
>   E l'inferno è certo. (*OV* 133)

But the 'Mottetti' move progressively away from the mere portrayal of an (albeit intense) erotic experience, as the figure of the beloved develops into a complex myth, an embodiment of possible existential, spiritual and political salvation in the atmosphere of growing historical negativity. Amidst the private agony of separation from the beloved, the momentary appearances of the figure of Clizia soon acquire several layers of meaning. Her privileged emblems of light ('barbaglio', 'fólgore') and wings or flight ('penne') begin to emerge as she appears in opposition to the darkness and oppressive enclosure all around. She represents a mysterious (and tendentially mystical) 'otherness' with regard to the phenomena of experience: 'Altro era il tuo stampo' (*OV* 141). A key moment in her transformation occurs in 'mottetto' 12:

> Ti libero la fronte dai ghiaccioli
> che raccogliesti traversando l'alte
> nebulose; hai le penne lacerate
> dai cicloni, ti desti a soprassalti.
> [...] (*OV* 144)

Here the woman's angelic attributes (flight and feathers) are introduced, though their power and redemptive sigificance are radically limited in this first instance by the images of vulnerability (passivity, sleep, torn wings), which place the woman on an equal footing with the *io*, who in fact ministers tenderly to her. Nevertheless, even this wounded angel bestows a privileged status on the *io*, who with his knowledge of her is set apart from the surrounding ignorance: 'e l'altre ombre che scantonano / nel vicolo non sanno che sei qui'. Humanity as 'ombre' places us once again in an infernal setting. But more importantly, this poem (though added to the second edition and probably written in 1940) can be seen as the first clear instance of Montale's *stilnovismo* in the definitive ordering of the collection.

The idea of a Montalean *stilnovismo*, widely adopted in the critical literature, is authorized by the poet himself on a number of occasions, for example in a 1961 letter to Glauco Cambon where he describes Clizia as she appears in 'Finisterre': 'Ma chi è costei? Certo, in origine, donna reale; ma qui e altrove, anzi dovunque, *visiting angel*, poco o punto materiale' (*OV* 945). Later, in the interview with Cima, he feels no need to elaborate on the fact that the women of his third book are 'dantesche, dantesche'.[24]

Clizia comes to the fore in the longer poems at the close of *Occasioni* as a figure with increasingly supernatural characteristics, who nevertheless manifests herself within historical reality to defend the poet's ethical and political values. In 'Elegia di Pico Farnese' (1939) her stern clearsightedness sets her apart from the surrounding ignorance and superstition ('Ben altro / è l'Amore'), marking out the figure of the poet as one of the privileged few, one of the ethically and historically elect amidst the mass of a debased humanity: 'distruggi le nere cantafavole e vegli / al trapasso dei pochi tra orde d'uomini-capre' (*OV* 176).[25] In 'Palio' (1939), against a present background of 'tempesta imminente' and amidst the 'ergotante balbuzie dei dannati', she preserves the memory of a lost time of authenticity ('C'era *il* giorno dei viventi'), and fixes her gaze on future renewal.[26] And in 'Nuove stanze' (1939) her 'occhi d'acciaio' enable the *io* to face the urgent threats represented by Fascism ('una tregenda / d'uomini che non sa questo tuo incenso') and the expectation of imminent war ('follìa di morte'). Once more her presence sets him apart from the ignorance of the masses and the savagery of history:

> [...] Ma resiste
> e vince il premio della solitaria
> veglia chi può con te allo specchio ustorio
> che accieca le pedine opporre i tuoi
> occhi d'acciaio. (*OV* 177)

In the course of this final section of *Occasioni*, Clizia has taken over from Arletta as the main *ispiratrice*. There are some elements of continuity between the two figures, especially with the projection of Clizia onto a non-human, supernatural plane, recalling the removal of Arletta into the world of the dead as a necessary condition of her function as a poetic entity. There are important differences in their function, however, as Grignani observes with regard to 'L'orto', in which the two figures are superimposed: Arletta, bound up with the world of childhood and memories, is incapable of projection into the future, whereas Clizia, with her 'etichetta solare-stilnovistica' brings a prophetic message of redemption.[27] Her function is inseparable from the expectation of future salvation.

In *La bufera e altro* the transformation of Clizia continues, with Montale's *stilnovismo* reaching its apogee in the woman's promotion from angel to Christ-bearer. In the opening section, 'Finisterre' (1940–2), her role as 'inconsapevole Cristòfora' (Montale's words to Cambon), means that she is definitively disembodied, removed from the 'quaggiù': 'Tuttavia è già fuori, mentre noi siamo *dentro*. Era *dentro* anche lei' (*OV* 946). At the same time, however, as she becomes a more rarefied, less concrete figure, historical reality looms larger in these poems than ever before, the *io* being still very much 'dentro', trapped in the hell of history, which explodes in the texts as an unmistakably Dantesque 'bufera'. The representation of this reality is intimately linked to that of the figure of Clizia. With the advent of war, the poet's need for salvation, for an 'other' reality, becomes more acute, and her departure in the opening poem into another, unknowable realm ('mi salutasti — per entrar nel buio') is a prerequisite for her subsequent apparitions, which then take on the idealized, rarefied quality of quasi-religious epiphanies. On 'Finisterre', Montale writes, 'Ho proiettato la Selvaggia o la Mandetta o la Delia (la chiami come vuole) dei *Mottetti* sullo sfondo di una guerra cosmica e terrestre, senza scopo e senza ragione, e mi sono affidato a lei, donna o nube, angelo o procellaria' (*SMAMS* 1483). So historical events form an integral part of the background, a necessary point of reference, but they are named only obliquely, as in the apocalyptic title itself, or in the image of the storm, or in such generic expressions as 'il folle mortorio'; circumspect images of chaos and destruction in the highly charged atmosphere of a personal, spiritual and historical crisis.

The myth of Clizia, through which are expressed the poet's hopes for political renewal and subsequently his bitter post-war disillusionment, culminates in what has been called the 'allegorismo cristologico' of 'Silvae', the fifth section of *Bufera*.[28] The longer poems of this section, ranging from 'Iride' and 'L'orto' to 'La primavera hitleriana' and 'L'ombra della magnolia' are some of the most difficult and complex ever written by Montale. The woman achieves her final transformation here as the poet moves from the invocation of a more or less private mystical salvation (with echoes of the *Vita nuova*) to that of a universal salvation to include humanity as a whole, more in keeping with the broader canvas of the *Commedia*. This salvation, obtained through the Christ-like sacrificial gesture of the woman, is an allegory of the political renewal earnestly expected by the poet and ultimately unrealized. In the dream-poem 'Iride', she becomes 'sempre più mitica e sovrumana [...] un po' come la Beatrice degli ultimi canti del Purgatorio'.[29] The ultimate consequence of this transfiguration is that the woman sacrifices her very identity. As the convergence of private mysticism and public history reaches a climax in 'La primavera hitleriana', Clizia's 'cieco sole' (the same, ultimately impotent, image as that of the sunflower in *Ossi*) must annihilate itself, must be transformed like the mythical nymph was, in order to have a function which can transcend that of strictly personal saviour for the privileged *io*:

> [...] Guarda ancora
> in alto, Clizia, è la tua sorte, tu
> che il non mutato amor mutata serbi,
> fino a che il cieco sole che in te porti
> si abbàcini nell'Altro e si distrugga
> in Lui, per tutti. (*OV* 249)

The poem is dated 1939–46, and it is likely that these dates represent a process of writing begun before the war (when the apocalyptic vision of Hitler as 'un messo infernale' clearly could not have been published) and completed, with the addition of the *post-eventum* prophecy of the last part, at the height of Montale's brief, optimistic *impegno* of 1945–6.[30] Thus an indignant historical polemic (including a denunciation of his own guilt by association—'più nessuno è incolpevole') combines here with perhaps the most unequivocally positive figuration of contemporary reality in all of Montale's poetry, the end of the war as a new dawn: 'un'alba che domani per tutti / si riaffacci'. The repetition of 'per tutti' is emphatic and unequivocal: the explicitly collective thrust of this text has rightly been seen by Franco Croce as representing 'un momento eccezionale' in Montale's poetic parabola. The critic also notes the exceptional absence here of the interior/exterior divide so central elsewhere. Also absent consequently is the distinction between masses and élite (including the *io*): all are caught up in the guilt of the exterior scene described. Similarly all must be redeemed, hence the need for a fundamental, 'religious' transformation of the figure of Clizia.[31]

But, as seen in the Introduction above, such heady enthusiasm did not last long. The poetic consequences of political disillusionment are soon felt in the abandonment of Clizia as an active, mythic embodiment of renewal. She functioned in *Bufera* as an absent figure of hope, of future salvation, but she cannot re-descend into reality. She cannot function when the element of expectation, the anticipation of imminent salvation, is no longer meaningful. When Montale's ideological vision of secular liberalism becomes un-sustainable, so does the highly charged symbolism associated with its incarnation in Clizia. In 'L'ombra della magnolia ...' (1947) his disillusionment is clear. She, the embodiment of his ideals and hopes, remains unbending, but 'gli altri arretrano / e piegano', as a wintery chill sets in and he takes his leave of her in the final line: 'Addio' (*OV* 252). The allegory of potential salvation now turns to one of frustration and defeat, as Clizia (both the real woman and the historical aspiration she represents) is clearly unattainable.[32]

Volpe

At the same time as the very possibility of public, political commitment fades for Montale, so the poetic *io* withdraws into the world of 'Madrigali privati' (mostly written in 1949). Here salvation of a sort is still represented by a woman, the earth-bound and earthy figure of 'la Volpe' (inspired by the young Maria Luisa Spaziani, whom the poet met in 1949: see Appendix). This woman, 'una controfigura di Clizia in chiave profana', is described by Montale to Guarnieri in explicitly Dantesque terms: 'Qui appare l'Antibeatrice come nella Vita Nuova; come la donna gentile che poi Dante volle gabellarci come Filosofia mentre si suppone che fosse altro'.[33] It is a moment of great intensity and renewed vitality on a personal level, as reflected in the sensuality and animal symbolism of these poems. Volpe bestows on the *io* the gift of an instinctive, at times rather dark, vitality, through the 'respiro di quel forte / e morbido tuo labbro che riesce, / nominando, a creare' (*OV* 258). But paradoxically, this moment of renewed participation in life, after the rarefied, spiritual adventure that preceded it, coincides with the poet's disillusioned disengagement from political questions. The *io*–Volpe relationship is played out entirely within the confines of concrete, earthly reality, but its focus is inwards: it excludes the other inhabitants of that reality ('con chi dividerò la mia scoperta, / dove seppellirò l'oro che porto [...]?'). Volpe's 'gift' in 'Anniversario' confirms the poet's alienation from contemporary history (the words 'per tutti' must surely be a calculated reference to the repeated formula of 'La primavera hitleriana'):

> [...] il dono che sognavo
> non per me ma per tutti
> appartiene a me solo, Dio diviso
> dagli uomini [...] (OV 264)

With the search for positive values in history frustrated, Montale opts to portray such values as lying within the confines of a private, erotic fulfilment. But this private form of salvation is short-lived, and before long, in 'Conclusioni provvisorie' (1953–4), the poet faces the possible extinction of poetry ('persistenza è solo l'estinzione') and the condition of imprisonment within an all-encompassing historical negativity. The impossibility in this context of any incarnation of positive values results in almost a decade of poetic silence.[34]

Mosca

The death in 1963 of Drusilla Tanzi, Montale's lifelong companion and eventually his wife, seems to have been the trigger for his return to poetic activity with the writing of the first 'Xenia' poems in 1964. Drusilla, whom Montale met in Florence in 1927, was known affectionately (if somewhat strangely) as 'Mosca', and this is the name by which she becomes the principal female presence in the poetry of *Satura* and later (see Appendix). While it is possible to draw a generic analogy between Mosca and Montale's previous female figures, for almost all of whom some form of absence seems a prerequisite for their poetic presence and symbolic transformation, Mosca's function and the values she represents are quite different to those of her predecessors. In the new historical context of the 1960s, there is for Montale no longer any meaningful absolute ideological value, any realistic political aspiration, that might be embodied in the figure of a saviour. Contemporary historical reality is now addressed in many texts without the mediation of a female interlocutor, through the less intense modes of irony and satire, or by direct polemical intervention (see Chapter 2 below). Mosca, unlike Arletta or Clizia, does not function in an allegory of historical salvation. Rather, the depiction of the relationship between her and the *io* concerns his complete alienation from any historical perspective (thus recalling, if anything, the role of Volpe).[35] This relationship, as portrayed in 'Xenia' at the outset of *Satura*, prepares the ground for two of the major thematic strands of that book: the depiction of the *io* directly in relation to the background of external, historical reality, and the quirky, speculative exploration of atemporal reality, the non-physical realm of the *oltrevita*.

Nonetheless, Mosca, like earlier female figures, is closely associated on a thematic level with certain positive values. The first appearance of the ghost in 'Xenia I' 1, revolves around her myopia, a characteristic of the real woman ('non avevi occhiali / non potevi vedermi'); but paradoxically one of her prime attributes as the series unfolds is a superior kind of clear-sightedness, an ability to perceive private and public contradictions and unmask hypocrisy. This is first introduced in XI 5:[36]

> Non ho mai capito se io fossi
> il tuo cane fedele e incimurrito
> o tu lo fossi per me.
> Per gli altri no, eri un insetto miope
> smarrito nel blabla
> dell'alta società. Erano ingenui
> quei furbi e non sapevano
> di essere loro il tuo zimbello:
> di esser visti anche al buio e smascherati
> da un tuo senso infallibile, dal tuo
> radar di pipistrello. (*OV* 285)

Mosca's apparent vulnerability ('insetto miope / smarrito') in the world at large (whose inauthenticity is immediately connoted by the comic 'blabla') is soon overturned in a text densely packed with antitheses and inversions. So the 'furbi' become 'ingenui', whose principal characteristic is their ignorance: 'non sapevano [...]'. Mosca, by contrast, is endowed with a superior ('infallibile') form of vision: despite darkness and myopia, she has the key ability to unmask others using a mysterious sixth sense. So a clear opposition is set up between Mosca and 'gli altri': the opposition between insight and ignorance, between truth and hypocrisy.

There are, however, further oppositions in this poem, springing from the presence of the *io* in the opening lines. On the one hand, the *io*, in his perplexity and uncertainty, is contrasted with 'gli altri' of line 4 with their false certainty: his privileged relationship with Mosca allows him to see beyond her exterior appearance, just as she sees what lies beneath the exterior of bourgeois social 'blabla'. But within the private area of their relationship, ambiguities remain: it is unclear who is the truly privileged one, who leads and who follows, in a relationship apparently fraught with tensions. Even the image of the dog (regardless of whom it is applied to) is ambiguous, both 'fedele e incimurrito'. But for all the uncertainty of their roles, a clear demarcation is set down between the couple, on the one hand, in their compact closeness (note the rapid chiastic succession in lines 1–3 of personal pronouns and possessive: *io–tuo–tu–me*[37]), and 'gli altri' on the other. This will be developed in other poems as the two figures become even more closely identified with each other in the face of external reality.

Mosca's clairvoyance is merciless and judgemental as she unmasks inauthenticity whether on a large or a small scale. Her 'parola' is paradoxically both 'stenta e imprudente' (XI 8). More than once her 'imprudently' frank judgement is associated with her laughter, as in XI, 11:

> Ricordare il tuo pianto (il mio era doppio)
> non vale a spenger lo scoppio delle tue risate.
> Erano come l'anticipo di un tuo privato
> Giudizio Universale, mai accaduto purtroppo. (*OV* 291)

Again, the memory of Mosca does not have unequivocally positive associations: her laughter is inseparable from her 'pianto' (this motif will return in XII 10 in the everyday oxymoron of 'piangere / dal ridere', where her laughter is directed at the *io*). An oxymoronic tension also spans the enjambement of lines 3–4, 'privato / Giudizio Universale', underlining the paradoxical nature of the values embodied in Mosca, whose lessons, though concerned with universal questions, remain a privileged secret to all but the *io*. And again, here, the two figures are closely linked in the possessives ('tuo [...] mio') of line 1.

At the close of 'Xenia I', her curious wisdom is contrasted with the facile assertions of conventional, public discourse in the anaphoric sequence of XI 14:

> Dicono che [...]
> [...]
> Dicono che [...]
> [...]
> negano che [...]
> [...]

Tu sola sapevi che il moto
non è diverso dalla stasi,
che il vuoto è il pieno e il sereno
è la più diffusa delle nubi. (*OV* 294)

So her privilege is spelled out in terms of knowledge of the equivalence of opposites. But the *io* has some access to this insight. So he understands the paradox of her life as a 'lungo viaggio / imprigionata tra le bende', until ultimately an explicit identity between the two figures is established: 'Eppure non mi dà riposo / sapere che in uno o in due noi siamo una sola cosa'. In this typically paradoxical lesson of Mosca, the use of the verb 'sapere' is highly significant. Given the 'Tu sola sapevi' earlier in the poem, it indicates the achievement by the *io* of a form of fusion with Mosca's knowledge. (This is subsequently confirmed in *Diario*: 'ora so / che [...] stasi o moto / in nulla differiscono'; *OV* 461.[38]) 'Sapere' has been a privileged Montalean word in the past, notably in 'Visita a Fadin' (in *Bufera*), another piece dealing with knowledge of the imponderable: 'Essere sempre tra i primi e *sapere*, ecco ciò che conta, anche se il perché della rappresentazione ci sfugge.' It was, and is here, a knowledge that transcends the merely rational dispensation of 'gli altri', leading the *io* into the realm of *l'Altro*.[39]

There is another side to Mosca's sharp insights, and this concerns the figure of the poet himself. As seen in the opening of XI 5, tensions persist within the private zone inhabited by the two central characters. Through these tensions, Mosca can act as a counterbalance to the pomposity or self-righteousness that from time to time threaten to characterize the *io*, here and elsewhere in *Satura*. Thus, for example, in XII 7 she deflates his philosophical ponderings:

'Non sono mai stato certo di essere al mondo'.
'Bella scoperta, m'hai risposto, e io?'.
[...] (*OV* 303)

Nevertheless, the sense of domestic intimacy in such an exchange, the gentle irony of her mockery, serve also to underline the closeness of the two figures. A further instance of Mosca's corrective role with regard to the *io* and (in this case) his attachment to his art, occurs in XI 6:

Non hai pensato mai di lasciar traccia
di te scrivendo prosa o versi. E fu
il tuo incanto — e dopo la mia nausea di me.

> Fu pure il mio terrore: di esser poi
> ricacciato da te nel gracidante
> limo dei neòteroi. (*OV* 286)

Just as she later encapsulates 'dolcezza e orrore in una sola musica' (XII 4), here 'il tuo incanto' is also 'il mio terrore', yet another antithetical pair reflecting the contradictions and tensions at work within and between the two figures of *io* and *tu*. The antithesis hinges around a central formula of reflexive self-deprecation, 'la mia nausea di me'. So the 'incanto-terrore' is placed in a highly interiorized sphere, where Mosca becomes a sort of *alter ego*: her potential contempt for the *io* a dramatic figuration of his self-doubt. The serene integrity of her silence is as opposed to the verbiage of poetic fashion as it is to the 'blabla' of high society.[40]

The memory of a visit to Lisbon (described extensively in a journalistic piece, now in *PR* 1060–5) provides another example of Mosca's iconoclastic function with regard to the figure of the *io* as poet, seen this time in a highly public role in XII 10:

> [...]
> La sera fui paragonato ai massimi
> lusitani dai nomi impronunciabili
> e al Carducci in aggiunta.
> Per nulla impressionata io ti vedevo piangere
> dal ridere nascosta in una folla
> forse annoiata ma compunta. (*OV* 306)

The last three lines, with *io* and *tu* surrounded by the 'folla', contain in microcosm the three-way system of relationships present throughout the series. Her mirth (tainted by the emphatically positioned 'piangere') is directed both at the somewhat ridiculous adulation and at him, its object. But though she is apparently lost in the midst of an indifferent and ultimately insincere ('annoiata ma compunta') social setting, she is linked to him by the personal (and in the context of Mosca, emblematic) bond of sight—'io ti vedevo'—which overcomes the banal, comical hypocrisy of their surroundings. On the whole, then, there is a clear division between, on the one hand, the *io* and Mosca, and on the other, external reality, the world and logic of 'gli altri'. Perhaps the most radical expression of this separation occurs in XII 13, where, with reference to those who would claim to know their 'pedigree' (their private, intimate history?), he declares: 'non erano essi stessi esistenti, / né noi per loro' (*OV* 309).

All of this occurs in the context (established with 'Botta e risposta I' at the opening of *Satura*, and fully elaborated in the subsequent sections) of the depiction of public life, historical and political reality, as an ethical wilderness: the grotesque, faecal 'nuova palta' of post-war hypocrisy, on which the *io* is cast adrift, surrounded by the 'formiconi degli approdi'. In this light, one of the functions of 'Xenia' is to set up what one may call a zone of authenticity within *Satura*, a zone in which the poet can save his personal and ideological values from the deluge. The corollary of this, however, is that these positive values now reside exclusively within this zone, and are definitively absent from the outer zone of contemporary reality. This inner zone includes the figure of Mosca, indeed is to a large extent presided over by her. Thus we can outline a new variant on the spatial division of interior and exterior zones ('IN' and 'ES', as posited by Marchese; see Introduction). In *Occasioni* and *Bufera*, the archetypal situation was of the *io* in his interior space besieged by a hostile external reality. Clizia moved between these two zones, whether appearing as a redemptive presence in the interior of 'Nuove stanze', or as the visiting angel of *Bufera*, where she came from a transcendent outer zone, beyond the immediate, negative exterior of historical reality. In any case, she brought to the enclosed inner space of the *io* a salvation that interacted with, sought to touch, and expected or aspired to alleviate, over time, the negativity of the surrounding external zone.

Now, in *Satura*, no further interaction is possible between the poet's inner zone and the immediately surrounding external reality. While these zones are still in part characterized spatially, as established through the domestic settings of 'Xenia' and other later texts (see Chapter 3 below), they exist principally on the level of personal, cultural and ideological values. The *tu*, in the form of Mosca, no longer brings salvation in from without by way of miraculous epiphanies. Rather, she is first and foremost the companion, as Lonardi writes, the 'con-sorte', a presence, albeit ghostly and intermittent, within the inner zone of the *io*.[41] Meanwhile, she also inhabits an 'other' outer zone, the atemporal 'oltrevita', but she never functions as an agent of interaction between the *io* and the vast area of inauthenticity that immediately surrounds him, the zone of 'gli altri', of 'la realtà [...] che si vede' (XII 5). The only communication she facilitates is an increasingly important upward, atemporal movement, from the shared zone of authenticity to the putative (but problematic) non-physical realm of *l'Altro*.

If there is a historical or ideological dimension to the figure of Mosca and the paradoxical thematic values associated with her, it lies in this system of relationships between her, the *io*, and external reality. In the last poem of 'Xenia II', the poet broadens the perspective to contemplate directly that external reality, represented in the image of the Florentine flood of 1966, which has submerged the relics of a vanished pre-war cultural universe (Pound, Valéry, Alain, ...) under an 'atroce morsura / di nafta e sterco'. In the context of the collection as a whole, this piece can be seen to prepare the way for the direct, unmediated consideration of this distasteful tide of reality in the following sections.[42] It also clarifies the system of relationships we have just referred to:

> [...]
> Non torba m'ha assediato, ma gli eventi
> di una realtà incredibile e mai creduta.
> Di fronte ad essi il mio coraggio fu il primo
> dei tuoi prestiti e forse non l'hai saputo. (*OV* 310)

The *io* is besieged by a hostile external world, trapped in his own inner zone, from where, however, he can bring to bear the benefit of Mosca's insight (in this case, knowledge of the ultimate insignificance of the besieging forces). Mosca is, however, powerless in the face of the catastrophe. Unlike Clizia in the 1930s, she does not embody, and cannot save, the cultural and ethical values represented by the artefacts listed. She is not a priestess of the religion of poetry and culture. Nevertheless, although the *io* is unable to act on his surroundings, to break the siege, the presence of Mosca alongside him provides him with a possible paradoxical *modus vivendi*: armed with her 'coraggio', he can now acknowledge, clear-sightedly and without illusions, the reality of the 'alluvione' that surrounds him, while never flinching from the need to condemn the negative, unacceptable nature of that reality. It is, writes Luperini, a survival strategy, a stance underlying Montale's resumption and continuation of poetic production: 'il coraggio [...] di sopravvivere nell'adeguamento e persino grazie all'adeguamento, riservandosi, come unico riscatto, lo smascheramento, la risata, dissacratrice e demistificante'.[43]

Changing Narrative Perspectives: from Clizia's Epiphanies to Mosca's Visits

One of the most important differences between the early volumes, from *Ossi* to *Bufera*, and the later collections in which the figure of Mosca comes to the fore, is the presence of overall narrative or quasi-narrative structures in the first three books and their almost complete absence thereafter.[44] This is evident in the structure of the individual collections. In *Ossi*, the poems are arranged in distinct sections, whose succession, while broadly reflecting the composition dates of single texts, also suggests a succession and development of thematic concerns, especially in the definitive 1928 edition, where the addition of important longer texts to the penultimate section reinforces the inter-personal, human dimension, representing a move away from that of the lyrical voice isolated in the landscape. This kind of diachronically conditioned structure is even more in evidence in *Occasioni*, where historical events are increasingly important as the background to the passage from the crepuscular cycle of Arletta to that of Clizia. In section IV of *Occasioni* the full chronological range of the volume is brought together in the progression from the time of 'Stanze' to that of 'Nuove stanze', reflecting a clear personal and historical development, expressed through the figures of women in relation to the *io*. There emerges in these books a dynamic system of oppositions (principally between *io* and *tu*), behind which Lonardi notes the presence of 'grandi coppie mitologiche' (e.g. Orpheus and Euridice, Daphne and Apollo), figures which support 'una linea di romanzo d'esperienza e d'amore a fine non lieto'.[45]

It is in *Bufera* that the narrative tendency becomes most pronounced. The structure of the collection again follows in its broad lines the chronological order of composition, but the arrangement of individual poems deviates significantly from this at various points, especially in later sections. The sequence of sections IV–VI, 'Flashes e dediche' (1948–54), 'Silvae' (1944–50) and 'Madrigali privati' (mostly 1949–50) clearly reflects the poet's desire to set up a dynamic opposition between the figures of Volpe and Clizia, culminating in the defeat of the latter, independently of the composition dates of some of the poems involved (hence the originally intended title, 'Romanzo', as revealed by the poet to Giovanni Macchia in 1949).[46] There is an ideal narrative order in the collection as a whole, leading from the initial absence of Clizia and her intermittent epiphanies in

'Finisterre', through the interferences of the figure of Volpe and the climactic returns of the 'Cristofora', to the final collapse of the myth of the saviour and the personal and historical retrenchment of the final poems. Indeed, within 'Silvae', some poems seem to have been positioned specifically to create the sense of a 'parabola', running from the abstract heights of 'Iride' to the 'guizzante immagine terragna dell'anguilla'.[47] As in the *Vita nuova* (a precedent directly invoked by the poet, as already seen), there is a carefully constructed narrative, a tale of development and crisis recounted through figures and symbols.

This narrative arc is inextricably bound up with the presence of female figures: it is principally through their development, interaction and changing relationships to the *io* that the sense of an overall progression is expressed. And, conversely, the female figures themselves acquire meaning and function principally as part of a narrative sequence. The figure of Clizia in particular, so often invoked in her absence and anxiously awaited, must be seen in the context of an outlook of tense expectation, of hopes and fears projected into the future, a tension inseparable from the historical circumstances of the late 1930s and early '40s. As this 'tensione dell'*attesa*' (as Luperini puts it) evaporates along with the poet's illusions after the war, so does the functionality of the novelistic, diachronic structure and the central role therein of the female figure.[48] The model of the 'romanzo' has run its course with the publication of *Bufera* in 1956, and when Montale comes back to writing verse in the mid-1960s he inevitably adopts new models, with far-reaching implications for the possible functions and attributes of the female interlocutor.

Maria Corti, writing on *Satura* in 1971 (the year of its publication) is quick to point out the clear 'distacco' between this collection and its three predecessors. While, on the one hand, she notes a substantial continuity of underlying ideological outlook, she also observes that this is now expressed through new literary structures, most notably that of 'diario poetico' (Corti was writing before Montale's use of the term 'diario' as a title).[49] This 'diaristic' character of *Satura* is contrasted with the narrative inclinations of the previous books: thus instead of situations and objects being linked by any 'catena di causalità o legge spazio-temporale', they are 'apparizioni istantanee di cose isolate e di attimi privilegiati', linked by the poetic structure itself, by their own organization within the book, not by any temporal or chronological order of events:

per cui si ha sì processo di sviluppo, ma solo tematico e simbolico, assolutamente cioè legato alla storia interiore del poeta all'atto in cui costruisce l'opera. Perciò si parla di 'diario poetico' [...]: si verifica cioè un passaggio dai contesti del passato evocato al contesto del presente, ovvero della poesia, della pagina scritta[50]

This move away from the representation of a temporal continuum within a historical context demands a new way of reading Montale's poetry. There is no overall narrative thrust, no search for conclusions, however provisional. Rather, the book builds into a composite portrait of a static psychological and ideological situation in which the possibility of progress is absent. This introduces a new level of difficulty for the reader: as Luperini observes, 'la lettera dei singoli testi è perlopiù sufficientemente esplicita, ma il loro messaggio conclusivo non per questo risulta chiaro (mentre nei primi tre libri succedeva esattamente il contrario)'.[51] *Satura* does not yield entirely to the mere recording of events or emotions in succession, as would a true diary. This further stage of structural levelling will be approached in the subsequent *Diario* and *Quaderno*, as indicated by the titles themselves.[52] In *Satura*, there is still a kind of structure, an organization of the texts into sections, and, especially in the two 'Xenia' sections, still a residue of symbolic meanings, though in a minor key, as befits the portrayal of Mosca. But the sense of an overall narrative movement is now absent, as positive or unequivocal formulations of meaning, even projected into a hypothetical future, are no longer possible.

In order to illustrate these changing narrative perspectives, it is interesting to compare some aspects of Clizia's epiphanies in 'Finisterre' with the later depiction of Mosca's 'silent visits', focusing in particular on the presence (or otherwise) of the element of *attesa* and how this functions in relation to narrative structures, whether on a large or small scale. The tension of *attesa* seen in the later poems of *Occasioni* took the form of foreboding, awareness of impending disaster, the looming 'nembo alle tue porte' of 'Nuove stanze'. It was also an awareness that the definitive transformation of Clizia was inevitable, that her departure for another realm was imminent, as seen in 'Palio': 'Il presente s'allontana / ed il traguardo è là [...] / [...] oltre lo sguardo / dell'uomo — e tu lo fissi' (*OV* 178). It was an expectation surrounded in ambivalence, as the future outcome included both a desired 'traguardo' and an inevitable separation. When the gathering storm finally breaks in the opening poem of *Bufera*, a turning point is reached in the nature of the *attesa*: Clizia as a human presence takes her leave and from this point on, removed from the space and time of the *io*, she herself becomes the object of hope, of the long desperate wait. The poetic *io* awaits her angelic visits as intimations of a possible future salvation.

The temporal dimension is central to the narrative character of this 'romanzo' of Clizia, and in the first section, 'Finisterre', dominated by the darkness of her absence, the texts are permeated with indicators of an openness to, and expectation of, future development. As the *io* addresses the absent *tu*, a resolution of his intolerable situation is repeatedly sought through the establishment of some form of communication with her:

> [...] la sera si fa lunga,
> la preghiera è supplizio e non ancora
> tra le rocce che sorgono t'è giunta
> la bottiglia dal mare. L'onda, vuota,
> si rompe sulla punta, a Finisterre.
> ('Su una lettera non scritta', *OV* 191)

Potential contact is projected into the future: in this case the key word is 'ancora': the barrier separating them is on one level physical (although of course the image of the sea in Montale always includes the sense of a metaphysical barrier), but also temporal. The scenario of 'La casa dei doganieri' is rewritten here, as contact with the *tu* is an anxiously awaited future possibility rather than a receding, irretrievable memory.

The sense of potential future change is reflected in the repeated use of images of dawn in association with the figure of Clizia in these poems, whose setting is predominantly the darkness of night, for example: 'Per un formicolìo d'albe' ('Su una lettera non scritta'); 'la tua fronte / si confonde con l'alba, la nasconde' ('La frangia dei capelli'); 'e già l'alba l'inostra / con un sussulto e rompe quelle brume' ('Il ventaglio'); 'o perigliosa / annunziatrice dell'alba' ('Giorno e notte'). These dawns, tokens of a desperate hope in the early 1940s, are all subsumed later in the great dawn at the close of 'La primavera hitleriana'. But for the time being, in 1940–3, 'Ben altro è sulla terra'. The dawn remains strictly a possibility while the poet is 'Nel sonno': '— tutto questo / *può* ritornarmi, [...] / [...] farmi desto / alla tua voce' (italics mine).

Varying degrees of uncertainty surround the attempts to re-establish contact in 'Finisterre'. Attempts in which the *tu* takes a more active role seem more likely to succeed, as in 'Gli orecchini', with its unequivocal future tense: 'La tua impronta / verrà di giù' (*OV* 194). However, the establishment of contact may be a problematic matter even for the powerful 'hand' of Clizia (recognizable here by the *senhal* of her gems):

> [...]
> come potrà la mano delle sete
> e delle gemme ritrovar tra i morti
> il suo fedele?
> ('Il tuo volo', *OV* 202)

Although the attitude of the *io* varies between optimism and pessimism regarding her eventual return, the texts are pervaded by the possibility of temporal, narrative development, as seen in the repeated use of future constructions and the powerful image of the dawn.

A typical epiphany of Clizia occurs in 'La frangia dei capelli' (one of a number of 'pseudosonetti' in 'Finisterre'[53]). Here, the realistic evocation of her distinctive physical traits is heavily overlaid with symbolic associations:

> La frangia dei capelli che ti vela
> la fronte puerile, tu distrarla
> con la mano non devi. Anch'essa parla
> di te, sulla mia strada è tutto il cielo,
> la sola luce con le giade ch'ài
> accerchiate sul polso, nel tumulto
> del sonno la cortina che gl'indulti
> tuoi distendono, l'ala onde tu vai,
> trasmigratrice Artemide ed illesa,
> tra le guerre dei nati-morti; e s'ora
> d'aeree lanugini s'infiora
> quel fondo, a marezzarlo sei tu, scesa
> d'un balzo, e irrequieta la tua fronte
> si confonde con l'alba, la nasconde. (*OV* 195)

The woman's initial presence is reduced to the essence of a gesture (the fringe and 'fronte' are the instantly recognizable signs of Clizia— see for example 'Voce giunta con le folaghe'). The simple realism of the metonymy is overwhelmed, however, by the dense series of associations ('metafore sublimanti')[54] which follows. Thus the fringe is disembodied and transformed into 'cielo', 'luce' and 'cortina', before finally becoming the all-important 'ala', one of the primary characteristics of Clizia as visiting angel.[55] We may note the addition of the attribute of crystalline hardness (another of her signs) in the form of her 'giade'. The entire cluster of symbols is then inserted into a complex setting made up of the poet's 'strada' (his existence within temporal reality), and 'il tumulto del sonno', against a background of apocalyptic disorder in the 'guerre dei nati-morti'. The distance separating the *io* and the *tu* is emphasized by her metamorphosis into the mythological Artemis, untouched by the historical convulsions in which he is immersed. The closing lines complete the process of disembodiment of the woman: her putative epiphany involves ethereal colour and light, even as her one remaining physical manifestation, her 'fronte', merges with the incorporeal image of the dawn. Her contact with the *io* is not direct, but only occurs implicitly as part of her beneficial action on the 'fondo' of surrounding, external reality. She comes to the *io* through the chaos of the negative zone of historical reality, remaining untainted by it, but nevertheless touching it with her redemptive luminosity.

This text does not narrate any event, realistic or fantastic. Clizia's gesture of the opening lines is the basis for an evocation of her persona, with its increasingly messianic implications, but even that minimal physical gesture is merely evoked by means of an admonition, not described as a reality. The only unqualified affirmations ('Anch'essa parla / di te, sulla mia strada è tutto il cielo') concern the ongoing meaning for the *io* of the 'frangia'. The final epiphany ('la tua fronte / si confonde con l'alba') is provisional, dependent on the hypothetical clause 's'ora d'aeree lanugini s'infiora'. There is no narration of past events, and only the image of dawn suggests potential future development. There is rather, within a complex series of syntactical subordinations (and subject to the strict constraints of the sonnet form), an aggregation of emblematic images—light, hardness, flight, descent from on high—which build into an iconic representation of the angel-woman. This in turn functions as a single, richly painted moment in the macro-narrative of the collection as a whole, a moment of anxious expectation, as the *io*, surrounded by the intolerable reality of the 'nati-morti', awaits a sign of salvation (the salvation that will eventually come tantalizingly close in the climactic texts of 'Silvae').

In 'Xenia' the scenario of visitation of the *io* by an absent female figure is broadly analogous to that of 'Finisterre', but the meaning and formal treatment of such situations are radically different, and indeed the differences can be seen to a large extent as paradigmatic of the thematic and formal innovations of *Satura* as a whole. Here, each text is indeed, as Corti notes, a 'frammento di un solo, lungo discorso'. But the discourse in question is diaristic rather than narrative. The presence of narrative structures is thus displaced from the level of the collection as a whole, to that of individual texts: 'ne nascono brevi sequenze quasi narrative, dove la moglie morta [...] si fa personaggio'.[56] In the first poem, the fantastic event of her apparition is described with the utmost simplicity:

> Caro piccolo insetto
> che chiamavano mosca non so perché,
> stasera quasi al buio
> mentre leggevo il Deuteroisaia,
> sei ricomparsa accanto a me,
> ma non avevi occhiali,
> non potevi vedermi
> né potevo io senza quel luccichìo
> riconoscere te nella foschia. (*OV* 281)

This is poetry far removed from the intense concentration and elaborate prosody of 'Finisterre'. The syntax is direct, without complex inversions or subordinations and the use of rhyme is sparing (confined to the single final rhyme *perché : me* and other imperfect or surreptitious examples such as *io : luccichìo : foschia*). This is Montale's 'poesia che apparentemente tende alla prosa e nello stesso tempo la rifiuta', the understated, half-spoken mode characteristic of this and later collections.[57] The main clause, lying at the centre of the poem, narrates the miraculous apparition in a matter-of-fact way, without recourse to complex, 'difficult' imagery and without the creation of an atmosphere of expectation or anticipation: 'Sei ricomparsa accanto a me'. The woman is not associated with images of flight (except ironically as 'mosca' and 'insetto') but with her glasses, the realistic, tangible sign of her disability, her limitations (but we have seen already that in 'Xenia' such physical limitations are easily overturned). In short, though the situation evoked (darkness, solitude) is in direct parallel with that of the earlier text, the woman's apparition here is 'non sublimante'.[58] The light associated with Clizia is now reduced to a diminutive 'luccichìo', which occurs only as a reflection of Mosca's glasses (and is, in any case, actually absent here). The prosaic, colloquial diction is interrupted only by the jump in register represented by the unexpected, precise erudition of 'Deuteroisaia', creating a rather surprising partial assonance with 'buio': an indication of Montale's stated intention to carefully 'refuse' mere prose, his constant tendency in *Satura* to catch the reader off guard.

Thematically, the poems of 'Xenia' can be divided broadly into two types. First are those that focus on the solitary figure of the *io* as he seeks and sometimes finds signs of the woman's reappearances (as in the text just seen) or of her continuing presence in unexpectedly meaningful objects and situations ('il desiderio di riaverti, fosse / pure in un solo gesto o un'abitudine'). This type tends to predominate in 'Xenia I', with a sort of resigned equilibrium being achieved in XI 8: 'Mi abituerò a sentirti o a decifrarti / nel ticchettìo della telescrivente'. The second type is more prevalent in 'Xenia II' (written entirely after the initial publication of XI, and to some extent modelled on it thematically and structurally[59]) where, this tenuous form of contact having been established, there are more pieces in which the poet recounts remembered, shared experiences, episodes from the past in which Mosca remains alive in memory. Here, straightforward narrative modes become more frequent, as for example in XII 3, where the loss of a shoehorn in Venice is recounted (an instance of the couple's shared attachment to totemic objects). In XII 4 there is an unusually obscure account of another remembered event, which can be clarified by reference to the variants (*OV* 984–5). Mosca, on emerging from an episode of 'delirio febbrile', has the curious presence of mind to make a pun on the name of her doctor (Mangàno), transposing it into *manganello* (a type of club used by Fascists):[60]

> Con astuzia,
> uscendo dalle fauci di Mongibello
> o da dentiere di ghiaccio
> rivelavi incredibili agnizioni.
>
> Se ne avvide Mangàno, il buon cerusico,
> quando, disoccultato, fu il randello
> delle camicie nere e ne sorrise.
>
> Così eri: anche sul ciglio del crepaccio
> dolcezza e orrore in una sola musica. (*OV* 300)

It is an instance of Mosca's astringent black humour, her ability to conjure 'incredibili agnizioni' out of moments of horror and crisis. Behind the uncharacteristic obscurity of the allusions, however, lies a syntactically direct miniature narrative. A pithy but complete instance of Mosca's unpredictable behaviour is recounted, framed by general memorial considerations. Thus the first four lines describe the background of the narrative event, and the last two act as a résumé and conclusion (bringing the structure to a close on the distant, understated assonance between 'astuzia' and 'musica'). At the centre, however, is a complete (albeit condensed) narrative in the past historic tense. Further micro-narratives (in which at times the *io* and Mosca are joined by other quirky characters) occur in the episode of the 'vinattiere' in XII 6 and 8 (originally one piece), the visit to Lisbon recalled in XII 10, or the contacts with 'il dottor Cap' and 'Celia' (XII 2 and 11).

The broad division of the texts into two types across the two series (a division that is by no means rigorous or airtight) does not, however, imply a significant sense of development over time. Nor does the increased presence of miniature narratives in XII imply the creation of a narrative movement in the second series as a whole. Rather the episodes tend to be self-contained, self-resolving. They are linked by the recurrence of thematic nuclei, in much the same way as individual texts are linked throughout *Satura*, forming a web of references and correspondences between motifs (for example, that of vision, impaired or enhanced, that of the 'viaggio' linked to hotels and exotic locations, or that of communication and its difficulties, by speech, telephone, 'telescrivente', etc.). These motifs combine in a non-linear structure, as do the episodes in which they are contained. As Grignani observes, the increased presence of 'narratività' does not give rise to 'realismo diaristico'; rather the poems form a 'costellazione di micro-strutture'.[61] Together they build into a quasi-dramatic portrait, a *tableau vivant* of the *io* in his relationship to Mosca, and their shared and definitive detachment from the world of 'gli altri'. It is, however, a non-dynamic, non-narrative situation, in which no possible future development can become the object of *attesa*.

'Xenia' constitutes the only major thematically defined structural division within *Satura*.[62] The figure of Mosca is not widely present in the two following 'Satura' sections, and does not have a significant role in the more public or directly polemical poems they contain, but rather functions there primarily in relation to the *io*, who is, along with her, besieged by historical and social reality. Thus, the arrangement of the 'Xenia' poems in a compact series, clearly demarcated from other texts dealing with broader historical issues, is a fitting structural figuration of the dichotomy between the inner zone of the *io* (and Mosca) and the surrounding flood-tide of contemporary life. This represents a radical change from the system of *La bufera*, where the woman functioned as the allegorical embodiment of historical aspirations, and where contemporary reality was present in the texts almost exclusively as filtered through the mechanism of the idealized love-story.

Satura as a whole, though it includes a comprehensive consideration of fundamental questions of history and time, does not constitute a journey in time but rather an atemporal overview of the poet's static intellectual and spiritual landscape, a space whose boundaries are mapped by the titles of the opening and closing poems, 'Il *tu*' and 'L'Altro' (to the exclusion of 'gli altri' and historical reality). Clearly these two titles assume special significance by virtue of their positioning, and taken together they suggest some sort of overall movement in the collection on a thematic level. Corti interprets this as follows: 'L'opera inizia con la lirica *Il "tu"* e termina con *L'Altro*, i due assenti protagonisti che aprono la via verso l'Ignoto.'[63] This interpretation seems open to correction, however: *l'Altro*, as an absent protagonist (some kind of *Deus absconditus*), surely represents nothing less than the 'Ignoto' itself. It is rather the *tu*, Mosca, who opens up for the *io*, from within the private zone of 'Xenia', the pathway towards this unknown Other. This potential movement away from the axis of historical time allows the poet the possibility of a detached perspective while still imprisoned in the 'viaggio' (in which, of course, any movement or progress is illusory):

> [...]
> Il mio [viaggio] dura tuttora, né più mi occorrono
> le coincidenze, le prenotazioni,
> le trappole, gli scorni di chi crede
> che la realtà sia quella che si vede. (XII 5)

Thus, *Satura* contains no narrative potential in the area of historical reality, from which the poet is irreversibly alienated. Movement towards the realm of 'l'Altro' is atemporal, and is associated with insights acquired through the figure of Mosca, who is outside of time and knows time's meaninglessness ('che il moto non è diverso dalla stasi'), and who cannot inspire the tension of *attesa*. Mosca's presence, whether in memory in the narration of self-contained episodes, or in the continuing manifestations of the ghost, neither allows nor requires further progress in time. This stasis is the poetic correlative of Montale's reluctant resignation to the permanence of historical negativity, a disillusioned realization that no historical progress can take place. It is a resignation translated, elsewhere in *Satura* and beyond, into the impotent and at times bitter genres of parody and satire.

Notes to Chapter 1

1. Luciano Rebay, 'Sull' "autobiografismo" di Montale', *Innovazioni tematiche espressive e linguistiche della letteratura italiana del novecento: atti dell'VIII Congresso dell'AISLLI, New York, 25–28 Aprile 1973* (Florence: Olschki, 1976), 73–83. See also Ettore Bonora, 'Anelli del ciclo di Arletta nelle Occasioni', *Le metafore del vero* (Rome: Bonacci, 1981), 9–38; Rosanna Bettarini, 'Appunti sul "Taccuino" del 1926 di Eugenio Montale', *Studi di filologia italiana* 36 (1978), 457–512.

2. Annalisa Cima, 'Le reazioni di Montale', *Eugenio Montale: profilo di un autore*, ed. A. Cima and C. Segre (Milan: Rizzoli, 1977), 192–201 at 195.

3. See Maria Antonietta Grignani, 'Occasioni diacroniche nella poesia', *Prologhi ed epiloghi sulla poesia di Eugenio Montale* (Ravenna: Longo, 1987), 49–70.

4. Angelo Jacomuzzi, 'Incontro: per una costante della poesia montaliana', *La poesia di Eugenio Montale: atti del Convegno ... settembre 1982*, 149–60 at 151.

5. Ibid., 156–7.

6. See Glauco Cambon, 'La lotta con Proteo', *Montale e l'Altro* (Milan: Bompiani, 1963), 115–37 at 118.

7. Arshi Pipa, *Montale and Dante* (Minneapolis: University of Minnesota Press, 1968), 16–42 at 41.

8. Cataldi, *Montale*, 30–1.

9. Luperini, *Storia di Montale*, 62–4.

10. The word 'senhal', meaning the 'cover-name' for the beloved in troubadour poetry, is used mistakenly by Montale to indicate a symbol or emblem of the woman. See 'Due sciacalli al guinzaglio', *SMAMS* 1489–93.

11. Rebay, 'Sull' "autobiografismo"', 76.

12. Guido Gozzano, *Tutte le poesie*, ed. Andrea Rocca (Milan: Mondadori, 1980), 175. For the publication dates of 'Le farfalle', see 371–4. See also Pipa, *Montale and Dante*, 46; Becker, *Eugenio Montale*, 57.

13. Rebay ('Sull' "autobiografismo"', 76) writes that Montale called Arletta 'una donna "crepuscolare", una donna segnata dalla morte'.

14. Becker, *Eugenio Montale*, 45.

15. See ibid., 75.

16. On the possible presence of Clizia in this poem, see Rebay, 'Sull' "autobiografismo"', 82; idem, 'Montale, Clizia e l'America', *La poesia di Eugenio Montale: atti del Convegno ... settembre 1982*, 218–308 at 295–8. Bonora (*Le metafore del vero*, 19), however, disputes this, dating the first appearance of Clizia to 1937.

17. Ibid., 20–1.

18. Elio Gioanola, 'La donna nella vita e nella poesia di Montale', *Studium* 86 (1990), 281–96 at 281–2.

19. Luperini, *Storia di Montale*, 73. Montale's declaration, quoted here by Luperini, occurs in the interview with Cima, 'Le reazioni di Montale', 194. See also Forti, *Eugenio Montale*, 144.
20. See Ettore Bonora, *Montale e altro Novecento* (Caltanisetta (Rome): Sciascia, 1989), 8.
21. On this 'fede', see the poet's comments in *OV* 902, and in Lorenzo Greco, *Montale commenta Montale*, 2nd edn. (Parma: Pratiche, 1990), 41.
22. For further details on Liuba, see Appendix. The apparatus of both of the major editions fails to clarify when exactly the note was added. *OV* (899) does not mention that it was ever absent, while *TP* (1087) makes it clear that it did not appear in the first edition.
    On this text, see also D'Arco Silvio Avalle's structural analysis in *Tre saggi su Montale*, 3rd edn. (Turin: Einaudi, 1972), 93–9.
23. On spatial relationships in 'Mottetti', see Marchese, *Visiting angel*, 111–19.
24. Cima, 'Le reazioni di Montale', 194.
25. For a detailed ideological reading, see Carpi, 'Analisi dell' "Elegia di Pico Farnese"', *Il poeta e la politica* (Naples: Liguori, 1978), 311–55.
26. On 'ergotante' ('cavilloso') see Isella's annotated edition of *Le occasioni* (Torino: Einaudi, 1996), 220. See also Andrea Zanzotto, 'La freccia dei diari', *La poesia di Eugenio Montale: atti del Convegno ... settembre 1982*, 52. Bonora ('Proposte per "Palio"', *Le metafore del vero*, 66–93 at 87) reads 'il giorno dei viventi' as a reference to 'l'Italia postrisorgimentale [...] l'età d'oro della democrazia liberale', as encapsulated in Croce's *Storia d'Italia dal 1871 al 1915*, a book whose historical analysis held great sway among intellectuals of Montale's generation.
27. Grignani, *Prologhi ed epiloghi*, 68. See also Gioanola, 'La donna ', 292.
28. Arshi Pipa, 'L'ultimo Montale', *La poesia di Eugenio Montale: atti del Convegno ... novembre 1982*, 241–64 at 257.
29. Glauco Cambon, 'Ancora su "Iride", frammento di Apocalisse', *La poesia di Eugenio Montale: atti del Convegno ... settembre 1982*, 227–44 at 232. See also Ettore Bonora, 'Un grande trittico al centro della *Bufera*', ibid., 95–114.
30. On this two-stage composition, see ibid., 97–8.
31. See Croce, 'La primavera hitleriana'.
32. See Claudio Scarpati, 'Sullo stilnovismo di Montale', *La poesia di Eugenio Montale: atti del Convegno ... settembre 1982*, 253–62 at 259. On Montale's definitive abandonment in the late '40s of any aspiration to join Irma Brandeis in America, see Rebay, 'Montale, Clizia e l'America', 286.
33. Greco, *Montale commenta Montale*, 60, 57.
34. 'E' la teoria stessa dell'incarnazione — cioè della conciliazione del valore con la vita — che si va sfaldando, rendendo precaria la sopravvivenza stessa della poesia': Luperini, *Montale o l'identità negata*, 162.
35. Luperini, *Storia di Montale*, 218.
36. The two series of 'Xenia' are referred to hereafter as XI and XII respectively, followed where necessary by an arabic numeral to indicate the individual poem.
37. On the proliferation of personal pronouns and possessives in 'Xenia', see Grignani, 'Storia di Xenia', *Prologhi ed epiloghi*, 85–115 at 100–2.
38. On this acquisition by the *io* of Mosca's knowledge, see Gilberto Lonardi, *Il Vecchio e il Giovane* (Bologna: Zanichelli, 1980), 200.

39. 'Visita a Fadin' contains significant thematic similarities with areas of *Satura* and subsequent collections (*OV* 217): 'Exit Fadin. E ora dire che non ci sei più e dire solo che sei entrato in un ordine diverso, per quanto quello in cui ci muoviamo noi ritardatari, così pazzesco com'è, sembri alla nostra ragione l'unica in cui la divinità può svolgere i suoi attributi, riconoscersi e saggiarsi nei limiti di un assunto di cui ignoriamo il significato.'

The piece also contains the phrase 'decenza quotidiana' (describing the lesson learned from the deceased), which has become something of a cliché to evoke Montale's ethical stance.

40. Bonora (*Montale e altro Novecento*, 25) sees in the 'neoteroi' a reference to the 'aloni di mistero cercati dai così detti poeti ermetici'.

41. Lonardi, *Il Vecchio e il Giovane*, 199.

42. See Franco Croce, 'L'ultimo Montale II: gli *Xenia*', *La rassegna della letteratura italiana* (1974), 378–401 at 392. See also Riccardo Castellana, 'L'alluvione', *Montale Readings*, ed. Éanna Ó Ceallacháin and Federica Pedriali, Italian Research Studies, 3 (Glasgow: University of Glasgow Press, 2000), 103–25.

43. Luperini, *Storia di Montale*, 220–1.

44. Fundamental observations on this can be found in Lonardi, '"Presto o tardi": fine del romanzo mitologico', *Il Vecchio e il Giovane*, 190–202, and in Luperini, 'Il viaggio dell'anguilla: o il "romanzo" delle "Silvae"', *Montale o l'identità negata*, 86–193.

45. Lonardi, *Il Vecchio e il Giovane*, 197.

46. Giovanni Macchia, 'Il romanzo di Clizia', *Saggi italiani* (Milan: Mondadori, 1983), 265–316.

47. Luperini, *Montale o l'identità negata*, 87. (On the question of 'romanzo' in general, see esp. 86–100.)

48. Luperini, *Storia di Montale*, 197.

49. Maria Corti, '*Satura* e il genere "diario poetico"', *Per conoscere Montale*, ed. Marco Forti (Milan: Mondadori, 1986), 349–72 at 350.

50. Ibid., 351.

51. Luperini, *Storia di Montale*, 212.

52. See Franco Croce, 'Satura', *La poesia di Eugenio Montale: atti del Convegno ... settembre 1982*, 353–80 at 354.

53. The term is Montale's: see *OV* 943.

54. Marchese, *Visiting angel*, 171.

55. On the importance of images of flight, wings, etc. see e.g. Avalle, *Tre saggi su Montale*, 36–41.

56. Corti, '*Satura* e il genere "diario poetico"', 355.

57. Montale's words are quoted by Corti (ibid.), who goes on to characterize 'Xenia' as a 'singolarissima poesia colloquiale', but also notes subsequently that 'il ricorso alla lingua d'oggi ha un suo modo sottile di essere eversivo' (369). Similarly, Pier Vincenzo Mengaldo, 'Primi appunti su *Satura*', *La tradizione del Novecento*, ed. P. V. Mengaldo (Milan: Feltrinelli, 1975), 335–58 at 353, observes: 'L'impressione che così spesso questa poesia di Montale provoca [...] di prosaico, di sliricato, probabilmente non resiste troppo [...] a un'analisi più approfondita; ma è anche vero che, cacciata dalla porta, rientra subito dalla finestra.'

58. Marchese, *Visiting angel*, 199.

59. On the history of the texts, see Grignani, *Prologhi ed epiloghi*, esp. 86–8.
60. See ibid., 93.
61. Ibid., 93, 97.
62. With the exception of 'Dopo una fuga', the sequence dedicated to a last amorous involvement with a young woman, which, like the cycles of Volpe and Mosca, tends at best towards a strictly private form of salvation, incomprehensible to others.
63. Corti, '*Satura* e il genere "diario poetico"', 353.

CHAPTER 2

Satura:
The Poetry of Public Discourse

At the time of writing *Satura* in the 1960s, Montale in his disillusionment has come to an awareness of a bitter truth: that of the woman's definitive absence, the absence of positive values from contemporary reality and the end of poetry as *romanzo*.[1] The problems of the historical world are treated at length in this collection in the sections 'Satura I' and 'Satura II' (where the figure of Mosca appears only rarely) and these problems continue to represent a significant thematic concern in the subsequent collections. However, the reality of the world in time, which was addressed in the earlier work through the mediation of a more or less complex angel-mythology, is now, in *Satura* and beyond, approached directly in a new type of public poetry, in which historical events and ideological debates are represented without the mediation of a female 'tu' figure. In this new dispensation, the poetic persona, though armed with Mosca's 'coraggio' as established in 'Xenia', is for the most part cast adrift alone against the backdrop of historical reality. He is represented as an increasingly isolated figure, for whom that reality, though now viewed directly, is bereft of meaning and value.

The Structure, Title and Themes of *Satura*

The sense of narrative progression found in *Occasioni* and *Bufera* is no longer present in *Satura*, whose structure reflects rather the absence of an overall narrative line. And yet, the poems in *Satura* do not merely follow chronological order, nor are they arranged at random. As shown by Grignani's detailed examination of the various stages of the text's development, the final ordering of the collection is the result of a lengthy process of refinement and revision, a process involving no fewer than seven draft indices, some of which differ radically from the definitive order.[2] The reasons for this final order, however, are by no means readily apparent, although there are certain clearly visible criteria behind the larger structural divisions of the book. The placing of 'Il tu' and 'Botta e risposta I' as a kind of opening manifesto recalls similar prefatory sections in *Ossi* and *Occasioni*. The 'Xenia' sequence, dedicated to a single female *tu*, occupies a structural position similar to that of 'Mottetti' in *Occasioni*, or 'Finisterre' in *Bufera*. The placing of 'Xenia' before 'Satura I' reflects the fact that the 'Xenia' poems were all written between 1964 and 1967, thus predating entirely the texts contained in the subsequent sections. But within each section of the book regard for chronological order or thematic patterns appears scant indeed. Thus for example the strategy of 'occultamento dei nessi tematici troppo espliciti' observed by Grignani in 'Xenia' can also be discerned in the ordering of 'Satura I', where all the poems belong to the period 1968–70 but are arranged without regard to their dates of composition or to any clear thematic order.[3] In both cases, the criteria employed seem to arise from the need to balance two opposing forces: first, the tendency to group components that treat the same material into thematic nuclei, and secondly, the desire to prevent such nuclei from becoming clearly defined subdivisions by breaking them up and interspersing them with apparently extraneous elements. Indeed, there appears to have been a conscious effort to conceal the existence of certain thematic and structural patterns within the various sections by the judicious rearrangement of material, an attempt to create a superficial impression of amorphous diversity, ungoverned by any evident organizing principle or system, while maintaining the sense that hidden structures lurk beneath the surface.

The presence of such clandestine patterns can be illustrated, for example, in the distribution within 'Satura I' of texts dealing with the major thematic areas of history and religion. 'La storia', near the beginning of the section, brings together two texts, dated respectively '28/4/69' and '10/7/69', in a basic formulation of Montale's ideas on the subject of history. These are developed and elaborated further by two poems at the end of the section, 'Dialogo' ('30/11/68') and 'Fanfara' ('1/4/69') (for the dates, see *OV* 992–8). As the dates show, this arrangement is entirely contrived, and its effect is to create two corresponding thematic centres at opposite ends of 'Satura I'. Similarly, as Luperini points out, four poems containing religious motifs or terminology are brought together around the centre of the section: 'La morte di Dio' ('15/4/69'), 'A un gesuita moderno' ('10/12/68'), 'Götterdämmerung' ('17/11/68') and 'Intercettazione telefonica' ('1969'; the 'religious' element in the last is somewhat superficial). This potential series is interrupted half-way through, however, by 'Nel fumo' ('18/12/69'), a personal memory of Mosca that would not have been out of place in 'Xenia' but in fact post-dates the four texts just mentioned. Thus, the emergence of a quasi-religious thematic nucleus at the centre of this section is held in check by the need to vary, to distribute themes (and registers) in carefully measured doses. We find this principle at work in the organization of *Satura* as a whole, leaving us with 'una sensazione di sovrabbondanza, di percorsi paralleli e intrecciati, di pluridimensionalità'.[4]

Thus, though the two 'Satura' series stop short of presenting clearly defined structural divisions based on content or style, they do not give the impression of an entirely undifferentiated mass of material. One is struck by the presence in 'Satura I' of manifesto-type poems whose titles point towards broad, abstract thematic concerns (e.g. 'Gerarchie', 'La storia', 'La poesia', 'Le rime'). These key poems, distributed singly or in small clusters, form as it were centres of gravity around which other texts can be seen to orbit, whether in close proximity or, by thematic affinity, at a distance. In this first series, the tone, though undoubtedly varied, tends on the whole to be more sober than in 'Satura II', where abstract ideas are tested against the rich diversity of specific phenomena. The difference in overall tonal and stylistic registers between the two 'Satura' sections was pointed out to Dante Isella by Montale himself, who spoke for example of a 'tono satirico-grottesco', present in both sections, but which 'da appena accennato in *Satura I* sarebbe diventato la dominante di *Satura II*'.[5] In fact, 'Satura I' can be seen in many ways as a microcosm of the longer second series, a sort of ideological preface, a concise digest of themes to be explored more freely and with greater stylistic variety in 'Satura II'.

The title *Satura* has several meanings, but probably the most significant one, from the original Latin, is that of a mixed or hybrid literary genre. This leads directly to the notion of satire, a word derived from 'satura' and linked to the presence in such a genre of a satirical element. Furthermore, related etymologically to the first sense is the Latin *satura lanx*, a dish composed of many and varied foodstuffs. (The latter meaning is specifically ruled out by the poet, but nevertheless, given the recurrence of gastronomic motifs, it does tend to assert objectively a claim to legitimacy.)[6] Finally, as an adjective ('[poesia] satura'), the title may indicate, as Zanzotto observes, an ironic sense of disgusted excess, of 'saturazione insopportabile, non-poterne-più'.[7]

The openness and deliberate ambiguity of the title are confirmed by Montale in an interview with Maria Corti:

Ma io ho giocato per il titolo un po' sull'equivoco, ma non escluderei che significasse anche satira, però le poesie satiriche in realtà sono poche, diciamo così. Invece come presentazione di poesie di tipo diverso, di intonazione e di argomento diverso, allora come, oserei dire, miscellanea, la parola poteva andare.[8]

What is clear is that *Satura* is conceived, both thematically and stylistically, as a miscellany. One major component of this miscellany is, of course, the thematic strand concerned with the evocation of Mosca, as represented most notably by 'Xenia'. It may be useful, however, given the minimal structural differentiation of the rest of the collection, to highlight the presence, here and in the subsequent collections, of at least two other main thematic areas: first—the subject of this chapter—a broad thematic strand concerned with the discussion of public issues, in which contemporary events and political and historical debates are explicitly present as never before in Montale's poetry; and secondly the exploration of the self, the attempt to outline a self-portrait, to define the parameters of the poetic *io* in relation to the world (see Chapter 3). Both strands are prominent in the opening programmatic poems 'Il *tu*' and 'Botta e risposta I'. Thus the volume begins with a discussion of the problematic nature of personal identity ('Il male / è che l'uccello preso nel paretaio / non sa se lui sia lui o uno dei troppi / suoi duplicati') and immediately proceeds to a consideration of the individual's relationship with history in the political allegory of 'Botta e risposta I'. Similarly, throughout the later sections 'Satura I' and 'Satura II', the representation of the *io* is constantly intertwined with Montale's new vein of explicitly public discourse. The overall focus of the poet's attention tends gradually to shift, however, as the collection progresses. While public discourse and historical themes occupy key positions in 'Satura I', they are increasingly overtaken in the later texts by on the one hand individual, personal concerns, and on the other more universal, metaphysical speculation. This pattern will become clearer in *Diario* and *Quaderno*, as the spatial setting of the poetry is increasingly the interior world of the home, with the exterior world of public discourse used as a kind of grotesque background or pedal note, against which the poet sketches his self-portraits and wryly contemplates the eternal mysteries.

'Satura I': The Emergence of Montale's Comic Realism

What I am calling the 'public' poetry of *Satura* can be divided in turn into two broad sub-categories. The first consists of poems dealing with history primarily as an abstraction or as a theoretical concern, while the second comprises texts that refer to contemporary events, ideological debates or political realities in a more immediate, sometimes polemical manner. 'Satura I', as a thematic microcosm of the collection as a whole, contains key texts that exemplify both of these categories.

Satura has been characterized by Becker as 'the satire of all systems', and in 'Satura I' Montale focuses extensively on systematic constructions of history.[9] Conventional historiographical ideas of progress in time, and indeed the notion of time itself as an irreversible linear phenomenon, are constant targets of Montale's attempts in *Satura* to question and undermine the principles of our perception and organization of reality. The two-part poem 'La storia' is central to the first 'Satura' series and is fundamental for an understanding of this radically sceptical approach. The poem, with its constant reiterations of negativity, is a typically Montalean anti-credo, whose lineage clearly runs back as far as *Ossi* and the famous refusal of certainties in 'Non chiederci la parola'. But now Montale's scepticism is even more far-reaching, as not only the facile certainty of history as progress, but also the very possibility of a negative certainty are seen to disintegrate:

> La storia non si snoda
> come una catena
> di anelli ininterrotta.
> In ogni caso
> molti anelli non tengono.
> La storia non contiene
> il prima e il dopo
> nulla che in lei borbotti
> a lento fuoco.
> La storia non è prodotta
> da chi la pensa e neppure

da chi l'ignora.
[...] (OV 315)

While one may not agree with Scrivano that Montale's procedure
here is purely rhetorical, concerned entirely with discourse rather
than with 'prospettive filosofiche', there is no doubt that the meaning
of this poem emerges as much on the level of rhetorical structures
as on that of substance or of the ideas enunciated.[10] The satirical
character of the piece relies, as Barberi-Squarotti points out, on the
contrast between its sententious rhetorical density (notably in the use
of anaphora and rhyme) and the apparently facile, gratuitous and
contradictory content of its assertions.[11] This poem is thus exemplary
of Montale's satirical approach in Satura, his use of irony, parody and
dissimulation to denounce meaninglessness and bad faith in the
historical world.

On the level of content, the basic proposition of the poem is clear:
the rejection of any notion of history as a chain of cause and effect.
However, the apparent sobriety of the opening statement is
immediately undermined in lines 4–5 by the shift to a tone of allusive
irony, as Montale re-uses a memorable metaphor from his own early
work in a characteristically demystificatory manner. The allusion to 'I
limoni' (Ossi) is unmistakeable: there the poet had sought 'il punto
morto del mondo, l'anello che non tiene', as he strove to transcend
the deterministic limits of our common perception of reality. Here,
however, his struggle is more radical, as the notion of determinism
itself is called into question. But following on the denial of history as
'catena', the almost parenthetic aside 'in ogni caso' represents a
prompt retreat from the certainty of that very denial. Logic is strained
in the process: history is not a chain but its links do not hold.
Meanwhile, the old, singularly miraculous 'anello che non tiene' is
replaced by the commonplace, unremarkable 'molti anelli'. Thus the
questioning of an apparent order, the challenge to a given version of
reality, manages to include within the scope of its irony the poet's own
youthful beliefs, the intensity of his early striving towards
transcendence. Here, as Montale questions all philosophical systems
that put their faith in progress or direction, relativism is absolute.

A similar rhetorical structure is evident in lines 6–9. Initially, the
bald, mechanical succession of 'prima' and 'dopo' is dismissed, much
like the earlier image of links in a chain. Immediately, however, this
dismissal is subsumed into the enigmatic image of the slowly bubbling

pot, which, while it supersedes with its all-embracing 'nulla' the question of chronological progress, once again provokes specific resonances within Montale's work. Culinary imagery is frequently associated in these later collections with the view of historical reality as grotesque or debased (the 'pâté' of 'Il sogno del prigioniero', the 'saltimbocca' of 'Botta e risposta I', more generic images such as the shapeless 'crème caramel' in 'Déconfiture non vuol dire', the 'nausea per l'odore di trifola' of 'Lettera a Malvolio').[12] Furthermore, the words used in this text echo precisely those of 'Xenia II' 6, where a similar image was employed to denote the existential 'hell' of an individual experience of reality ('non basta / esserci stati dentro a lento fuoco?'). It is difficult, then, to assign a precise or unequivocal meaning to this bubbling pot, but it seems clear that Montale is once again including his own metaphors, his sceptical formulations of historical negativity, within the scope of his satirical sententiousness.[13] Meaning is denied to the image even as it is used, leaving us with the nihilism of the basic proposition: 'La storia non contiene [...] nulla'.

So the poem continues as a series of negations and counter-negations: 'La storia non è prodotta / da chi la pensa e neppure / da chi l'ignora.' If the first part of the statement is reasonably clear (history is not, in idealistic terms, a product of the mind, of the spirit), the second part brings us back into the realm of rhetorical absurdity, as the initial affirmation seems spontaneously to provoke its opposite, in a triumph of form over meaning. As the texture of the poem grows denser in the following lines, the interweaving of denials and affirmations ('non si fa strada, si ostina / detesta il poco a poco, non procede / né recede, si sposta di binario') pushes constantly at the limits of the logical, until the poem denies the very possibility of meaning, not only for the concept of history, but for all rational constructs and the discourse that contains them. Ultimately the poem's scepticism turns inwards on itself, with the realization of the futility of this entire cognitive and rhetorical process: 'Accorgersene non serve / a farla più vera e più giusta'. Such questioning of the validity of intellectual or poetic activity frequently accompanies the poet's more 'public' pronouncements and, as we will see elsewhere, feeds into the ambivalence surrounding the figure of the poetic *io*.

Formally, this first part of 'La storia' contains several characteristic features of the public vein of *Satura*. The predominance of short lines, ranging from *quinari* to *novenari*, gives rise to a light, rapid rhythm whose movement is underlined by the anaphoric repetition of 'La storia non [...]'. This repetition also highlights the existence within the text of a succession of brief, epigrammatic, seemingly definitive formulae, a device employed widely by Montale throughout *Satura* and later, as he experiments with a range of comic, satirical or parodistic tones, assuming attitudes of mock solemnity, or ostensibly preaching exhaustive, comprehensive truths, while in fact merely playing with words (another good example is the first poem in 'Satura I', 'Gerarchie'). The presence of rhyme is initially understated, but is significant, and is supported by a dense network of phonic echoes. Assonance and consonance abound (*catena–contiene–procede*; *ininterrotta–borbotti–prodotta*; *giustifica–intrinseca*), along with internal rhymes (*fuoco–poco*; *procede–recede*; *ignora–deplora*) and a number of perfect end rhymes (*binario–orario*; *somministra–magistra*; *frusta–giusta*), whose concentration in the closing lines tends to highlight again the mock epigrammatic character of the text. This phonic network contributes greatly to the poem's formal unity, while acting as a counterweight to the almost oxymoronic tensions in the progression of ideas.

Such stylistic procedures will emerge as constant elements of what appears on the surface as the lighter or more playful register in *Satura* (a register employed however with serious critical intent, to deal satirically with the ideas and events of contemporary life). It is just one of a repertoire of distinct styles present in the collection, as pointed out by Mengaldo, who distinguishes 'l'emergere di [1] una nuova misura ritmica e formale, la misura balzante e scorrevole, da scherzo musicale, delle filastrocche, accanto a [2] quella grave e permeante, affidata a versi distesi, a lungo respiro, delle liriche più meditative e a [3] quella contratta e come miniaturizzata delle "occasioni-mottetti"' (the numbering is mine).[14] If one takes this latter 'misura miniaturizzata' as referring primarily to 'Xenia' (and to a small number of analogous texts), then the two parts of 'La storia' can be seen to represent perfectly the other two, more widespread rhythmic and tonal registers of the collection: the *filastrocca* of part I balanced and offset by the slower, more meditative second part.

In 'La storia II', having established that neither history nor the ratiocinative process can teach us anything, the poet turns to the 'broken links' in the alleged chain of determinism, through which the exceptional individual can perhaps escape in order to survive. In doing so, he introduces into the text another of the main thematic elements

of the collection, that of portrayal of the poetic *io*, the tentative
construction of an identity (although this remains largely implicit and
indirect here):

> La storia non è poi
> la devastante ruspa che si dice.
> Lascia sottopassaggi, cripte, buche
> e nascondigli. C'è chi sopravvive.
> [...]
> La storia gratta il fondo
> come una rete a strascico
> con qualche strappo e più di un pesce sfugge.
> [...] (*OV* 316)

The possibility of escape is, of course, yet another long-standing
Montalean theme (established in *Ossi* with 'In limine', of which there
are clear textual echoes here). But the dramatic imperative of that
earlier escape ('tu balza fuori, fuggi!') is here transformed into
something less urgent, a limbo of survival, which in various forms we
find repeatedly evoked in these later works, whether as the state to
which the *io* aspires or as that to which he is condemned. Comparison
with 'In limine' highlights the ambiguity of the situation depicted in
the present text. Here, 'più di un pesce sfugge': it is not clear whether
the *io* is among them, whereas in the earlier poem escape was explicity
desired for the *tu* and impossible for the *io*. Survival and escape are
now purely accidental matters in the face of a 'storia-sorte' which, in
Ramat's words, represents a kind of 'fatalità casuale', quite unlike the
Leopardian 'fatalità necessaria' of *Ossi*.[15] Indeed now the very
desirablility of 'escape' is uncertain: those within the net believe
themselves to be free, while the 'scampato', ignorant of his freedom,
derives no perceptible advantage from it:

> [...] non sembra particolarmente felice.
> Ignora di essere fuori, nessuno gliene ha parlato.
> Gli altri, nel sacco, si credono
> più liberi di lui.

However, despite the ignorance of the 'scampato' regarding his
condition, it is clear at the end that there is a qualitative distinction
between him and the 'others' who believe in their freedom. 'Gli altri'
are characterized by blithe self-delusion (as seen earlier in 'Xenia I' 5:
'Erano ingenui / quei furbi'), while by contrast the uneasy, isolated
ignorance of the 'scampato' can be clearly identified with the

problematic existential outlook attributed elsewhere to the figure of the poet himself.

The shift of emphasis in this second part of the poem, from general abstractions onto the individual, the survivor and his 'nascondigli', is accompanied formally by a notable change in metre and rhythm. In keeping with the more meditative vein to which it belongs, the piece is dominated by hendecasyllables and longer lines, as the brief epigrammatic statements of part I are expanded into fuller, more articulated sections. The anaphoric repetition of 'La storia [...]' remains, but now it marks just three broader divisions in the text, and occurs twice in the affirmative rather than the negative. Even the first occurrence of the words ('La storia non è poi [...]'), immediately points to a more subtle exploration of the issues raised in part I. So Montale's relativism now seeks to overturn even the negative tone and almost nihilistic conclusions of the first part. The more sparing use of rhyme also contributes to the slowing down of the rhythm here. The perfect rhymes, *dice–felice* and *distrugge–sfugge*, are both spread out over the strophic division, and so are maintained at a 'decent' distance (as playfully expounded in 'Le rime', *OV* 326), unlike in 'La storia I', where the density of rhyme and assonance contributed to the creation of compact (if contradictory) assertions and apparently definitive formulae. The overall effect of the more measured use of rhyme in 'La storia II', and of the prosaic rhythm of the longer hypermetric lines (e.g. ll. 13–14), is the avoidance of the kind of *cantilena* pattern that emerged in part I, and characterizes the more overtly satirical components of the collection as a whole. 'La storia II' on the other hand, leads us towards the more introspective element of *Satura*, the exploration of problems concerning primarily the individual, beyond or 'outside' history, areas of exploration clearly demarcated from historical inauthenticity in this poem by the formal and rhetorical structures employed.

Taken as a whole, 'La storia' exemplifies several key aspects of *Satura*. It introduces as a major thematic concern the direct, explicit discussion of theoretical issues linked to public, collective life. It also establishes unequivocally the poet's stance of sceptical relativism with regard to such issues, his rejection of all linear, deterministic theories that might support historical models of progress or of clear-cut cause and effect. Such models of order, satirized in the formal banality of the *filastrocca*, are rejected in favour of the chaotic fluidity of human experience, the unpredictable individual experience of time and the world postulated in the second part.

There are also examples in 'Satura I' of the second, closely related vein of public poetry in which abstract philosophical notions are combined with a more polemical consideration of contemporary ideologies, debates and events, a vein that borders at times on direct historical commentary or chronicle, as the poet takes up a highly critical stance with regard to the world around him. This polemical vein clearly springs from the same matrix as many of Montale's journalistic prose writings of the 1950s and '60s. His professional activity as a journalist brought him into closer and more frequent contact than ever before with the banalities of media discourse, the debased languages of political debate and the consumer society. In a 1961 article he refers, for example, to the disappearance of actual opinions from public debate (specifically as mediated by television) and their replacement by mere 'fiato di voce':

chiacchiere prive di consistenza ma dotate di una provvisoria efficacia. Coloro che reggono la vita pubblica (politici, amministratori, uomini d'affari) non potrebbero impunemente mostrarsi a vuoto di idee generali, di opinioni; e quanto più il vuoto è reale tanto più essi sono tenuti a coprirlo col vento della loro verbosità. ('Il mercato del nulla'; *SMAMS* 265)

Prose writings such as this lend themselves readily to the task of providing commentary and elaboration on the poetry of *Satura*: they can help to flesh out the ideological subtext of many poems and constitute a rich background source of thematic variants and glosses (they have frequently been used to this end in the critical literature). It can also be argued, however, that Montale's prose writings exercise a degree of stylistic influence, sometimes general, sometimes more specific, on his verse-production of these later years. It was in his prose, ranging from the more literary components of *Farfalla di Dinard* to shorter, more ephemeral and more truly journalistic pieces such as those published under the heading 'La storia vera' (signed 'Alastor'; now in *PR*), that Montale first employed a comic style in the 1940s and '50s, some twenty years before such a style would be widely adopted in his verse. And indeed, by the time of *Satura*, one can find some cases of close and direct interdependence between poetry and prose, as highlighted by the fact that examples of the two genres are frequently published together in the *Corriere della sera* in the late 1960s and early '70s. Thus it is no coincidence that as part of the huge lexical upheaval in Montale's verse introduced by *Satura*, the languages of ideological debate, media commentary and banal public discourse of all kinds begin to play a highly visible role (ranging from terms such as 'storicismo dialettico' to 'pubblica opinione', from 'consiglio d'amministrazione' to 'politica, pornografia'). As Cambon writes, 'Montale has never been so discursive, so polemical, so explicit in his formulations and so aggressively demotic, even journalistic, in his lexicon.'[16] This new breadth of lexical range emerges as one of the most visible components of the style with which he addresses public themes in *Satura*, a style that might be characterized as Montale's comic realism.

In 'Satura I', the most extreme application of this style occurs in 'Fanfara'. The apparently uncontrolled prolixity of this poem, far removed from the terse economy of Montale's most intense lyrics, is an integral part of his choice of satire and parody as the appropriate responses to the widespread diffusion of cliché, flawed thinking and intellectual bad faith. If the poet can no longer produce positive, mythic figures in the quest for individual or collective truths, he is still left with the possibility of denouncing falsehood and deception, if necessary by his own adoption of dissimulation, of the masks of inauthenticity, or as Contini observes 'impastando al controcanto le parole della moda'.[17] Satire is the means by which he now attempts to 'exorcize' the tragedy of contemporary life.[18] Corti, highlighting Montale's satirical intent in *Satura*, notes that between the rhetorical excesses of the world of media and advertising on the one hand and those of serious literature on the other 'Montale sceglie una terza via, quella aperta alla letteratura italiana nel lontano Duecento da scrittori come Guittone, in cui l'oltranza retorica si fa strumento di satira etico-politica'.[19] Montale himself suggests, in an article written in 1969, not long after the composition of poems such as 'Fanfara' and 'Piove', that satire may now be the only possible kind of 'poesia civile'.[20] Thus in 'Fanfara' the theoretical principle underlying 'La storia' (the rejection of all systematic, progressive models of history) now forms the basis of a direct satirical attack on a clearly definable target: those elements within the Western liberal intelligentsia who have apparently uncritically embraced Marxian ideology and rhetoric. Here, in the wake of the events of 1968, there is clearly a strong element of continuity with Montale's long-standing aversion to Marxism, as previously seen in the prose writings of the late 1940s and early '50s.

The title 'Fanfara' is an apt prelude to the arrogant posturing portrayed in the poem (an earlier title was 'Marcia trionfale'). The complex, all-embracing negations deployed in 'La storia', with their understated irony, are replaced by the straightforward satire of brash meaninglessness. In this it is quite likely that there is also an element of parody of current poetic fashions: in his 1968 review of Zanzotto's *La beltà* (where he writes enthusiastically of the latter's 'felice commistione lessicale' and skilful deployment of, among other devices, 'balbettamenti, interiezioni e soprattutto iterazioni'), Montale concludes gloomily: 'Avrà purtroppo imitatori perché può sembrare facile e "moderno" imbussolare parole, costrutti e interiezioni, agitare "prima dell'uso" e poi buttar tutto sul foglio.'[21] The complete absence of punctuation in 'Fanfara' sets the scene for just such an arbitrary enunciation of words emptied of sense. The poem begins with a lower-case letter and continues as an uninterrupted list of clichés and terminology rather than concepts, without any syntactical organization into logical arguments or even meaningful assertions:

> lo storicismo dialettico
> materialista
> autofago
> progressivo
> immanente
> irreversibile
> sempre dentro
> mai fuori
> mai fallibile
> [...] (*OV* 328)

One term leads to another in rapid succession, without the clear development of any actual idea, only the mock glorification of the poet's *bête noir*, 'lo storicismo', through the dense use of empty rhetorical devices.[22] The strophic divisions highlight the asyndetic accumulation of substantives of which the poem is composed ('lo storicismo [...] la meraviglia [...] il salto [...] l'eternità [...]'), each of which is followed by a series of qualifiers and subordinate clauses in which meaning is sacrificed to mere verbosity. The poem mimics the dull hypnotic effect of a religious litany, highlighting Montale's scorn for the purveyors of dialectical materialism as dogma. This self-sustaining model of history as self-perpetuating progress was already attacked in 'La storia', which, as Scrivano observes, constitutes the essential theoretical pretext for this text's seemingly playful 'filastrocca accusatoria'.[23] Thus the preaching voice of 'Fanfara' is constantly undermined by quiet negations of the earlier text ('progressivo' and 'irreversibile' immediately recall the earlier 'non procede / né recede, si sposta di binario', while the sequence 'immanente / [...] / sempre dentro / mai fuori' mirrors and distorts 'la storia non è intrinseca / perché è fuori'). Meanwhile, the systematic shortening of lines to a single word represents a radicalization of the structure of 'La storia I' and leads to a rapidity of movement that underlines the profound insignificance and vacuity with which the poet seeks to invest the terminology of 'lo storicismo'. The inconsequential character of the content is stressed by the use of simple, grammatical rhymes and assonances in extended sequences throughout the poem: *materialista–papisti–frontisti–progressista; irreversibile–fallibile–credibili–tascabile–responsabili; individuale–universale–morale–eventuale–provvidenziali–funzionale–intellettuale.* The resulting emphasis on the proliferation of abstract, polysyllabic terms, so incongruous within the light rhythmic *cantilena* framework, tends paradoxically to diminish their potential value and weight. Conceptual distinctions seem to collapse under the pressure of alliteration and rhyme, as opposing terms are assimilated: 'il salto quantitativo / macché qualitativo'. (This is typical of a more widespread use of similar 'impoverished' phonic patterns in *Satura* and later, as discussed by Rebecca West.)[24]

However, this predominantly comic poem has its darker side, reflecting the seriousness of the poet's intentions. Thus in the second stanza the 'meraviglia sintetica' of dialectics is turned into a caricature of the miracle of the loaves and the fishes, but with a distinctly hollow note in the description of its outcome, grating against the facile music of the rhyme, as the universal 'meraviglia' leads to 'il digiuno / che nutre tutti / e nessuno'. The most notable shift towards a darker tone occurs when the poet contemplates the disappearance of the individual, in a world where free intellectual endeavour is equated with the primitive mystifications of religion or witchcraft:

> [...]
> la morte
> del buon selvaggio
> delle opinioni
> delle incerte certezze
> delle epifanie
> delle carestie
> dell'individuo non funzionale
> del prete dello stregone
> dell'intellettuale
> [...]

Given the centrality of the individual (and the intellectual) to Montale's idea of freedom, the political and philosophical urgency that fuels this satire scarcely needs further comment.

As well as addressing such general issues, Montale's satirical or comic manner also contains direct references to specific individuals or events. While such allusions are limited in this poem, one emerges clearly in the sixth stanza, where 'noosfera' constitutes a precise textual link to another poem in 'Satura I', 'A un gesuita moderno' (*OV* 320). In both cases the object of Montale's scorn is the theology of the Jesuit Pierre Teilhard de Chardin (1881–1955), who combined mysticism with Darwinian evolutionary theory, linking humanity's spiritual development in a continuum with the biological development of the species. This quasi-scientific cosmology relied heavily on the notion of progress in time, an easy target for Montale's derision. Here in 'Fanfara', however, in keeping with the broad scope of his scepticism, he multiplies the objects of his polemic, using the reference to Teilhard as part of his satirical attack on the Marxist materialists. Their intellectual poverty is parodied through the absence of rational or theoretical argument in their facile dismissal of Teilhard's theories as merely one of the 'bubbole / che spacciano i papisti / modernisti'. A further specific allusion, this time more urgently historical, occurs in the penultimate stanza, where the tone becomes bitterly ironic:

> [...]
> la guerra
> quando sia progressista
> perché invade
> violenta non violenta
> secondo accade
> ma sia l'ultima
> e lo è sempre
> per sua costituzione
> [...]

This is an unmistakable reference to the Soviet invasion of Czechoslovakia in 1968 ('Fanfara' was written sometime late in 1968 or early in 1969).[25] Similarly, the earlier reference to the death of opinions and of the intellectual must surely be read in the light of the horrors of the Chinese Cultural Revolution and the widespread influence of Maoism in Western left-wing circles.

In the closing lines, the poem's various utterances, none of which contains any clearly organized argument, are brought together as a nebulous whole ('tutto questo') to form some sort of self-evident truth, to which, apparently, objections of any kind would be inappropriate:

> [...]
> tu dimmi
> disingaggiato amico
> a tutto questo
> hai da fare obiezioni?

The peremptory nature of the final question is in keeping with the lack of argument or ideas in the poem as a whole. It can only be met with ironic silence by the 'disingaggiato amico', the poet's mute mouthpiece: it is after all impossible to object coherently to incoherent discourse. The lack of a response forces the reader's attention back to the litany recited, and highlights by contrast its empty, arrogant triumphalism.

The close of 'Fanfara' introduces implicitly the idea of a quasi-dramatic dialogue, the presence of two voices or characters engaged in philosophical or ideological disputation. The dramatic and satirical potential of this dialogic structure is exploited more fully and frankly in the penultimate poem in 'Satura I', 'Dialogo'. Here arguments reflecting Montale's own position are put to a blinkered ideologue, a proponent of history as system, who ultimately has no answers other than blind dogma. In order to clarify the two positions, the poem is transcribed here along with an indication of the two voices as 'A' and 'B':

> [A]   'Se l'uomo è nella storia non è niente.
>   La storia è un *marché aux puces*, non un sistema'.
> [B]   'Provvidenza e sistema sono tutt'uno
>   e il Provvidente è l'uomo'.
> [A]   'Dunque è provvidenziale
>   anche la pestilenza'.
> [B]   'La peste è il negativo del positivo,
>   è l'uomo che trasuda il suo contrario'.
> [A]   'Sempre avvolto però nel suo sudario'.
> [B]   'Il sistema ternario
>   secerne il male e lo espelle,
>   mentre il binario se lo porta dietro'.

[A]   'Ma il ternario lo mette sottovetro
        e se vince lo adora'.
[B]   'Vade retro,
        Satana!'. (*OV* 327)

Speaker A's dismissal of the idea that history is a system that might somehow serve humanity identifies him immediately as expressing the poet's own outlook. B's response, that the system is created by Man, is a Marxist variant of the Hegelian concept of providence, whereby Man in history is an agent of the providential system itself. Speaker A objects however that in such a system, 'la pestilenza' (a figure of the chance event, the unforeseen negative force, 'il male') is also providential and, therefore, inevitable, implying that this 'Providence' is less than benign. B's reply is confident, unwavering: the existence of historical negativity is not denied, but it must be understood within the dialectical system. It is the negative that gives definition to the positive, as part of a process of development by which Man's imperfections are brought to the surface, literally sweated out. A's retort is bitterly sarcastic, as the poet's black humour characteristically chooses rhyme and assonance as the vehicles of his polemic, twisting 'trasuda' into Man's 'sudario': a dialectical model contains the negative by definition, and any change it allows is merely movement within a closed system. For Montale, the 'sudario' is the system itself, in which Man remains trapped, the victim, wrapped in his own funeral shroud, just as in line 1 his envisaged position 'nella storia' meant his annihilation.[26] Speaker B is unmoved: the system expells 'il male' having brought it to the surface. A binary system (e.g. a Manichean opposition of good and evil) is static, whereas the ternary dialectical system is movement towards good. A's final objection returns to the hypothesis of a negative outcome within the providential system, where 'il male', seen as inevitable, is paradoxically privileged. In a deterministic system where all historical change must be for the better, the unthinkable victory of the negative must be hailed as progress, 'il male' enthroned and adored, as rigid ideology triumphs over human experience. Speaker B, turned aside at last from his single-minded recitation of ideological orthodoxy by the shock of such heresy, can only reply with the blind faith of the zealot.

In this poem, as in its companion piece 'Fanfara', Montale deploys the formal armoury of his comic manner to satirical effect (note for example the use of the rudimentary musicality of repetition, along with the use of rhyme, as between *provvidenza–pestilenza, contrario–sudario–ternario*, to deflate and undermine the ideologue's pomposity). Throughout the poem, the self-assured tone of speaker B's pronouncements contrasts with the subtler, more ironic approach of the other. Each of A's declarations is linked to his opponent's previous statement: the opening 'Se l'uomo [...]' appearing to continue an ongoing debate, followed by 'Dunque [...]', 'Sempre avvolto però [...]', 'Ma il ternario [...]', each of which explicitly counters the point previously raised. On the other hand the voice of the ideologue, while possibly coherent in its arguments, has been closed within the parameters of its own system and the arguments deployed fail even to engage syntactically with those of speaker A. When pressed, speaker B has finally had to resort to undisguised dogmatism, rendered satirically by the poet with the religious formula (indeed, Macrì calls this ideologue 'il prete neohegeliano provvidenzialista').[27]

The form chosen, that of a more or less explicit dialogue, while by no means common in Montale's poetry, can nevertheless be seen to have significant resonances in his prose writings. A 1964 piece, 'Peripatetici', included by the author in *Auto da fé*, bears clear structural and thematic similarities to 'Dialogo' as Montale presents an overheard dialogue between two wandering 'philosophers' (as suggested ironically in the title). Here are the opening lines:

L'importante è di sapere se l'uomo sarà il padrone del suo avvenire o se l'avvenire sarà il padrone dell'uomo. *Tertium non datur.*

'La prima ipotesi è il progresso, la seconda è la catastrofe. Ma il progresso potrebbe coincidere con la catastrofe. Si avrebbe allora un progresso antiprogressista e il trionfo dell'ipotesi escatologica. Ma potrebbe anche darsi che il progresso biologico-tecnico-sociale riduca l'uomo in una condizione catastrofica del tutto normale e permanente.'

'Può esistere una catastrofe senza una soluzione?'

'Quando ne manchi il desiderio, la soluzione potrebbe essere differita quasi all'infinito. [...]' (*SMAMS* 350)

As in 'Dialogo', the topic discussed by these disembodied voices involves the future of humanity and whether this is to be seen pessimistically or optimistically. The language is heavy with mocking abstractions, including elements of absurd paradox, such as 'progresso antiprogressista'. The piece constitutes a miniature dramatic scene, in which, however, the two voices are ethically indistinguishable in their obtuse philosophical musings, a scene whose absurdity is intended to satirize the death of real opinions and meaningful debate, as deplored repeatedly by the poet in these years. As such, it may well have provided a structural model, whether conscious or otherwise, for 'Dialogo'. The fact that 'Peripatetici' predates the poem by some five years need not preclude this possibility, not least in the light of an even longer-term persistence of the same paradigm in Montale's prose. Thus in 'Peripatetica' (1945), we find another overheard conversation:

Bardolfo (asciugandosi un occhio ammaccato): "Maledizione! I soliti elementi reazionari!"
Cirillo: "Posso esserLe utile in qualcosa?"
Bardolfo: "Grazie, è un'inezia. Un contrasto di idee al congresso del partito illiberale, di cui faccio parte. Anche Lei viene di là?"
Cirillo: "Passo di qui per caso. Dunque Lei è vittima di uno scambio ... di opinioni. [...]" (*PR* 653)

Political views of doubtful sincerity and highly questionable coherence are presented satirically as the piece unfolds: the supporter of the 'partito illiberale' is ultimately matched in his absurd incoherence by his interlocutor, the founder of the 'reazionari indipendenti di sinistra', who are 'per l'ordine e il disordine [...] per l'autorità e per la libertà'. Yet another dialogue along similar lines is to be found in 'Nel parco' (also dating to 1945), the 'recording' of a conversation supposedly overheard in 1943 between two Fascists as they tried hastily to distance themselves from the disgraced Mussolini (*PR* 650–2). Again, here, the intent is satirical as the two voices surpass one another in their extreme political and intellectual bad faith.

So the model of a dramatic dialogue written with comic or satirical intent has a long history in Montale's prose. It is in 'Dialogo' that it finally surfaces explicitly in verse form, but its presence can also be detected elsewhere, notably in the 'Botta e risposta' series, where the poet's persona doggedly defends the besieged ideological space he now occupies. The dialogue form also occurs in several of the 'Xenia' poems (e.g., I 10, II 7, II 8), which can be seen perhaps to provide a structural precedent in verse for 'Dialogo'. Later, a less obvious but highly significant example of the same dialogic model occurs in 'Lettera a Malvolio' (in *Diario*), where we hear just one side of a bitterly polemical debate. The latter poem, indeed, can be read as the long-awaited response to 'Fanfara', whose 'disingaggiato amico' finally expounds his 'obiezioni' and justifies his silence as 'un rispettabile / prendere le distanze' (*OV* 456—see Chapter 3 below). Thus dialogues and polemics, whether overt or merely implicit, contribute to the construction of what Ramat calls Montale's 'progetto comico'; that is, *Satura* seen not only as 'comic' poetry, but poetry tending towards 'commedia', where the world appears as a kind of Pirandellian spectacle of the absurd.[28]

Variations on Public Themes in 'Satura II'

In 'Satura II', the last and longest section of the book, Montale returns to public, historical themes and polemics in numerous poems, echoing and re-examining the basic thematic repertoire of 'Satura I' in a greater variety of musical registers. The problematic question of temporal progression arises repeatedly, for example in 'Tempo e tempi' (*OV* 342), which continues the abstract, theorizing vein of 'La storia', or in the more frankly comical 'Auf Wiedersehen':

> hasta la vista, à bientôt, I'll be seeing you, appuntamenti
> ridicoli perché si sa che chi s'è visto s'è visto.
> La verità è che nulla si era veduto
> e che un accadimento non è mai accaduto.
> [...] (*OV* 353)

Here the poet mocks the aspiration to even a minimal degree of predicability of future events, based on the mistaken belief in knowledge or understanding of the past. Thus the notion of time as a conveniently structured continuum, allowing revisions and repetitions, is rejected. Any attempt to structure past events is an 'inganno', but such delusions are essential to allow speculation on the future:

> [...]
> Ma senza questo inganno sarebbe inesplicabile
> l'ardua speculazione che mira alle riforme
> essendo il *ri* pleonastico là dove
> manca la forma.

It is a generic critique of the vanity of human intellectual endeavour, of attempts to control or codify reality (yet placed firmly in the sphere of public life, collective history, by the focus on 'riforme').

This text offers a good example of another direction of formal innovation in *Satura*: the use of uncompromisingly prosaic rhythms, at the opposite extreme of the metrical spectrum from the *filastrocca* model, but converging with this in their anti-lyrical intent. (Other instances range from the spoken register of parts of 'Xenia', to the hypermetric lines of 'Dopo una fuga', to the extreme case of 'Due prose veneziane'.) Here, as in some of the examples mentioned, such rhythms are accompanied by the ostentatious introduction of foreign terminology, creating dissonant musical effects. However, the rhythmic tendency towards prose is offset in part by the widespread presence of unexpected rhyme and assonance. Thus in the first four lines one can discern the presence of two phonic sequences: *hasta–vista–visto–visto–verità–era veduto*; and *bientôt–appuntamenti–accadimento–accaduto*, converging in the end rhyme *veduto–accaduto*. The foreign words are playfully integrated, and indeed are used at the outset to establish some of the principal elements of the rich phonic texture. Rhythmically and metrically then, this text is far removed from the manner of the *filastrocca*. However, it belongs none the less to the comic style, with the poet's propensity for word-play projected, as it were, from the vertical axis of short, rhyming lines onto the horizontal axis of prosaic rhythm.

Shorter lines and *cantilena* rhythm return in 'È ridicolo credere', where, in the second stanza, familiar theoretical problems of knowledge and time are addressed:

> [...]
> è ridicolo
> ipotecare il tempo
> e lo è altrettanto
> immaginare un tempo
> suddiviso in più tempi
> [...] (*OV* 363)

The approach again is abstract and speculative, the ideological implications indirect. We cannot foresee humanity's evolution, cannot pre-empt the future, which is just one of the nonsensical subdivisions of time. The deeply sceptical approach to all intellectual constructs is accompanied by some familiar formal features: *settenari* and shorter lines dominate, and a facile musicality arises out of the repetition of 'tempo/tempi' (for example in the second and fourth of the lines quoted, where the identical rhythm is underlined further by the internal assonance of the two infinitives). Such theoretical musings on time and history have, on one level, direct ideological implications regarding the view of contemporary reality espoused in *Satura*. They are also inseparable, on another level, from the portrayal of the poet's persona as an isolated (whether privileged or impoverished) outsider. This depiction of the *io* as a figure outside time, extraneous to history and the world, is, as we shall see, another key element in Montale's figuration of historical negativity in these later collections.

Along with the theoretical approach to history, Montale continues however to develop the vein of more immediate, polemical commentary in 'Satura II', where at times indeed the poems contain elements of direct contemporary chronicle. 'Piove', for example, with its unabashed parody of D'Annunzio, belongs unequivocally to the comic or satirical manner and gives voice once again to the poet's jaundiced world view. It also belongs, peripherally, to the Mosca cycle ('Piove / sulla tua tomba [...]') and is one of the texts through which her influence extends into the later part of *Satura*, where she, along with the poet's own figure, stands in clear opposition to the inauthenticity of public life. Her absence here is a metaphor for the absence of meaning in the world, where 'l'assenza / è universale'. The nihilistic side of Montale's scepticism is manifested again in this poem, but this time in the context of specific public events:

> [...]
> Piove
> sul nulla che si fa
> in queste ore di sciopero
> generale.
> [...] (*OV* 337)

So the poet muses upon a particular situation at a particular time ('in *queste* ore'), in a procedure which will become more prominent in the increasingly diaristic collections to follow. But such reaction to specific events is still inseparable from the theorizing, conceptual satire of poems such as 'La storia' or 'Dialogo'. Not only does the rain of the poet's ironic indifference (Forti calls it a 'pioggia dissacratoria'[29]) fall on events and objects, but also on ideas:

> [...]
> Piove sui nuovi epistèmi
> del primate a due piedi,
> sull'uomo indiato, sul cielo
> ominizzato, sul ceffo
> dei teologi in tuta
> o paludati,

> piove sul progresso
> della contestazione,
> piove sui works in regress,
> piove
> sui cipressi malati
> del cimitero, sgocciola
> sulla pubblica opinione.
> [...]

The wide range of the targets of Montale's derision is matched by the range of his linguistic inventiveness. The satire of ideologies and dogmas gives rise both to learned, literary coinages ('epistèmi' or the pseudo-Dantesque 'indiato [...] ominizzato') and to the grotesquely comical ('sul ceffo / dei teologi in tuta'). These are combined with the banal, intermediate register of current media discourse ('progresso / della contestazione', 'pubblica opinione'), where the poet's irony damns the 'contestazione' through its association with the discredited notion of progress, and his disdain for mass opinion is contained in the contemptuous 'sgocciola' (rendered all the more forceful, after the extensive reiteration of the verb 'piove', by its position at the end of the line rather than the beginning). Meanwhile, a jibe at the inauthenticity of contemporary high culture uses and mocks the latter's fashionable international jargon with 'works in regress' (the combination of word-play with the use of foreign terminology underlining very strongly the poet's aversion to any concept of progress). Elsewhere in the same text, his own literary legend, in the form of the 'ossi di seppia', is subject to the same unflattering rainfall. Thus Montale's scepticism, theoretically formulated elsewhere, is here applied comprehensively to the multiple phenomena of contemporary reality. Thematic strands become intertwined, as in the entire series of 'Satura II', but one can always discern elements of continuity with key texts in 'Satura I'. So, the rhythmic and phonic features of 'Piove' (short lines and a dense but playful musical texture) belong unmistakeably to the line of satirical *filastrocche* traced from 'La storia I'. (It is interesting to note that 'Piove' was written just six days after 'La storia I'.[30])

Much later in 'Satura II', 'Nel silenzio' opens with another reference to current public events: 'Oggi è sciopero generale' (*OV* 404). Once more the strike is used by Montale as an image of general inertia and absence: 'Nella strada non passa nessuno'. The initial specific temporal indication 'oggi' is repeated at the close and underlined in line 4 by 'Da qualche giorno': poetry seems to approach the condition of chronicle. Here again, however, the image of the strike is used in a poem concerned with wider problems (the absence and silence of Mosca, the 'sonno universale' of death and the miraculous suspension of time), so that the banality of the chronicled event is transformed by its link to other major Montalean themes (see Chapter 3 below for a fuller reading of this text).

Current events come into the foreground in 'Fine del '68' whose title immediately declares it to be part of a diary or chronicle, as underlined by its original appearance at the foot of one of Montale's *Corriere della sera* articles, a piece with which, as we shall see, it has close textual links. What is remarkable here is not only that Montale comments directly on an identifiable event, but that it is an event of worldwide public and media interest. Written on 31 December 1968, the poem is inspired by the Apollo 8 mission, which captured the popular imagination as, for the first time, three astronauts orbited the moon. More precisely, one can safely presume that it was inspired by a specific image, that of a distant earth rising above the rim of the moon's horizon, which was to become an instantly recognizable media icon of the period. The image was published as a still photograph in the *Corriere della sera* on the day the poem was written, suggesting a possible case of direct inspiration of a poetic text by a press report, but it is just as likely that the inspiration came from, or was reinforced by a television broadcast of the image, in a film clip famously accompanied by an emotional reading of the opening of *Genesis*, finishing with a salute to the 'good earth' by one of the astronauts. (This hypothesis would add this text to the group of poems, discussed in Chapter 3 below, in which external reality impinges on the poet's world via the television screen.) In any case, it is an image that brings the poem firmly into the realm of public commentary, of media discourse. Furthermore, it is an archetypal image of the kind of confident scientific and technological progress about which Montale was so sceptical. But it is juxtaposed here in a fine balance with the evocation of darker, more uncertain portents. Out of the poet's contemplation of the spectacle of the contemporary world, there emerges a bemused meditation on the human condition:

> Ho contemplato dalla luna, o quasi,
> il modesto pianeta che contiene

> filosofia, teologia, politica,
> pornografia, letteratura, scienze
> palesi o arcane. Dentro c'è anche l'uomo,
> ed io tra questi. E tutto è molto strano.
> [...] (*OV* 366)

These lines could stand as an epigraph for the entire collection. The extraterrestrial viewpoint becomes here a sort of ivory tower for the new technological age, an appropriate figuration of the poet's aristocratic detachment, which allows him, literally, to look down on the world, to reduce, at a glance, the planet and humanity to a uniform level of insignificance. Of course the poet must include his own persona in this glance, and so the whole range of his concerns in *Satura* is represented here: from grand abstractions to individual self-consciousness, including the 'letteratura' through which the latter is expressed, all combined to form the object of his ironic bewilderment.

The meditative tone set by the opening 'Ho contemplato' is reinforced by the strong predominance of hendecasyllables, which, along with other longer lines, as seen elsewhere, are characteristic of the more contemplative vein of *Satura*'s public verse. But any suggestion of solemnity is undermined by the poet's irony, even from the end of line 1, with the addition of 'o quasi'. The catalogue of human activity is mocked by the typically comical use of a facile but incongruous rhyme sequence: *filosofia–teologia–pornografia*.[31] Humanity's status is that of a mere afterthought ('c'è anche l'uomo'), and any notion of privilege in the vantage point of the *io* is negated as he is reduced to a component of this insignificant whole, 'ed io tra questi'. Not for the first time, Montale's pessimistic relativism recalls that of Leopardi, as the twentieth-century poet's lunar meditation wryly echos the sincere bewilderment of the wandering shepherd's question, 'ed io che sono?'.

In the second stanza the tone changes, as the poet alludes initially to the empty frivolity of New Year celebrations and then to less auspicious aspects of contemporary history. The irony grows darker and more bitter as fireworks give way to other, more sinister explosions:

> [...] Forse di bombe o peggio,
> ma non qui dove sto. Se uno muore
> non importa a nessuno purché sia
> sconosciuto e lontano.

A brief examination of the context in which the poem first appeared can cast interesting light on these lines, and indeed on the text as a whole. 'Fine del '68' was published, shortly after its composition, in the *Corriere* of 12 January 1969, along with an article in the 'Variazioni' series (such articles were often accompanied by previously unpublished poems during these years).[32] The tone and content of the article provide a clear illustration of Montale's state of mind at the time and point to a close interdependence between poetry and journalistic prose. Like most of the 'Variazioni' pieces (many of which are now in *Prose e racconti*), the article consists of several more or less unconnected sections. A personal and cultural memoir of the 1920s is followed by a sardonic account of light entertainment on television (ranging from 'giovani donne in mutande' to 'il loro, il nostro, il mio, il vostro Pippo Baudo'), followed in turn by a consideration of the high-pitched excesses of popular music (characterized, in an ironic reference to the moon race, as 'l'allunaggio alla "seconda ottava"')[33]. Then however, Montale's humour turns decidedly blacker:

L'uomo non ha più molto interesse per l'umanità. L'uomo si annoia spaventosamente. I giornali sono poveri di notizie e del resto solo un italiano su dieci legge un giornale. Le guerre per il momento sono poche e lontane. Hanno il solo vantaggio di render meno certa la vera grande guerra, quella per cui si spendono miliardi. Per evitarla, è vero. Ma una volta che siano creati gli strumenti perché non usarli? (*PR* 1114)

The tone hovers between the darkly pessimistic and the ironically flippant. The alleged shortage of news must be seen in the context of serious international crises in Vietnam and the Middle East, along with continuing social and political unrest in Italy and elsewhere in Europe in the wake of the traumatic upheavals of 1968. The statement that wars are 'poche e lontane' has a mock complacency that leads directly back to the closing lines of the poem and the grim sarcasm of the poetic persona's feigned indifference for the suffering individual ('non importa a nessuno purché sia / sconosciuto e lontano'): there is a clear semantic and tonal correspondence here between the two texts.

The prose piece then goes on to ridicule the sciences and other disciplines in a repetitive rhetorical sequence:

Non so se questa universale noia sia un fatto nuovo nella storia dell'umanità. Non chiedetelo ai sociologi, cultori di una scienza inventata per creare nuove cattedre universitarie. Non chiedetelo ai filosofi, convinti come sono che la filosofia è morta; ma allora che stanno a fare? Non chiedetelo agli ecclesiastici, decisi a rendere meno noiosa e più spiccia ogni forma del rito. Non chiedetelo a medici, psicologi, psicanalisti.

Here in effect, he gives a full, satirical elaboration on the 'scienze palesi o arcane' listed in the poetic text. The emphatic use of an anaphoric structure in the prose mirrors the widespread reliance on such rhetorical devices in the more satirical or comic poems. Meanwhile, the poet's profound existential anguish feeds into the nihilistic conclusions of the newspaper article:

Nessuno di questi potrà spiegarvi perché quando due o tre persone si trovano insieme per qualche mezz'ora, esse si guardano allibite e si pongono l'angosciosa domanda: che cosa facciamo? quasicché ogni genere di scemenza sia preferibile al non far nulla, mentre è certo che questo nulla può essere un tutto.

The close correspondence between the two texts as originally published together allows us a fuller insight into the depth and breadth of the poet's sense of alienation from contemporary society, the necessary background to the comic poetry of *Satura*. In 'Fine del '68', this alienation is expressed initially in the familiar stance of ironic detachment, but a more pessimistic note is unmistakable in the accumulation of expressions of negativity in the closing lines, reinforced by the alliteration and assonance of *n* and *o* ('non qui [...] / non importa a nessuno [...] / sconosciuto [...]'). Here the emphasis has shifted from the vicissitudes of humanity as a whole to the isolated suffering of the individual ('se *uno* muore'). Finally, the single perfect end-rhyme in this text serves to highlight the sense of alienation and estrangement expressed at the close: *strano–lontano*. So the poetic voice returns to a perspective of distance and detachment, but it is a different detachment to that of the initial extraterrestrial musings. Having descended into the reality of the 'modest planet', Montale imparts one of the principal lessons of *Satura*: behind the mask of the collective *commedia* lies the universal isolation of the individual.

Notes to Chapter 2

1. See Lonardi, *Il Vecchio e il Giovane*, 201.
2. See Grignani, '*Satura*: da miscellanea a libro', *Prologhi ed epiloghi*, 117–37.
3. Ibid., 96.
4. Luperini, *Storia di Montale*, 208–10.
5. Dante Isella, *Ancora sulla struttura di Satura* (Naples: Edizioni Scientifiche Italiane, 1990), 23.

6. Montale writes: 'Il titolo ha tre o quattro significati. Escluso quello di appetitosi *avantgoûts*, desidero che li mantenga tutti' (*OV* 973).

7. Andrea Zanzotto, 'In margine a *Satura*', *Nuovi Argomenti*, nos. 23–4 (1971), 215–20 at 219. Zanzotto's interpretation of the title here is richly subtle. On the meaning of 'Satura' see also West, *Eugenio Montale: Poet on the Edge*, 95, and Luperini, *Storia di Montale*, 206–7.

8. '*Satura* di Eugenio Montale' [interview with Maria Corti], in *Eugenio Montale: immagini di una vita*, ed. Franco Contorbia (Milan: Mondadori, 1996), 267.

9. See Becker, *Eugenio Montale*, 124.

10. Riccardo Scrivano, 'La storia', *Letture montaliane*, 299–320 at 299.

11. Giorgio Bàrberi-Squarotti, 'La storia', ibid., 283–96 at 285.

12. On culinary and related imagery see Giuliano Gramigna, 'Il pâté degli iddii pestilenziali', *La poesia di Eugenio Montale: atti del Convegno ... novembre 1982*, 511–18.

13. Bàrberi-Squarotti sees the bubbling pot perhaps too unequivocally, as an image of 'l'oppressione, la violenza' ('La storia', 288). Nevertheless, it does recur later with this specific connotation in 'Botta e risposta III'.

14. Mengaldo, 'Primi appunti su *Satura*', 348.

15. Silvio Ramat, '*Satura*, il progetto comico', *L'acacia ferita e altri studi su Montale* (Venice: Marsilio, 1986), 145–83 at 160.

16. Cambon, *Eugenio Montale's Poetry*, 220. Similarly, Marchese (*Visiting angel*, 245) writes of 'un lessico marcato dagli usi settoriali tipici dei mass media'. See also Mengaldo, 'Primi appunti su *Satura*', 354–5.

17. Gianfranco Contini, *Una lunga fedeltà: scritti su Eugenio Montale* (Turin: Einaudi, 1974), 98.

18. Bàrberi-Squarotti, 'La storia', 296.

19. Corti, '*Satura* e il genere "diario poetico"', 370.

20. 'Resta la vena della satira', *SM* 2926–7. Here he alludes dismissively to the 'molti poeti contestatori' of the time, who can be in fact be counted among the targets of his own poetic satire.

21. *SM* 2891–5 at 2895. On Montale's later work in relationship to Zanzotto (and Sereni) see also Luperini, *Storia di Montale*, 200–1, and Mengaldo, 'Primi appunti su *Satura*', 357.

22. On the rhetorical density of 'Fanfara', 'Gerarchie' and 'Dialogo', see Corti, '*Satura* e il genere "diario poetico"', 369–71.

23. Scrivano, 'La storia', 312–13.

24. West, *Eugenio Montale: Poet on the Edge*, 99–104.

25. The contemporary reference is confirmed in Greco, *Montale commenta Montale*, 62. The precise date of the poem is unclear. It is given as '1/4/69' in *OV* (998), but Grignani (*Prologhi ed epiloghi*, 121) notes the possible existence of an earlier draft as early as Dec. 1968.

26. The Leopardian overtones of this deeply pessimistic view have been pointed out by Scrivano ('La storia', 314): 'È il punto massimo del leopardismo di Montale: come per Leopardi, anche per Montale la felicità universale, se pur non fosse [...] un mito illusorio, non rimedia l'infelicità di uno'. One might add that it is surely the wry, ironic Leopardi of the *Operette morali* whose voice echos through Montale's later verse, especially at moments of quasi-dramatic dialogue such as this.

27. Oreste Macrì, 'L'"angelo nero" e il demonismo nella poesia montaliana', *L'Albero* 23/54 (1975), 3–75 at 42.
28. '[...] una commedia. *Sui generis*, ovviamente: bilanciata fra prosa e verso, fra dialogo e monologo; ma commedia essenzialmente.' See Ramat, *L'acacia ferita*, 167.
29. Forti, *Eugenio Montale*, 393.
30. The poems are dated '4/5/69' and '28/4/69' respectively; see *OV* 992 and 1001.
31. There may be an ironic echo of Goethe's *Faust* in this list of human intellectual endeavour. Consider Faust's opening words : 'Habe nun, ach! Philosophie, / Juristerei und Medezin, / Und leider auch Theologie! / Durchaus studiert, mit heißem Bemühn.' I am grateful to Professor Patrick Boyde for pointing out this possible allusion.
32. The 'Variazioni' article of 30 Nov. 1968, for example is accompanied by the untitled 'Dialogo' (described as the work of an anonymous 'nemico della dialettica'), while the article of 11 Apr. 1969 ends with 'Auf Wiedersehen' (under the original title 'La vera gibigianna'). See *PR* 1108, 1125.
33. Other sceptical or ironic allusions to the Apollo programme occur in 'Luna e poesia' (17 July 1969) and 'I naufraghi del cielo' (28 Apr. 1970) (see *SM* 2927–31, 2956–8). There is also a similar reference in a poem originally attached to another 'Variazioni' piece in Nov. 1969, 'Surrogati', now among the *Poesie disperse* in *OV*. Here 'gli allunamenti, d'interesse sempre / decrescente' are reduced to a uniform level of insignificance with 'le guerre (ma locali, che non ci tocchino) [...] le lotterie, le canzonette, il calcio' (*OV* 807).

CHAPTER 3

The Poet's Persona:
Isolation and Withdrawal

Images of isolation are characteristic of what may broadly be termed the autobiographical strand in *Satura* and the later collections, especially in those texts that explicitly present self-portraits. Montale's earlier poetry of tenacious resistance and opposition is now replaced by the poetry of impotent (and at times bitter) protest, a protest from within the society and the intellectual class so unflatteringly represented. Images of isolation, of withdrawal and of mere survival are the only means by which the poetic *io* can now assert his difference, his tenuous integrity in the face of a debased public life. Such images of the isolated self, while counterbalancing the overwhelmingly negative portrayal of the contemporary world, are themselves often rather ambiguous in their connotations. While Montale vigorously condemns the inauthenticity that surrounds him, he is equally uncompromising in his attitude to his own poetic persona, whose contradictions and limitations he repeatedly exposes. Thus questioning, self-doubt and, often, self-deprecation characterize his portrayal of the self, whether in relation to recent history, contemporary reality or his own poetic past.

'Botta e risposta': Ambiguous Self-Portraits

The representation of the *io* is one of the central concerns of the 'Botta e risposta' series, three poems that, taken together, constitute a multi-faceted and at times contradictory self-portrait (the texts were, in fact, composed over several years).[1] Indeed, these poems can be seen as part of a longer series of major self-portraits, going back at least as far as 'Il sogno del prigioniero' at the end of *Bufera* (but whose ultimate roots are found in 'Arsenio' in *Ossi*, as signalled explicitly at the start of the first 'Botta') and continuing in texts such as 'Lettera a Malvolio' or 'A questo punto' in *Diario*. Thus, as Forti observes, 'Botta e risposta I', acting as a kind of bridge between the third and fourth books, picks up and develops elements that were already present in the closing texts of *Bufera*, while, on the other hand, Franco Croce remarks that 'Lettera a Malvolio' can be seen as a sort of 'Botta e risposta IV', thus continuing the series into the fifth collection.[2] Within *Satura*, however, the 'Botta e risposta' series emerges as a clearly defined, self-contained entity. Apart from the cohesion deliberately indicated in the repeated use of the title, the poems are notable for their length (amidst other generally shorter texts) and their explicit structural and thematic similarities. In fact, the series constitutes one of the few clearly visible structural components of the book. An examination of each of these three self-portraits will help to delineate the features of the new poetic persona created by Montale in *Satura*, a persona whose presence and voice continue to be identifiable throughout the later collections.

'Botta e risposta I', placed at the opening of the book, has been the object of a great deal of interpretation and some lively critical and ideological polemics since it first appeared in an essentially private publication in 1962. Indeed, even in the early 1970s, not long after the poem's more public appearance in *Satura*, when Montale was questioned by Guarnieri as to the controversial identity of 'Lui' in the text, he was able to reply (with characteristic evasiveness) 'se n'è parlato tanto'.[3] What does seem clear is that the poem offers a kind of summation of aspects of the poet's life and times at a crucial point in his career, what West calls 'a great synthesis involving both past and future poetic goals and motifs'.[4] Furthermore, it seems most likely, as Jacomuzzi argues, that this poetic narrative of imprisonment in the Augean stables and subsequent liberation requires some kind of allegorical interpretation.[5] What is less clear however, is the precise nature of the events and processes to which the allegory refers:

> Uscito appena dall'adolescenza
> per metà della vita fui gettato
> nelle stalle d'Augìa.
> Non vi trovai duemila bovi, né
> mai vi scorsi animali;
> pure nei corridoi, sempre più folti
> di letame, si camminava male

> e il respiro mancava; ma vi crescevano
> di giorno in giorno i muggiti umani.
>
> Lui non fu mai veduto.
> La geldra però lo attendeva
> per il presentat-arm
> [...] (*OV* 277)

On the one hand, the poem has been interpreted as a straightforward historical allegory, an 'autobiografia politica in versi', or, broadly speaking, an account of the author's experience of the Fascist dictatorship and the anticlimactic post-war settlement.[6] Other critics, however, have offered more complex readings, questioning the simple correspondence between the stages of the narrative and major historical events, and suggesting that the degrading years of 'prigionia' may represent primarily a personal poetic and existential experience.[7] One of the most problematic questions has been that of the identity of 'Lui'. He is seen by Forti as a kind of personification of historical negativity, 'una presenza infernale: simultaneamente Dio e demonio, possibile e mai veduto salvatore e tiranno; una sola, grottesca immagine del negativo che accentua in sé un passato — politico, esistenziale, religioso — di comuni vergogne senza appello'.[8] For Jacomuzzi, on the other hand, 'Lui' is a kind of *deus absconditus*, the target of the poet's polemic precisely because of his absence, 'la figura di una frustrata attesa teologica' (in this perhaps prefiguring the problematic relationship with 'L'Altro'—see Chapter 4 below).[9] Clearly this figure, like this part of the text as a whole, is ultimately highly ambiguous. As Branca observes (in an article that, while it emphatically rejects a simple historical interpretation, simultaneously emphasizes the poem's historical roots): 'Anche "Le Stalle" [this poem] presentano dunque [...] un plurisemantismo, una plurileggibilità autobiografica. Vanno lette, sì, in senso metastorico e esistenziale ma senza escludere riflessi e riferimenti storici, che ci sono sempre anche nella poesia più metafisica'.[10] Such a reading, open and multifaceted but also firmly aware of the historical context, offers probably the most useful key to understanding the text.

However, leaving aside the controversies over the interpretation of this first part of the *risposta*, there seems little doubt that the last two stanzas of the poem refer directly to the political situation of post-war Italy, and reflect Montale's deep disillusionment with the country's failure, as he saw it, to realize the potential for true democratic and civic renewal:

A liberarci, a chiuder gli intricati
cunicoli in un lago, bastò un attimo
allo stravolto Alfeo. Chi l'attendeva
ormai? Che senso aveva quella nuova
palta? e il respirare altre ed equali
zaffate? e il vorticare sopra zattere
di sterco? ed era sole quella sudicia
esca di scolaticcio sui fumaioli,
erano uomini forse,
veri uomini vivi,
i formiconi degli approdi?
. . . .
                          (Penso
che forse non mi leggi più. Ma ora
tu sai tutto di me,
della mia prigionia e del mio dopo;
ora sai che non può nascere l'aquila
dal topo).

Montale's disgust at the mass politics practised by the two dominant
ideologies (an outlook formulated directly in his prose writings and
satirically in numerous other poems in *Satura*) is expressed here in
images and language whose scatological nature and crude energy
mark unequivocally, and with a shock for the reader, the passage from
his earlier to his later work. And, in the context of this fiercely
polemical vision of putrefaction and inhumanity, the poet concludes
by offering a self-portrait, framed in terms of exaggerated humility
and self-abasement. Negativity in the new dispensation is not
confined to the external world. Already, in the 'botta', his
correspondent had chided the *io* for his 'torpore / di sonnambulo',
and the closing image of the 'risposta' appears to confirm such a
reductive, unheroic characterization.

This image of the 'topo' is highly ambiguous (indeed, for the
English-speaking reader, the word itself is intrinsically ambiguous,
since it does not distinguish between the concepts of 'mouse' and
'rat', with their very different connotations). It marks, on the one
hand, an acceptance by the *io* of his own devalued status, a
renunciation of any aspiration to liberating flight (with all its positive
connotations from Montale's poetic past, ranging from the divine
indifference of the 'falco alto levato' in *Ossi*, to the many flights of
female figures, especially Clizia). Indeed, a foreshadowing of the
io–topo motif can be seen in several of the Volpe poems in *Bufera*,

where, with Clizia superseded, the poet's persona was already portrayed in the debased guise of 'rospo / uscito dalla fogna' ('Hai dato il mio nome', *OV* 258), or surrounded by 'lunghe strida / di sorci' ('Argyll Tour', *OV* 226), or ready to plunge into the sewers at the woman's command in 'Vento sulla Mezzaluna' (*OV* 227).[11] This embracing of personal and artistic limitations is one of the main foundations on which the poet goes on to build his self-portrait in *Satura*, where a full awareness of the impotence of the *io* and a willingness to declare this openly, to apparently reveal all ('tu sai tutto di me'), go hand in hand with resignation to the deeply problematic nature of the poet's art, and indeed to its possible irrelevance ('forse non mi leggi più'). (Questions related to the status and function of poetry are addressed elsewhere in numerous texts, for example 'La poesia' and 'Le rime' in 'Satura I'.)

On the other hand, however, the inadequacies of the *io/topo* exist on an entirely different level to the historical negativity denounced in the grotesque faecal imagery of the 'nuova palta'. Admittedly, on the face of it, the image of the 'topo' might seem to place the poetic persona on a level of degradation comparable to that of the entire post-war swamp and its inhabitants. After all, the mouse or rat is more immediately associated with the semantic area of the 'palta' and the 'zattere di sterco' than are the strange 'formiconi'. There are, however, very strong formal indicators of a clear separation between 'topo' and 'palta' here: the allegorical narrative ends with the extended indication of ellipsis, and the closing lines, addressed directly in the second person to the correspondent, are enclosed in a parenthesis that further isolates them from preceding material. In fact the imagery of the final lines, placed outside the closed system of the allegory, must be read in the broader context of Montale's poetry as a whole. There are numerous 'topi' in the poet's bestiary, but only once does the word have unequivocally negative connotations, when, in 'Madrigali fiorentini' the routed fascists, 'padroni d'ieri (di sempre?)' are characterized as 'topi di chiavica' (*OV* 207). Elsewhere, for example, there is Dora Markus's saving amulet, 'un topo bianco, d'avorio' (*Occasioni*), there are the 'topi familiari' of the poet's childhood home in 'Proda di Versilia' (*Bufera*), the same re-evoked later (not without irony) in 'Sotto la pergola' (*Quaderno*): 'Sulla pergola povera di foglie / vanno e vengono i topi in perfetto equilibrio' (*OV* 543). And also in *Quaderno*, in 'La verità', 'topi' offer a kind of minimal truth ('La verità è nei rosicchiamenti / delle tarme e dei topi'; *OV* 582), an integrity that stands in clear opposition to 'la logorrea schifa dei dialettici'. In *Altri versi*, we find the poet wryly speculating as to whether 'il topo che ha messo casa nel solaio' may not be just as well-equipped with 'autocoscienza' as he is (*OV* 659). These 'topi' then, though by no means uniform in their connotations, have in common an association with the idiosyncratic value of individual truths, the authenticity of individual experience, although this, like all values, is treated with increasing irony and ambiguity in the later works. But it is clear that in the last examples cited, the 'topo', as a detached observer of chaotic reality, shares some of the positive characteristics of the figure of the ageing poet himself.

In order to understand the relationship between this *io/topo* and the 'nuova palta', one must look within the allegorical narrative itself. Clearly, the initial position of the *io* is one of enforced inclusion in the mire of history: 'fui gettato [...]'. Nor does this change substantially. What does change, however, is his sense of his place within the community of this faecal world, within whose confines he moves from a position of belonging (albeit belonging to a degraded, humiliated community: 'badilanti infiacchiti colti in fallo / dai bargelli del brago'), to a clear position of detachment from collectivity. Thus in the post-war 'palta' his point of view from the spinning raft sets him apart from the 'formiconi degli approdi': while it clearly continues to include him in the fetid swamp, this position is also an embodiment of his detachment, his sense of 'inappartenenza' ('Xenia I' 14) in a meaningless world, the uncontrolled 'vorticare' a figure of his powerlessness to act upon that reality. The image of 'formiconi' typifies the poet's sense of aristocratic disdain and superiority over 'a contemptible collectivity', seen as 'un'amorfa entità massificata'.[12] Indeed, the same disdain inspires Montale more than once to use a similar image in his prose writings of this period. Thus for example, in 'La gente capisce' (1964), we find the following dismissive reference to mass entertainment: 'C'è la televisione, capace di vuotare le strade di ogni città ogni volta che un romanzo d'appendice a lungo metraggio venga offerto al formicaio dei "teleaudioutenti"'.[13]

Thus the close of 'Botta e risposta I', with the figure of the humble or degraded 'topo', is not an unequivocal act of self-debasement on the part of the *io*. The image is, as Zanzotto observes, less abject than it may seem.[14] Rather it represents a complex reappraisal of the powers and limitations of the poetic voice and of its relationship with society. While it denies the poetic persona the heroic role of 'aquila', it also represents an assertion of truth, of individual lucidity, over collective delusions. The *io* knows that self-denunciation, the declaration of his own impotence, is now a necessary part of his condemnation of a reality that contains him. As Franco Croce observes, 'Montale denuncia i suoi limiti ma non se ne fa piedistallo. Protesta contro la tirannide, ma protesta anche contro di sé, "topo", che la tirannide ha marcato per sempre.'[15] As in 'Fine del '68', he is both of the world and detached from it, isolated within the collective morass.

The reappraisal of the poet's relationship with society is taken up again some seven years later in 'Botta e risposta II', where a detached awareness of his own isolation is combined with his resigned immersion in the collective 'formicaio'. In the 'botta', the poet's correspondent, writing from her decadent retreat in Ascona, calls for a new disengagement on the part of the *io*: '"Il solipsismo non è il tuo forte, come si dice. / Se fosse vero saresti qui, insabbiato / in questa Capri nordica"' (*OV* 346). Here, as Croce notes, the roles of *io* and *tu* are apparently reversed: 'Montale, se nella prima ['Botta e risposta I'] rispondeva a un invito implicito a *s'engager*, qui risponde a un invito, esplicito, a *se désengager*, a essere davvero solipsista'.[16] The 'risposta' takes the form of an investigation, through personal and artistic memory, of the poet's purported solipsism and of how he can reconcile this with the present reality of life amidst the vulgarity of 'policromi estivanti' (a reference to his regular *villeggiatura* in these latter years in Forte dei Marmi, treated with similar ironic disdain elsewhere).[17] His self-examination once again includes his own poetic past, as he evokes ironically imagery from 'Meriggiare pallido e assorto', from the truly solipsistic phase represented by *Ossi*: 'Sto curvo su slabbrature e crepe del terreno / entomologo-ecologo di me stesso'. He then recalls a visit of his own to the the rarefied heights of Ascona (a visit treated journalistically elsewhere[18]), wryly acknowledging his own past dealings with the world of the ivory tower advocated by his correspondent. But now he rejects all this, declining the woman's invitation in a tone of superior disdain: 'E ora tutto è cambiato, un formicaio / vale l'altro ma questo mi attira di più'. Thus the terms of his reply evoke the imagery of 'Botta e risposta I' (already present here in the opening lines in the entomologically observed 'formicone'), but now de-dramatized, the object of indifference rather than disgust, as the *io* is resigned to submitting to the collective existence.

This is not, of course, to say that Montale now proposes to embrace the values (or pseudo-values) of the 'formicaio'. A sense of the ethical and intellectual superiority of the *io*, despite his diminished status, remains clear in this rather complex self-portrait. On the one hand, he rejects as 'mean' the philosopher Porphyry's élitist paradise of 'immarcescibili avari' (adding, lest we rush to find the source, that 'questo il greco / non lo disse e non è il caso di leggerlo').[19] Meanwhile, however, he continues to affirm his own difference from the throng. Like Mosca, he is one of the few 'bozze scorrette che il Proto / non degnò d'uno sguardo'. Having thus hesitated over whether or not he belongs to a privileged élite, the poetic persona eventually seems to imply that he does, but also, as Cambon observes, 'turns the weapons of irony against himself in the self-deflating posture we had already noticed in "Botta e risposta I"'.[20] So his difference is expressed in terms of withdrawal, self-abasement and lucid awareness of the 'buio' which is descending on him and his ilk:

> [...]
> Non per tutti, Porfirio, ma per i dàtteri
> di mare che noi siamo, incapsulati
> in uno scoglio. Ora neppure attendo
> che mi liberi un colpo di martello.
> [...] (OV 348)

Once again, resignation to imprisonment and impotence characterizes the figure of the *io*.

A similar image of defensive detachment and withdrawal, tinged with ironic self-mockery, brings this self-portrait to a close. On the one hand, he remains an inhabitant of the 'formicaio', as depicted in frankly comical and self-deprecating terms: 'questo butterato / sabbiume di policromi / estivanti ed io in mezzo, più arlecchino / degli altri'. Thus the element of inclusion in a negative reality, seen elsewhere, is maintained here. But, on the other hand, that inclusion, as before, is balanced by the motif of enclosure and withdrawal, as his very immersion in the world of 'gli altri' highlights his difference, his 'inappartenenza':

> [...]
> Nel buio e nella risacca più non m'immergo, resisto
> ben vivo vicino alla proda, mi basto come mai prima
> m'era accaduto. È questione
> d'orgoglio e temperamento. Sto attento a tutto. Se occorre,

spire di zampironi tentano di salvarmi
dalle zanzare che pinzano, tanto più sveglie di me.

While these lines undoubtedly recall the distant past of 'Falsetto' (*Ossi*), where the 'razza di chi rimane a terra' watched enviously as Esterina embraced the sea, they now rule out any sense of ambition on the part of the *io* to participate in the surrounding reality ('mi basto [...]'). Here, the speaker's activities and aspirations are reduced to a minimum: silent observation from within a hostile reality and a minimal degree of self-preservation, as the *io* defends himself against the hostilities of mere 'zanzare', possibly a comic reduction of the earlier 'formiconi', now no more than a source of irritation. Meanwhile, the mosquitos' main attribute, their wakefulness, highlights another constant element in these self-portraits: his torpor, that of the 'tardi risvegliato' of 'Botta e risposta I', a motif developed elsewhere in images of senile 'dormiveglia'.

The minimal aspiration to survival is pursued further in 'Botta e risposta III', where, however, it is explored in direct relation to contemporary history, giving rise to a rare but fleeting moment of unambiguous moral and ethical tension in this series. The 'botta', a letter from Kifissia, introduces the urgent historical reality of resurgent right-wing dictatorship (the poem was written in 1968, the second year of the military regime in Greece).[21] This reality, however, is consigned to the circumspection of metaphor (in keeping with the apprehensive tone of the correspondent's letter): 'Già la pentola bolliva / e a stento bolle ancora mentre scrivo' (*OV* 360). The image resonates clearly with the whole vein of culinary motifs used repeatedly in the portrayal of historical and political negativity in this series of self-portraits and beyond.[22] These culinary motifs are further underpinned throughout the later works by a related network of images of general putrefaction. Thus, for example, in the present text, the poet recalls being offered 'triglie [...] marce' during a visit to Greece, reinforcing the impression that a background of corruption and decay constantly threatens the integrity of the poet's persona.

Here in the 'botta', indeed, the *io* is initially portrayed in an attitude of vulnerability and retreat ('Ho riveduto il tetro dormitorio / dove ti rifugiasti'), as his correspondent recalls the poet's difficulty in finding a room in an Athens hotel, full because of a royal wedding.[23] But the characterization of the *io* as a 'povero malnato' at the mercy of the great and powerful must clearly be read ironically (Montale's worldly familiarity with places such as the 'King George' is amply documented in other poems of these years).[24] The problems he encountered during his Athenian sojourn were of an entirely different order to the malevolent 'bollore' of dictatorship that now threatens the correspondent, which she tries to muffle with the 'suono dolce' of her harpsichord, the fragile voice of art, of culture. Yet the two figures are linked, however tenuously, by their need for some kind of refuge.

This motif of 'rifugio' is taken up and elaborated in the 'risposta' as the poet's persona replies to the correspondent's gentle ironizing with an understated but heartfelt profession of faith in the power of language, of poetry, to counter the threat of 'persecuzioni, manette', and to offer a secret, individual form of survival:

> [...] le ombre che si nascondono
> tra le parole, imprendibili,
> mai palesate, mai scritte,
> mai dette per intero,
> le sole che non temono
> contravvenzioni,
> persecuzioni, manette,
> non hanno né un prima né un dopo
> perché sono l'essenza della memoria.
> Hanno una forma di sopravvivenza
> che non interessa la storia,
> [...] (OV 361)

One can hear what Forti calls 'la voce del maggior recitativo montaliano' (albeit 'intimizzata') in the close-knit phonic texture of these lines, their avoidance of the flatly prosaic rhythms of 'Botta e risposta II' and other texts.[25] This underlines a rare moment of confidence in language as authentic individual expression, and, implicitly, confidence in the poet's art. One might even read into these lines an oblique allusion to the necessary political reticence of Montale's own work of an earlier period, but the 'ombre' to which he now refers are more than just the areas of obscurity and allusivity that a poet might exploit to circumvent censorship. They are, rather, the privileged internal zone in which an individual, personal truth can remain untouched by the external forces of history. This safe haven of authenticity, of the reality of individual identity ('l'essenza della memoria'), accessed through the interstices of language, is also a personal temporal dimension, placed in direct opposition to conventional historical time. So political 'persecuzioni' can be seen as just one more hostile emanation from the old enemy, Time itself, and the atemporal 'ombre' another formulation of the 'nascondigli' of 'La storia II'.

This privileged space or hiding place is defined more openly in the second stanza, where the poet's attempt to 'trovare spazio' (one of the main 'tactical' concerns of *Satura* according to Ramat, along with the need to 'assumere un volto'[26]) seems to have been successful:

> [...]
> E posso dirti senza orgoglio
> [...]
> che c'è tra il martire e il coniglio,
> tra la galera e l'esilio,
> un luogo dove l'inerme
> lubrifica le sue armi,
> poche ma durature.
> [...]

The lines are striking for their tone of quiet assurance, as the *io* affirms a positive possibility of resistance, with, in Croce's words, 'uno scatto di agonismo', quite out of keeping with the resigned scepticism of the other two 'Botta e risposta' texts.[27] Is this then, as Ramat asks, the sign of a new confidence, a new *impegno*, 'la sede morale della nuova resistenza montaliana?'[28] The answer, though by no means unequivocal, tends ultimately in this poem towards the negative. Even within these richly musical lines, the speaker's faith in his 'weapons' (which, one may tentatively assume, include the instruments of poetry) is formulated in the context of an oxymoronic tension between 'armi' and 'inerme'. And in the following stanzas, contradictions in the poet's self-portrait accumulate as the construction of a possible ethical 'habitat' is seen to be deeply problematic in the context of contemporary Italy. Thus while resistance to open oppression ('Resistere al vincitore') may have been superseded by the more difficult resistance to the falsifications of post-war Italy ('resistere al peggio che simula il meglio'), even this new 'resistance' is 'un inganno', there is no escape from a profoundly contaminated reality. Authentic values, even for the individual, reside in the past (for example in a memory of Greece, when he was still 'un nume', still 'nel divino', even if 'in abito turistico'). Now the *io* is immersed in the amorphous mass of contemporary political reality, where apparent divisions are meaningless:

[...] Ora
vivo dentro due chiese che si spappolano,
dissacrate da sempre, mercuriali,
dove i pesci che a gara vi boccheggiano
sono del tutto eguali.
[...]

Just as in 'Piccolo testamento' (*Bufera*), where he spurned equally
'chierico rosso, o nero', the speaker here declares his contempt for the
dominant, ethically indistinguishable, ideologies (the political
references were much more explicit in an earlier draft—see *OV* 1017).
But for all his ethical detachment, he is inescapably contained in this
reality: 'vivo dentro [...]'. Once again an image of inclusion, albeit
unwilling inclusion, negates any unequivocal ethical superiority to
which the *io* may aspire. He is contaminated by the morass around
him, and unsure as to whether he himself deserves the 'pietà' he
applies to that external reality.

The concluding lines bring us back to the important question of
the value of poetry itself. It seems that the act of writing, a possible
refuge from hostile forces, is ultimately a marginal pursuit, of dubious
significance. Here, there is a parallel with 'Botta e risposta I', where
the *io* had questioned the usefulness of his writing ('forse non mi leggi
più'). But now the problem is more radical, as it concerns the
continuation even of attempted communication, the continuation of
correspondence:

[...] Lascio irrisolto
il problema, sigillo questa lettera
e la metto da parte. La ventura
e la censura hanno in comune solo
la rima. E non è molto.

Thus, with a characteristic note of de-dramatizing banality (the simple
rhyme, *censura–ventura*, whose significance, along with that of all
rhyme, is immediately minimized), Montale counters the danger that
he might slip into a pompous vatic mode in his attitude of civic
indignation. The dismissal of 'la rima' is just part of the tendency to
constantly devalue the poetic voice itself. And yet, there remains the
openness to 'la ventura', to the possibility of the positive (in *Ossi*,
'ventura' was, memorably, one word for Montale's 'miracle': 'svanire
/ è dunque la ventura delle venture'). It is an exiguous 'forma di
sopravvivenza' that sets the *io* (and his correspondent: 'in questo mi

rassomigli [...]') apart from the tyranny of 'la storia'. Ultimately, however, Montale retreats in this self-portrait from the momentary 'agonismo' seen above, and settles once more on a model of enclosure and withdrawal ('sigillo questa lettera / e la metto da parte') as the only possible strategy of 'resistance' to the reality in which he is trapped.

This is the stance that he defends a few years later when he comes to write 'Lettera a Malvolio' (*Diario*), a sort of 'risposta senza botta', where the *io* responds to accusations of cowardice by a new interlocutor:

> Non s'è trattato mai di una mia fuga, Malvolio,
> [...]
>
>   No,
> non si trattò mai d'una fuga
> ma solo di un rispettabile
> prendere le distanze. (*OV* 456)

There is, behind Montale's ostensibly dignified tone, more than a hint of ironic self-mockery here, reinforced in the following lines by the rather unheroic depiction of his strategy at an earlier time, 'dapprima' (under Fascism), when it was easy to 'rendersi invisibili, / forse esserlo'. As in previous self-portraits, the role of 'topo' is embraced by the *io*, along with all the ambiguities that this entails. However, notwithstanding this element of self-deprecating irony, a note of marked and heartfelt antagonism is present from the beginning of 'Lettera a Malvolio'. The precise identity of Montale's interlocutor is not clear (and is ultimately of limited importance), but it may indeed, as is widely presumed, be Pasolini, who had written a withering ideological critique of *Satura*.[29] The *io*, accused of having a flair for 'il peggio', turns the charge back against his unnamed accuser in a gesture of bitter recrimination: 'Questa è una virtù che tu possiedi'. This sets the tone for a text in which various motifs, images and rhetorical structures already found in the three 'Botta e risposta' poems are brought together in a fiercely polemical synthesis. For his adversary (whoever this may be), the poet's detachment from public life apparently represents an unacceptable relinquishing of responsibility. This charge offers Montale the pretext for a vigourous defence of his position and a scathing attack on the spurious certainties of the *engagé* intellectual (what one critic calls 'il coro compatto degli intellettuali borghesi in crisi').[30] If the conclusion of

'Botta e risposta III' seemed to portray the poet's isolation in terms of pessimism and defeat, this is coloured now with a new note of passion and defiance in the face of what the poet sees as the facile dogmatism and bad faith of the times.

The pessimistic view of contemporary historical reality is not only sustained here, but given a new definitive formulation, in terms that explicitly recall the bleak vision of 'Botta e risposta I' and simultaneously confirm its validity and render it absolute and enduring:

> Ma dopo che le stalle si vuotarono
> l'onore e l'indecenza stretti in un solo patto
> fondarono l'ossimoro permanente
> e non fu più questione
> di fughe e di ripari. [...]

Nevertheless, if escape is impossible, imprisonment permanent, Montale also confirms in this poem the existence of a valid model of detachment, a slender possibility of hope sought in paradox, of withdrawal from the world while remaining in the world:

> [...]
> Ma lascia andare le fughe ora che appena si può
> cercare la speranza nel suo negativo.
> Lascia che la mia fuga immobile possa dire
> forza a qualcuno o a me stesso che la partita è aperta,
> [...]

'Fuga immobile': his retreat, as befits the age of oxymoron, is not a retreat, it is a continuing presence, but also a dogged refusal to participate and conform, to accept defeat. In this context, his ambition with regard to his fellow man is strictly limited: not 'dare' but '*dire* forza', the mere continuation of discourse.

In this series of self-portraits as a whole (as elsewhere in *Satura*), the values and attitudes attributed to the poet's persona are often contradictory: on the one hand the *io* is portrayed as ethically superior to the surrounding mass, lucid in his denunciation of falsehood and hypocrisy; on the other hand, he is a debased and impotent figure, unsure of the validity of his own beliefs and actions, trapped in his own 'torpore'. The range of images employed reflects these tensions: figures of isolation, defensive withdrawal and detachment from a negative reality are constantly challenged by images of imprisonment, enclosure, contamination and belonging, giving rise to a widespread presence of paradox and oxymoron. And indeed, if oxymoron is, as Mengaldo asserts, the 'fundamental' rhetorical figure employed in Montale's later works, it is appropriate that the characteristic condition and attitude of the poet's persona with regard to historical reality in these works is itself a paradox, a condition of 'partecipazione e distacco' of simultaneous *impegno* and withdrawal.[31] Having already examined (in Chapter 2) several texts in *Satura* dominated by an element of polemical 'partecipazione', we will now turn to a series of poems (especially in *Diario* and *Quaderno*) where the element of 'distacco' comes to the fore, as expressed in particular through a cohesive group of images centred on the space of the home, the place from which, increasingly, the lyrical persona conducts his detached but attentive observation of the world.

The Retreat: The Domestic Space from *Satura* to *Quaderno*

In his 1971 review of *Satura*, Pasolini refers in passing to the circumstances of Montale's existence as one might perceive them through his poetry: 'Egli ha fatto trapelare nei suoi tre libri [...] che la sua vita, se si vuol proprio dedurlo, si svolge tra un appartamento elegante ma non eccezionale e un soggiorno in qualche albergo di prima categoria'.[32] The idea of this axis of location between the home and the quasi-public space of the hotel is taken up by Elisabetta Graziosi, who explores at some length what she calls the 'spazio turistico' of the hotel and other similar locations.[33] Graziosi largely ignores the 'spazio domestico' however, and it is this space that becomes the key setting for the poetry of *Diario* and *Quaderno*. There is a clear shift in the poetic locations used after *Satura*. There, the 'spazio turistico' is still indeed very much in evidence (for example in numerous texts in 'Xenia', or in the sequence 'Dopo una fuga'). Subsequently, however, poems with a clear setting outside the home become harder to find, and a count of the texts in which a physical setting as a *present* reality is either stated explicitly or clearly implied (i.e. a setting involving neither distant memory nor fantasy) reveals that the home is by far the single most frequently occurring poetic location in the following two collections. Twenty-three poems in *Diario* and *Quaderno* can be identified as having a domestic interior setting, while all other identifiable locations taken together account for only thirteen texts.[34] Thus, while most poems have no specific setting, the predominance of the domestic scene among those that do tends clearly to establish this as the spatial focus of these collections. From *Diario* onwards, Montale's apartment in via Bigli in Milan becomes the key physical space in his poetry, as the poetic voice now speaks almost exclusively from within the clearly delineated and physically restricting boundaries of the home. As Luperini observes: 'La scena è quasi del tutto deserta di eventi, di paesaggi e di cose; si riduce a qualche interno, alla cornice di una finestra, allo spazio di un balcone ove talvolta si posano merli o piccioni.'[35] As the dominant spatial image, the home (along with its contents and peculiar fauna) soon acquires a number of figurative connotations closely linked to the representation of the poetic *io* and his values.

It is in *Satura* that the domestic space first emerges as an image with clearly recognizable features and connotations. It is the implicit setting for a number of the 'Xenia' poems, e.g. 'Xenia I' 1 and 2, where the poet's solitude, 'quasi al buio', reading, strongly suggests a domestic setting. In others we are given fleeting glimpses of his intimate surroundings: we see the portraits of Mosca (XI 13: 'tu eri / la bimba scarruffata che mi guarda / "in posa" nell'ovale di un ritratto.') and of Mosca's father (XII 13: 'Ho appeso nella mia stanza il dagherròtipo / di tuo padre bambino'). In 'Satura II' a number of texts evoke indirectly the physical setting from which the solitary *io* observes the world: he looks out of a closed window for example in 'Vedo un uccello fermo sulla grondaia', and in 'Piove', as he peruses his tax papers, he watches the raindrops 'qui dal balcone aperto' (*OV* 343, 337). In 'Nel silenzio' the setting is made more explicit, the silence of the title being that of the empty apartment in which the lyrical voice is heard:

> Oggi è sciopero generale.
> Nella strada non passa nessuno.
> Solo una radiolina dall'altra parte del muro.
> Da qualche giorno deve abitarci qualcuno.
> Mi chiedo che ne sarà della produzione.
> La primavera stessa tarda alquanto a prodursi.
> Hanno spento in anticipo il termosifone.
> Si sono accorti ch'è inutile il servizio postale.
> [...] (*OV* 404)

The poetic persona is cut off from the outside world and from human contact (though the once metaphysical barrier of the wall, now domesticated, cannot quite separate him from the sound of unseen neighbours). The structure, with each line coinciding with a single grammatical period, is unusually inert, reflecting the dull monotony of the situation (Pellini suggests that this is a specific parody of Franco Fortini, poet laureate of Italian Marxism).[36] The silence is that of non-communication, of a world which no longer addresses the *io* in any meaningful way. (In this context, the muffled 'radiolina' could perhaps be read as a muted reference to Mosca's cryptic communications in 'Xenia' via the telex or telephone, but more probably embodies the constant 'blabla' of the world at large.)

The silence of the title is also that of Mosca and of the dead in general, whose 'agitazione', paradoxically, consists of an unaccustomed stillness:

> [...]
> Non è gran male il ritardo delle funzioni normali.
> È d'obbligo che qualche ingranaggio non ingrani.
> Anche i morti si sono messi in agitazione.
> Anch'essi fanno parte del silenzio totale.
> Tu stai sotto una lapide. Risvegliarti non vale
> perché sei sempre desta. Anche oggi ch'è sonno
> universale.

Even in her silence she is a presence, 'sempre desta', seemingly the only vital presence in the otherwise empty, universal silence of the poet's shrunken world (and, appropriately, her appearance brings about the only break in the relentless structural uniformity of the text). At the centre of the poem, acting as a hinge between this world and the world of the dead, of Mosca, is another variant on the familiar motif of the unforeseeable event, the suspension of 'funzioni normali' echoing the dysfunction in the 'congegni' of 'Tempo e tempi', the tear in the net of 'La storia II'. Thus 'Nel silenzio' combines elements of the meditative vein (represented by those two poems) with echoes of the Mosca cycle (for example, the paradoxical merging of opposites—sleep and wakefulness—the prosaic rhythm and paratactic structure), and weaves them in a rich and subtle counterpoint with the more diaristic elements of commentary on contemporary reality and the private chronicle of the minutiae of domestic life.

In the next poem in *Satura*, 'Luci e colori', the poet's room is again the setting for one of Mosca's 'visite mute'. Here, not only does she appear as the familiar ghost, glimpsed in a 'lampeggio di lenti', but her visit coinicides with the appearance of a 'vermiciattolo / che arrancava a disagio' on the bedside rug. This curious, vaguely repulsive apparition seems to be the only tangible sign of her presence, and given the other unflattering images associated with her elswhere (not least in her bizarre pet name) it is not perhaps too far-fetched to see the creature as an emblem of her. In this context, what Montale does with the 'vermiciattolo' is interesting, as it may, by association, suggest the beginning of the difficult process of liberation from the persistent presence of the ghost:

> [...] Non riuscì facile farlo
> slittare su un pezzo di carta e buttarlo giù vivo
> nel cortile. Tu stessa non devi pesare di più. (*OV* 405)

Especially in the light of the explicit comparison in the closing line, it seems significant that the instrument of this liberation is paper, the medium of the poet's art, through which he has, in a sense been freeing himself from Mosca's presence since 'Xenia'.[37] But what is perhaps more immediately interesting, in view of Montale's subsequent use of the domestic space as an image, is that here for the first time we look out onto the courtyard below. Thus, already in *Satura* there begins to take shape a general outline of the poet's physical surroundings: an urban apartment overlooking a courtyard, a view of life whose restricted horizons will be found repeatedly in the later collections.

The domestic space becomes the most recognizable setting in *Diario* and *Quaderno*, and with it comes a cluster of recurrent images: the window, the balcony, birds outside and, within, the grudgingly accepted presence of the television screen, all presided over by the figure of the poet's housekeeper, Gina. Early in *Diario*, 'Rosso su rosso' sets the scene:

> È quasi primavera e già i corimbi
> salgono alla finestra che dà sul cortile.
> Sarà presto un assedio di foglie e di formiche.
> Un coleottero tenta di attraversare il libretto
> delle mie Imposte Dirette, rosso su rosso. Magari
> potesse stingere anche sul contenuto. È suonato
> il mezzogiorno, trilla qualche telefono
> e una radio borbotta duecento morti
> sull'autostrada, il record della Pasquetta. (*OV* 422)

Here one finds a number of familiar elements from the poems just examined in *Satura*. The window and courtyard again delimit the space. In 'Luci e colori' the 'vermiciattolo' was ejected into the courtyard, while here the insect world stages an incursion from outside (with contrasting lexical registers in 'formiche' and 'coleottero'). The tax documents recall those of 'Piove'. The distant or muted sounds of instruments of communication, telephone and radio, echo the unseen neighbour's 'radiolina' of 'Nel silenzio'. The season is spring, as in 'Nel silenzio'. There, however, the poet had transferred the paralysis of the general strike onto the very movement of the seasons. There was a temporal dysfunction, a quasi-magical event, involving a suspension of the normal passage of time, and that dysfunction was the key to the world of 'i morti' facilitating the *io*'s heightened awareness of the presence of Mosca, of her wakefulness in the universal torpor. Here in 'Rosso su rosso', however, there are only the unremarkable temporal indications of 'primavera', 'mezzogiorno' and 'Pasquetta', in keeping with Montale's new diaristic mode in which the passing of time is marked increasingly by the chronicling of day-to-day events. Mosca is no longer present: Easter has brought no resurrection, only the senseless slaughter of the 'Pasquetta', the unremarkable horror of two hundred road deaths, a gruesome echo of the earlier 'morti [...] in agitazione'. They are a part of the meaningless phenomena of an outside world beyond the poet's home, brought to him by the impersonal 'borbottare' of the media, of public life at one remove.

Most significantly, however, here for the first time the *io* is depicted completely alone in the domestic setting, unattended even by the ghost of Mosca. She does return sporadically in *Diario* and *Quaderno*, but her role in these domestic poems is soon taken over, at least in part, by a new guardian angel, 'la Gina', the figure of Montale's devoted housekeeper. Gina first appears in a poem whose setting closely resembles that of 'Rosso su rosso', 'Nel cortile'. The title itself defines the spatial boundaries of the scene, but here the courtyard becomes the stage for a somewhat more complex spectacle of emblematic figures and itself acquires a figurative significance. The poet reiterates his urban isolation ('la città si svuota'), as centre stage is occupied by a newly prominent member of the Montalean bestiary:

> [...]
> È dalle Idi di marzo che un vecchio merlo si posa
> sul davanzale a beccare chicchi di riso e briciole.
> [...] (*OV* 425)

Whereas in the past winged creatures have been associated in varying degrees with the supernatural qualities of Clizia, Volpe or Mosca, this blackbird, a recurrent presence in these final collections, displays none of the angelic or clairvoyant attributes of Montale's *ispiratrici*. Rather it appears to embody some of the qualities of the poet's own persona. ('Merlo' was a name given habitually to Montale in the idiolect employed in his private dealings with Mosca and others, as seen for example in the correspondence with Contini.[38]) Poised on the window-ledge, it belongs neither fully to the interior nor to the exterior scene, a situation characteristic of Montale's marginal and indeed ambiguous positions. Apart from old age, its main attribute seems to be a kind of aloofness: it spurns the 'cortile' below, which is of no interest to it, containing as it does the cast-offs and refuse of contemporary man:

> [...]
> Non utile per lui scendere nel cortile
> ingombro di tante macchine casse sacchi racchette.
> [...]

At this point it is useful to compare these lines with a passage from 'Le acque alte' in *Diario del '72*. That poem describes the erosion of meaning and individual identity wrought by time (represented by water), as the poet looks out apparently onto the same courtyard (its contents are almost identical to those of the other 'cortile'):

> [...]
> Parve che la ribollente zavorra su cui mi affaccio
> rottami, casse, macchine ammassate
> giù nel cortile,
> la fumosa colata che se ne va
> per conto suo e ignora la nostra esistenza,
> parve che tutto questo fosse la prova del nove
> che siamo qui per qualcosa un trabocchetto o uno scopo.
> Parve, non pare ...
> [...] (*OV* 465)

A figurative function of the 'cortile' and its contents begins to emerge. It is explicitly the poet's own persona who looks down with disdain on the 'rottami' below. The 'fumosa colata', the molten flow of which they are a part, can be identified with the 'acque' of the title. These in turn have already been established in lines 13–14 of the same text as a figure of time as it operates its 'flaccido / gonfio risciacquamento':

> Le acque si riprendono
> ciò che hanno dato: le asseconda il loro
> invisibile doppio, il tempo; [...]

The 'zavorra' then, the clutter and dross in the courtyard, is what remains of the once meaningful spectacle of the world in time. But now the illusion of meaning is gone: 'Parve, non pare ...'. The specific exterior of the 'cortile' becomes the latest embodiment of what Marchese calls 'l'esterno negativo della prospettiva montaliana, un esterno caotico di relitti', viewed here by the poetic persona through the emblematic 'frontier' of the window.[39] It is precisely on this frontier, 'sul davanzale', on the border between the inner and outer zones, that the poet places the blackbird of 'Nel cortile', indifferent to the useless wreckage below (clearly the same 'rottami' as in 'Le acque alte'), intent only on practical minutiae, 'briciole', at the edge of the poet's apartment. Given the figurative function of the 'cortile' just outlined, it is easy to identify the bird's quiet detachment with the attitude of the poet himself and to see its marginal position, belonging fully to neither zone, as another figuration of the poet's ambivalent withdrawal from the world.

Other figures are also seen on the edge of the courtyard's abyss in 'Nel cortile'. The poet's neighbours (an 'antiquario in vestaglia', a 'grande Oncologo') sit comfortably in his repertoire of *grandi borghesi* and mildly eccentric individuals (as present for example in *Farfalla di Dinard* and elsewhere). But between the two, there is another, incongruous presence:

> [...] Da un altro osservatorio
> un ragazzino rossiccio che tira ai piccioni col flòbert.
> [...] (*OV* 425)

This constitutes a precise allusion within Montale's creative universe. In *Farfalla di Dinard*, Montale evokes his own boyhood use of just such a weapon (a type of air-gun), as the protagonist of 'Il bello viene dopo' recalls a favourite pastime of his childhood, hunting small birds with his companions (when he was not hunting eels in dried-up streams): 'I miei amici avevano fionde all'elastico (vulgo *cacciafrusti*) ma io disponevo di un Flobert ch'ero riuscito a caricare con tre o quattro microscopici pallini' (*PR* 49). Indeed hunting is a recurrent theme in this first part of *Farfalla di Dinard* and seems to have constituted an early form of magical, though not entirely unproblematic experience in Montale's youth (see also 'La busacca' in the same book).[40] In this light, another piece of the old man's world falls into place. Memories of childhood and youth provide a positive note in the poetry of these years, in counterpoint with the disillusioned discourse on contemporary life and ideas. Thus the little boy with his 'flòbert' (shooting at pigeons, antagonists, as we shall see below, of the blackbird), uncontaminated by the chaos below, is a direct link between the window, the home, and the world of memory, a link that bypasses or ignores the debased, meaningless present.

In the closing lines of this poem Gina finally makes her appearance in the context of a typically unremarkable domestic anecdote, as she is wakened by celebrations in the neighbouring apartment:

> [...]
> Tanti gli stappamenti di sciampagna,
> i flash, le risa, gli urli dei gratulanti
> che anche la Gina fu destata e corse
> tutta eccitata a dirmi: ce l'ha fatta! (*OV* 425)

Characteristically of the later Montale, the episode reduces once symbolically laden terms like 'avvampare', 'luci' and 'flash' to the mere trappings of *mondanità*. One of Gina's functions is to comment (her words, as elsewhere, are reported directly) on the minor events in the poet's domestic life, and certain criticism has focused on the supposed bourgeois condescension in Montale's portrayal of her.[41] But her presence, presiding over the home in *Diario*, is unmistakably reminiscent in its functions of the presence/absence of Mosca in *Satura*. Gina appears, albeit in the background, as a source of companionship and support (but also of mildly ironic interjections) in the increasing absence of the ghost, and, as will emerge below, ultimately acquires some minor quasi-magical, positive connotations of her own.

In 'Al mio grillo' at the end of *Diario del '72* she appears almost as a manifestation of Mosca, or at any rate, the guardian of her memory, as the 'povero insetto' of 'Xenia' appears in the form of another insect. Gina's voice, whether quoted directly (as in line 1) or indirectly ('fa un disastro', line 4), adds another element to the rich variety of tonal registers employed in the comic style of these later collections:

> Che direbbe il mio grillo
> dice la Gina osservando il merlo
> che becca larve e bruchi dentro i vasi
> da fiori del balcone e fa un disastro.

> Ma il più bello è che il grillo eri tu
> finché vivesti e lo sapemmo in pochi.
> Tu senza occhietti a spillo di cui porto
> un doppio, un vero insetto di celluloide
> con due palline che sarebbero gli occhi,
> due pistilli e ci guarda da un canterano.
> [...] (*OV* 507)

In the opening lines a clear opposition is set up between the rapacious blackbird and the 'grillo', and figurative functions can be assigned implicitly to the bird and explicitly to the insect. The latter, it emerges in the course of the poem, is, at least on one level, some kind of plastic representation of a cricket, placed on a piece of furniture in the room (lines 8–10). There is also the suggestion, however, that the poet carries this 'grillo' with him ('porto'), and so one may see it as the latest in a long line of totemic creatures in Montale, though this 'insetto di celluloide' stands in clear contrast with earlier, more durable amulets such as Dora Markus's 'topo d'avorio' or Mosca's 'bulldog di legno'. The identification already outlined between the 'merlo' of 'Nel cortile' and the figure of the poet allows us to read into this poem a re-evocation of the sometimes tense and quasi-antagonistic relationship between the figures of the poet and Mosca as portrayed in 'Xenia'. As the bird wreaks destruction on 'larve e bruchi' (we recall the association of Mosca with the 'vermiciattolo' of 'Luci e colori'), it is Gina who sides with the unfortunate insects. After the poet's recollection of Mosca ('il grillo eri tu'), the present cricket is identified as her 'double' or counterpart, and Gina's role becomes explicitly to act vicariously for Mosca:

> [...]
> Che ne direbbe il grillo d'allora del suo sosia
> e del merlo? È per lei che sono qui
> dice la Gina e scaccia con la scopa il merlaccio.
> Poi s'alzano le prime saracinesche. È giorno.

The meaning of her gesture in chasing away the bird is ambivalent. She is certainly paying homage to the memory of Mosca, and her action is taken in defence of creatures reminiscent of Mosca's mixture of helplessness and winged freedom. But in the process she becomes the antagonist of a figure already established as sympathetic to the poet, the 'merlo', now (probably in her words) 'merlaccio'. Gina's unpretentious voice acts as a counterpoint to the poet's interior monologue, just as Mosca's memory has since 'Xenia' repeatedly impinged on his consciousness, causing him to question his values and self-esteem (see for example XI 6). For though the poetic persona may despise the world and its values, he still, however precariously, exists within it. Unlike his various *ispiratrici*, he is still condemned to be part of the debased reality of everyday life, where, as documented in these poetic diaries, no unequivocal value persists. Mere persistence is all, as day, with its return to banal reality, follows the potentially liberating realm of half-light (associated, in other related texts, with more authentic realities of memory and dream).

Gina intervenes in defence of another winged creature in 'Il rondone' (*OV* 436) and again the presence of Mosca is evoked: the swift of the title is crippled: 'non poteva volare'. The domestic setting becomes a sanctuary for the injured bird, brought in from the outside world of the 'marciapiede'. Here a number of previous inhabitants of Montale's poetic aviary are called to mind. The bird's 'ali ingrommate di catrame' may recall the 'penne lacerate' of 'Mottetti' 12 or the sooty wings of 'L'angelo nero' in *Satura*, and indeed, as Fortini notes, they echo precisely those of the winged *ispiratrice* in 'Sulla colonna più alta' (*Bufera*).[42] But the memory of Mosca persists in the bird's vision, as Gina nurses it tenderly: 'Lui la guardava quasi riconoscente / da un occhio solo'. The closing lines, with the bird's departure 'senza salutare', echo another long-standing theme of Montale's:

> Che fretta aveva fu il commento. E dire
> che l'abbiamo salvato dai gatti. Ma ora forse
> potrà cavarsela.

It is a variation in a minor key on the theme of vicarious salvation in *Ossi*: 'Il tuo cuore che non m'ode / salpa già forse per l'eterno' ('Casa sul mare'). In the present poem the situation is translated into domestic terms, into Gina's colloquial diction (or that of the 'cameriera del piano di sopra'), but again the *io* is condemned to stay behind, abandoned on the shores of a despised reality. Gina's intervention is in the role of guardian angel, but of a modest domestic type. As elsewhere in *Diario*, such importance as is bestowed upon trivial events springs in part from the strict spatial restriction of a world where poetic images must be forged out of material available within the boundaries of the poet's home and 'cortile'.

The motif of the 'merlo' recurs at intervals throughout *Quaderno*. In 'La solitudine' (*OV* 532), the now familiar scene of the window-ledge is repeated, with the added (and somewhat less distinguished) presence of some pigeons. In contrast with the solitary blackbird, the pigeons' gregarious character is highlighted, their 'agitazione' stemming from 'obblighi corporativi'. There is a mildly satirical tone in this use of industrial-relations terminology ('Al mio ritorno l'ordine si rifà / con supplemento di briciole'), in keeping with the wider use in these collections of the discourse of such public domains as journalism or bureaucracy. But the blackbird remains apart, at once privileged and marginalized: its special position of independence is no guarantee against the others' gaining the upper hand, as restated in epigrammatic form in *Altri versi*, in a pithy jocular image of the exclusion and defeat of the individual:

> Quel bischero del merlo è arrivato tardi.
> I piccioni hanno già mangiato tutto. (*OV* 632)

The type of routine sketched in these poems is also evoked in 'Ho sparso di becchime il davanzale' (*OV* 552), and with its repetition it comes to be seen as part of a minor nightly domestic ritual (see also *OV* 656). Its morning sequel ('il concerto di domani all'alba') is assured. And equally assured is the imminence of sleep, with its dream-vision of 'la sfilata dei morti'. The feeding of the birds then forms part of a wider ritual of solitude, a prelude to the memorial vision of the dead, thus bringing the birds into the circle of those Montalean domestic lares associated with the past.

In 'Appunti' later in *Quaderno*, the blackbird appears again. Here Montale is in his eschatological mode, considering the afterlife and the struggle between good and evil, as personified in the Zoroastrian figures of Ahura Mazda and Ahriman. But at the end of the poem the reader learns of its setting, nocturnal and domestic, through this separately headed section:

> [...]
>
> GINA ALL'ALBA MI DICE
>
> il merlo è sulla frasca
> e dondola
> felice. (*OV* 570)

In 'Ho sparso di becchime' the poet's night-time ritual led on to the world of dreams, of colloquy with the dead. Here, the overall direction of thematic movement is reversed. From his meditation on the great questions of the afterlife, the *io* returns to the concrete, the world of daily routine, as Gina's voice brings him back down to earth, back to the careful transcription of everyday objects and events.

In these poems of urban domesticity and old age, long-established themes are treated using the figures and language available within the spatial limits of the home and 'cortile' (viewed through the window). But the figure of the poet is also, on occasion, portrayed in a purely interior setting, without reference to the immediate external world, and here Montale makes repeated use of the image of television as a technological window on the world, thus widening the thematic range available in his commentaries on contemporary life, while the *io* remains enclosed within the emblematic space of the home (the poet acquired his first television set in 1967, though disparaging references to the medium occur in the prose writings much earlier; see for example *SMAMS* 230, 298).[43] The use of the image of the television screen, the postmodern icon par excellence, also raises some interesting questions regarding Montale's relationship with contemporary culture.

The voice of the media has already been heard in 'Rosso su rosso', where an intrusive radio brought an image of meaningless death into Montale's private world. But in 'El Desdichado', the image brought by television is less dramatic. Indeed, it is precisely its undramatic character to which Montale points with disdain:

> Sto seguendo sul video la Carmen di Karajan
> disossata con cura, troppo amabile.
> [...] (*OV* 427)

While his critique seems aimed at least in part at Karajan's clinical interpretation, it is also clear that even the sanctuary of the home (earlier titles were 'Indoor' and 'Nel chiuso') now affords no protection against the banal, sanitized forms of high culture purveyed by the mass-communication industry. The definitive title, meaning 'the disinherited' (which referred to striking workers outside the window in an early draft—see *OV* 1058–60), clearly alludes to Gérard de Nerval's well-known sonnet, but is perhaps best understood here as expressing the sense of cultural impoverishment and alienation inherent in the poem.[44] The outside world encroaches also through the troublesome accumulation of unanswered post: 'Buste color mattone, gonfie, in pila sul tavolo / imprigionano urla e lamentazioni'. The precise nature of these importunate voices is unclear (given Montale's status as senator and public figure the possibilities of political or cultural petitions of some sort are endless);

however, one possibility, corroborated by textual variants, is that they
may be unsolicited typescripts, presumably of verse (see *OV* 1059).
But what is clear is that they, like the televised opera, fail to
communicate, provoking only a momentary mechanical illumination
by the 'paralume mobile' before falling back into darkness and silence.
Under the levelling effect of cultural mass-production, de-dramatized
melodrama competes with human voices (literary texts?) that have
become coarsened and have lost their communicative potential:

> [...]
> Potessi mettermi in coda tra voi chiederei l'elemosina
>
> di una parola che non potete darmi
> perché voi conoscete soltanto il grido,
>
> un grido che si spunta
> in un'aria infeltrita, vi si aggiunge
>
> e non parla.

Similar language was used by Montale ten years earlier in an article in
which the absence of true communication was juxtaposed explicitly
with the impoverishment of public media discourse:

> Mai sono esistiti tanti mezzi di comunicare, né così facili né così irresistibili.
> L'importante è che fra questi mezzi sia sacrificata la parola, che ha il torto di
> [...] pretendere a qualche durevole verità. L'industria della comunicazione
> sarebbe minata alla base se i mezzi espressivi pretendessero di avere qualche
> durata nel tempo. Quel che occorre non è il linguaggio, ma l'interiezione,
> l'accenno, il grido, il lampo, l'arabesco che nasce e muore nel giro di pochi
> istanti. (*SMAMS* 268–9)

This is not the only prose piece to be echoed in this poem. In
'"Agganciare" il lettore' (1963) Montale writes of the increasingly
passive consumption of art in a world in which 'la solitudine di massa
ha reso vana ogni differenza tra il dentro e il fuori'. Discussing the
negative effects of 'mezzi audiovisivi', he refers to 'l'arte che s'intrude
nel vostro domicilio, il capolavoro che giunge per pacco postale
perché l'editore "ha scelto per voi"' (*SMAMS* 308–9). Although the
details are different, the sense of cultural siege is identical.

Television appears again in 'Il fuoco' (*OV* 433), where it is used by
Montale to epitomize the banality of contemporary public life, the
paucity of ideas in the world portrayed by the media. The poet
ironizes on a would-be prophet of doom, 'un Geremia apparso sul
video', whose words ring hollow in a world definitively bereft of any
higher truth, where 'non c'è modo / che scendano dal cielo lingue di

fuoco'. Here again the physical restriction of the poet's environment is made clear, his immediate vision of the world and its woes extending only far enough to see 'qualche bombetta fumogena all'angolo di via Bigli' (troubled times continue to constitute an important pedal note). In this situation television is one means by which the public sphere can re-enter his poetry, bringing him face to face with these 'farneticanti in doppiopetto o in sottana'. It also brings other images, not least from the world of sport (repeatedly derided as mindless mass spectacle in the prose writings—see *SMAMS* 217–18). In 'Il tuffatore' (*OV* 430) the distinctly televisual image of a diver shown in slow motion becomes the pretext for a rarefied discussion of existential and quasi-religious questions.[45] (It is difficult not to see this 'tuffatore' as a distant poetic descendant of Esterina, but her carefree abandon is here replaced by the cold technical perfection of his dive, whose 'cifra' is subjected to the analytical gaze of the camera.) Elsewhere, in 'La fama e il fisco', the poet considers another attempted popularization of art by television:

> Mi hanno telefonato per chiedermi che penso
> di Didone e altre dive oggi resurte
> alla tv;
> [...] (*OV* 467)

Television becomes an archetype of cultural distortion, unable to deal appropriately with traditional high culture. There is an unbridgeable gap between the ever more elusive 'classici' and television, which exalts inauthenticity in the sordid spectacle of mass consumer culture: 'Nulla resta di classico fuori delle bottiglie / brandite come stocchi da un ciarlatano del video'.

Even in the poet's home then the world of contemporary absurdity and inauthenticity continues to impinge. The public world treated so extensively in *Satura* constantly infiltrates the domestic day-to-day existence of *Diario* and *Quaderno*. This infiltration, which is of course primarily a function of the poet's own continuing, active meditations on that public world, is given a tangible figuration in images of television, radio, the telephone, even the postal service. The use of such images allows Montale to develop his own poetic persona as that of a virtual recluse, while representing physically the presence of contemporary mass culture. They are the poetic correlatives of an outlook characterized by Nascimbeni as 'il cauto distacco di chi non smette mai di osservare'.[46]

Indeed Montale's inclusion of the image of television within the privileged poetic space of the home is symptomatic of the ambivalence in his relationship with contemporary culture as a whole (as reflected elsewhere in the ambivalent portrayal of his own persona). On the one hand, he appears disdainful of what he sees as widespread cultural barbarism and repeatedly distances himself from it. In 1961, for example, he writes of the threat posed by the new dominance of 'visual' culture to those, like him, who wish to maintain a true clarity of vision: 'vorrei solo non andasse del tutto estinta la rara sottospecie degli uomini che tengono gli occhi aperti. Nella nuova civiltà visiva sono i più minacciati' (*SMAMS* 248). In prose and verse, he denounces both the non-communicative 'grido che [...] non parla' of contemporary high culture and the visual debasement of mass culture, from an apparently 'reactionary' position. But on the other hand he remains deeply involved with intellectual and aesthetic problems underlying contemporary culture.

As Oreste Macrì notes, even as the poet condemns contemporary fashions of 'mutismo' and 'incomunicazione' he acknowledges a degree of 'co-responsibility' in the propagation of the cultural industry of alienation.[47] In 1964, reviewing Eco's *Apocalittici e integrati*, Montale questions the simplistic labelling of the 'apocalittici' (those who abhor the new 'civiltà di massa' and its means of communication) as reactionaries, noting that 'gli apocalittici sono ben consapevoli della loro strana condizione di protestatari *contro i mezzi* e pur *dentro i mezzi*' (*SMAMS*, 299). It is a similar strange condition that leads Montale subsequently to practise the sort of stylistic crypto-radicalism perceived by Zanzotto in the poetry of the 1970s, with its 'darsi e dirsi come "medietà" e quasi atonia (ora) nei movimenti del suo stile, pur covando in essa tutti gli slogamenti, le fratture, i pestaggi della sintassi, della grammatica, del vocabolario, che in altri autori erano apparsi [...] in primo piano'.[48] So Montale successfully mimics elements of the experimentalism of the avant-garde while elsewhere debunking its pretensions and simultaneously questioning its (and his own) authenticity. It is a procedure that sits comfortably in the age of postmodernity. As Cataldi observes: 'Il Montale ultimo fa i conti con questa realtà postmoderna, ma non aderisce al suo orizzonte'.[49] The poet's jaundiced glance at the TV screen is a fitting image of such an attitude.

Perhaps the strongest connotation of the home as poetic space seen so far in these works is that of a retreat, a refuge of authenticity from

which the *io* looks out on a world of meaningless chaos. As such, it is
the principal site of intellectual activity, in which are examined not
only current events in the external world, but also the inner world of
the self, in an increasingly atemporal dimension. The new centrality
of the home in the poems also reflects the biological and social reality
of the ageing process. Montale reached the age of seventy-five in
October 1971, and with the resulting natural decrease in physical
mobility Montale the traveller fades from the repertoire of the poet's
personae in these collections. So, as well as a retreat, the home can be
seen increasingly as a kind of prison for the *io*.[50] In 'Il sogno del
prigioniero' the existential prisoner of the 1950s was unsure of his
ultimate fate: 'ignoro se sarò al festino / farcitore o farcito'. In 'Il
principe della Festa' in 1972, the poet considers the spectacle of the
world beyond the window in language which closely recalls the lines
just quoted: 'Ignoro se sia festa o macelleria / quello che scorgo se mi
affaccio alla finestra' (*OV* 486). The allusion to the earlier poem and
to the condition of imprisonment seems clear, but what has changed
is the nature of the poet's perplexity, as he speculates in this text on
the character of an unknown deity and other cosmic questions. Now
imprisonment of a sort is an accepted condition as the poet surveys
the world from his window. But confinement in the prison of the
home can encourage other freedoms and open other windows: with
the restriction of spatial horizons, there is an increasing tendency to
explore alternative temporal dimensions, whether the hypothetical
future of an 'other' life or personal memories of the distant past (see
Chapters 4 and 5 below).

Memory, though a possible means of escape from the tyranny of
time, can also become a chain, a constraint, as in 'I nascondigli' (*Diario
del '71*). At the opening of this poem a sense of reduced or even
evanescent vitality places the *io* at the threshold of the unknown other
dimension, prompting him to look for physical links with the past to
which he can cling (recalling again earlier amulets such as that of
'Dora Markus'):

> Quando non sono certo di essere vivo
> la certezza è a due passi ma costa pena
> ritrovarli gli oggetti, una pipa, il cagnuccio
> di legno di mia moglie, un necrologio
> del fratello di lei, tre o quattro occhiali
> di lei ancora! [...] (*OV* 426)

Though there is no direct reference to a specific physical setting here, all the evidence points to that of the home: the opening line, which recalls that of 'Xenia II' 7, and the list of objects connected with the figure of Mosca combine to place the persona implicitly in the domestic setting where her ghost has previously appeared. The memory of Mosca impinges on his consciousness (the process is not without suffering: 'costa pena [...]'), and it does so through the rediscovery of a series of objects that are heavily laden with poetic memories of her, a résumé of the paraphernalia of her previous appearances: the wooden bulldog, seen in 'Ballata scritta in una clinica'; her brother's obituary, recalling 'Xenia I' 13; her spectacles, privileged emblem of her paradoxical insights. But this is no actual manifestation of her ghost. She is clearly absent, referred to throughout in the third person, in contrast with the second person employed in 'Xenia' and elsewhere. The emphasis is rather on the objects themselves, whose listing dominates the first half of the poem. Yet, as they are listed, their only apparently noteworthy attribute is their association with her, underlined by repetition and by the unusual resort to an exclamation mark: 'di mia moglie [...] / [...] di lei [...] / di lei ancora! [...]'. They acquire significance through this association and through the memories they evoke and represent. Yet they retain their objective autonomy. There is no epiphany of Mosca (as in 'Xenia'), but her memory is used to validate certain items, in which memory itself is objectified.

In the second half of the poem these 'carabattole' (worthless trinkets—note Montale's constant tendency to deflate whatever risks sounding too portentous) achieve an even greater centrality, becoming active protagonists in an encounter between the poet and memory:

> [...] Mutano alloggio, entrano
> nei buchi più nascosti, ad ogni ora
> hanno rischiato il secchio della spazzatura.
> Complottando tra loro si sono organizzati
> per sostenermi, sanno più di me
> il filo che li lega a chi vorrebbe
> e non osa disfarsene. [...]

At this point the objects become embodiments of memory itself. Later, in the *Quaderno*, we shall find Montale attributing the same kind of autonomy overtly to memory as an abstract entity: 'Il guaio è che il ricordo non è gerarchico, / ... / C'è il caso che si stacchi e viva per conto suo' ('I pressepapiers', *OV* 566). In the same way the objects in 'I nascondigli' take on an arbitrary life of their own, and there results a tension between them and the poetic persona. Their constant shifting from one hiding-place to another surrounds them with an air of deviousness, and his own attitude to them contains a significant element of hostility, as seen in the constant threat of the waste-basket, his suppressed desire to 'disfarsene'. Yet positive connotations go hand in hand with these negative ones. After all, it is he who has sought them out for the 'certezza' they give him, and if they plot, it is in order to 'sustain' him, as they tie him to a distant past.

A further indication of the autonomous and arbitrary character of these object-memories is the exclusion from their ranks of the 'Gubelin automatico [...] sempre rifiutato' (a Swiss watch: see 'Il mio cronometro svizzero', *Altri versi*, *OV* 692). Its credentials initially seem sound, in terms of association with 'lei'. Yet perhaps it is in the very nature of an automatic watch to be incompatible with objects whose clandestine paths, whose 'nascondigli' are a figure of the tricks and tenacity of memory, in defiance of linear time. In any case the notion of linear time is undermined once again as the poem closes on the image of the ill-functioning timepiece.

> [...]
> Lo comprammo a Lucerna e lei disse
> piove troppo a Lucerna non funzionerà mai.
> E infatti ...

Thus in this poem the home, through its contents, the objects of an existence once shared with Mosca, functions as gateway to the timeless zone of the remembered past. The emotional intensity of that shared past, radiating as it were from the 'Xenia' poems, gives these objects an exemplary value, allowing the poet to investigate through them the nature and contradictions of memory, which operates as a means of intensifying life, identity and 'certezza', of 'tying' the poet within time, and of subverting time's progress.

Elsewhere Montale's poetic forays into the past conjure other domestic ghosts. Apart from the association of the apartment with the presence of Mosca, there already exists a much earlier link in Montale's work between the home and the poet's 'ancestral' dead (including the recurring figure of the domestic servant). For example

in 'L'arca' (*Bufera*) the memory of the dead ('i miei morti, / i miei cani
fidati, le mie vecchie / serve') has its focus in the kitchen where their
'volti ossuti' are reflected in the copper pot. Similarly in 'Proda di
Versilia' (*Bufera*) the memory of the dead evokes images of childhood,
his room 'accanto alla cucina' with, on the other side of the wall, 'care
ombre' at the kitchen sink. It is this past, the distant past, which
Montale enters through the gateway of the home in 'Il giorno dei
morti' (*Quaderno*):

> La Gina ha acceso un candelotto per i suoi morti.
> L'ha acceso in cucina, i morti sono tanti e non vicini.
> Bisogna risalire a quando era bambina
> e il caffelatte era un pugno di castagne secche.
> Bisogna ricreare un padre piccolo e vecchio
> e le sue scarpinate per trovarle un poco di vino dolce.
> [...] (*OV* 526)

The presence of Gina immediately conveys a precise sense of place
and time: the apartment of the poet's old age, which, however, is cited
directly only in the form of the 'cucina', as the site of her All-Souls'
devotion. There is an echo here of the purgatorial motif of the
opening stanza of 'Proda di Versilia' ('I miei morti che prego perché
preghino / per me'). Thus Gina joins the ranks of Montale's domestic
lares as he journeys through her (through her words, which become
images, memories) into the past. In the rich phonic texture of this
poem, the memorial pathway from the appearance of Gina to the
topos of childhood finds a precise correlative in the twin strands of the
internal rhyme sequence: *Gina–cucina–vicini–bambina–vino–vini–
porcellini*.[51] It is through the key-word and image 'cucina', with its
resonances and implications from earlier poems, that Montale, along
with the figure of Gina, gains access to the realm of distant memory.
That world of her childhood memories which he recreates is one of
warm domesticity, epitomized by the homely images of 'caffelatte',
'castagne secche' and 'vino dolce'.[52] Against this background of frugal
comfort Montale rehearses the values associated elsewhere with his
own childhood, focussing ultimately on the integrity of an individual
history, indifferent to other 'morti' not illuminated by the flame of
private memory. These latter may include 'qualche vivente,
semivivente prossimo / al traghetto' (probably the figure of the poet
himself) who along with the long-dead 'maestra' forms part of a
throng which is ultimately insignificant to Gina:

> [...] È una folla che non è niente
> perché non ha portato al pascolo i porcellini.

The value of the individual past is as irreducible as it is inexplicable to others.

The poet encounters his own 'morti' in 'Ho sparso di becchime il davanzale' (*Quaderno*, *OV* 552). The conclusion here, 'Abbiamo / fatto del nostro meglio per peggiorare il mondo', reflects on one level a yearning for the values of the past, inspired by the ghosts of the dead. But there is also in this poem a more ironic view of these figures from the past and of the processes of memory. In this piece, the apartment (with its attendant birds, as seen already) is again the setting for a memorial/oneiric procession of the dead. But the vision and the speaker's response to it are ambiguous. In keeping with the arbitrary character of memory, the ghosts include 'grandi e piccoli'. To assign a greater or lesser value to one or another of them is problematic: 'Arduo distinguere / tra chi vorrei o non vorrei che fosse / ritornato tra noi'. Above all he is aware of the deceptions of memory, the danger of idealization, inherent in his re-evocation of figures from the past. The unreal permanence of these ghostly figures may hide a reality of decay:

> [...]
> sembrano inalterabili per un di più
> di sublimata corruzione. [...]

That this decay has been sublimated reflects the poet's viewpoint through the distortions of memory, which tends to fix the past in a spurious state of grace in direct contrast with the present. In this context the closing line ('Abbiamo / fatto del nostro meglio per peggiorare il mondo') appears in a highly ironic light.

A distrust of memory and its tricks recurs in 'Quel che resta (se resta)' (*Quaderno*). The recollection of 'la vecchia serva' is another occasion to query the seemingly illogical priorities of memory:

> la vecchia serva analfabeta
> e barbuta chissà dov'è sepolta
> [...]
> chissà perché la ricordo
> più di tutto e di tutti
> se entrasse ora nella mia stanza
> avrebbe centotrent'anni e griderei di spavento. (*OV* 587)

In what is almost certainly a parodic allusion to Baudelaire's 'La servante au grand cœur' (whose 'âme pieuse' appears to the poet 'tapie en un coin de ma chambre'), Montale insists here on debunking any idealization of the past, any elevation of the ghost to a sacred status.[53] The self-directed irony of his mock terror points up the discrepancy between his attempt to create an ideal of remembered authenticity (the simple homely wisdom of the servant who 'ne sapeva più di noi') and the absurd, grotesque reality of a long-dead old woman.

However, these lines also underline one of the main features of the home as a poetic setting: its status as a potentially timeless zone, a stage peopled by ghosts and memories. This is further confirmed in 'Ribaltamento' (*Quaderno*). Here the poet's room is a space where the lines between reality, memory and dream are thinly drawn. What begins apparently as a present reality turns out finally to be an old man's dream or daydream of falling into a garden pond as a child. (Montale's description of the poem as 'il ricordo di un pauroso sogno [...] fatto a poco più di due anni' (*OV* 1133) would appear to contradict this interpretation. However, the reading of the text as an old man's dream seems more satisfactory, as supported by the 'ancora' of line 5.)[54] The 'vasca' is surely that which appears in *Ossi* in 'Vasca' and 'Cigola la carrucola', making this a particularly effective, if understated, use of 'autocitazione' by Montale.[55] In the two earlier poems (*OV* 45 and 71), the emergence of an image or a memory was described in terms of the fleeting appearance at the water's surface of something that then sank again. In this context the title of the later text, 'Ribaltamento', takes on another layer of meaning, as here the direction of movement is reversed and the poet descends into the realms of memory and the subconscious in a vain search for some meaning (the title may also, of course, refer to the process by which the old man appears increasingly child-like). Montale initially lures his reader into viewing the childhood incident from within its own time. The use of verbs in the present tense throughout the poem contributes to the blurring of distinctions between past and present. It is only in the closing physical gesture, in which dream and reality coincide, that we become fully aware of the setting in the poet's old age: as he reaches down, apparently to see whether there is still water in the pool, his hand unexpectedly finds the floor of his room:

> [...]
> Chissà se c'è ancora acqua. Curvo il braccio
> e tocco il pavimento della mia stanza. (*OV* 586)

The point of contact between dream and reality involves the tangible fabric of the room itself.

In the poems examined here the home has functioned primarily as a retreat, a place of refuge. In keeping with this and with its association with sleep or dreams, we tend to see it in the half-light of evening or daybreak, often through the lens of a kind of *dormiveglia* (described by Lonardi as a deliberate 'fiction' adopted by Montale in his later works).[56] But specific temporal indications are rare and the overall impression is of a space in which conventional time is suspended. In 'La pendola a carillon' (*Diario del '72*), another remembered or imagined household object, an antique chiming clock, speaks to the poet's persona before grinding to a stop:

> [...] Io ch'ero
> il Tempo lo abbandono. Ed a te che sei l'unico
> mio ascoltatore dico cerca di vivere
> nel fuordeltempo, quello che nessuno
> può misurare. [...] (*OV* 477)

In *Diario* and *Quaderno* as a whole, the sanctuary of the home comes to represent the gateway into this space outside of Time for the *io*. On switching his glance from the outside world, predominantly a zone of negativity viewed through the window, to the interior world of individual integrity (but also necessarily of questioning and self-doubt), he also turns away from the historically measured time he has sought to debunk since *Satura*. This shift of the poetic centre of gravity away from the outside, historical world into the home coincides with the new dominance, from *Diario* onwards, of a thematic strand centred on perennial, ahistorical cosmic questions, discussed with varying degrees of ironic distance and comic *sprezzatura*. The narrowing of the poet's physical horizons after *Satura* goes hand in hand with the opening up of this broad thematic area of pseudo-religious, philosophical and cosmological speculation that provides the material, the vocabulary and the imagery for some of Montale's last disenchanted musings on the historical world.

Notes to Chapter 3

1. 'Botta e risposta I' was written in 1961, whereas numbers II and III both date to 1968 (see *OV* 977, 1005, 1014).
2. See Forti, *Eugenio Montale*, 354; F. Croce, '*Satura*', 363.
3. Greco, *Montale commenta Montale*, 61.

4. West, *Eugenio Montale: Poet on the Edge*, 105. Franco Croce, 'Due nuove poesie di Montale', *Rassegna della letteratura italiana* 67 (1963), 493–506 at 499, calls the poem 'una "summa" della esperienza umana del poeta'. See also Andrea Zanzotto, 'Da "Botta e risposta I" a *Satura*', *Eugenio Montale: profilo di un autore*, ed. Cima and Segre, 115–23 at 115.

5. Angelo Jacomuzzi, 'Le Stalle di Augía', *La poesia di Montale*, 58–91.

6. See Carpi, *Montale dopo il fascismo*, 131; Cambon, *Eugenio Montale's Poetry*, 210.

7. See e.g. Jacomuzzi, *La poesia di Montale*, 65. Mario Martelli's exhaustive reading in *Il rovescio della poesia: interpretazioni montaliane* (Milan: Longanesi, 1977), attempts to rule out categorically a historical interpretation. While Martelli's thesis provides useful insights on the 'Botta' as a manifesto for poetic renewal, his reading seems too unequivocal at times, too unwilling to acknowledge the rich ambiguity of such a multi-layered text.

8. Forti, *Eugenio Montale*, 356. See also Pier Vincenzo Mengaldo, 'La "Lettera a Malvolio"', *Eugenio Montale: profilo di un autore*, ed. Cima and Segre, 134–67 at 154.

9. Jacomuzzi, *La poesia di Montale*, 88. Similarly, for West (*Eugenio Montale: Poet on the Edge*, 70), it is 'a divinity that never appeared'.

10. Vittore Branca, 'Montale nelle Stalle di Augía', *La poesia di Eugenio Montale: atti del Convegno ... novembre 1982*, 465–72 at 470.

11. 'Argyll Tour' and 'Vento sulla Mezzaluna', though both dated '1948' by the poet (i.e., bearing the year of the remembered Scottish trip and thus apparently antedating the encounter with Volpe in 1949), have recently been shown by Grignani to have been back-dated and to belong in fact to the Volpe cycle. See Maria Antonietta Grignani, *Dislocazioni: epifanie e metamorfosi in Montale* (Lecce: Piero Manni, 1998), 54–61. See also eadem, '"Se t'hanno assomigliato" e altro', *Montale Readings*, ed. Éanna Ó Ceallacháin and Federica Pedriali, Italian Research Studies, 3 (Glasgow: University of Glasgow Press, 2000), 53–75. In *Farfalla di Dinard*, the image of the rat recurs, but this time in what is most probably a (rather unflattering) portrayal of Mosca, in 'Sera difficile' (*PR* 153–4).

12. See respectively, Becker, *Eugenio Montale*, 121; Zanzotto, 'Da "Botta e risposta I" a *Satura*', 119.

13. *SMAMS* 345. See also 'Oggi e domani' (1962), where he writes of the 'termitaio umano' (*SMAMS* 215), and 'Uomini oggettuali' (1965), where he derides aspirations to find some new form of literary expression for 'l'uomo alienato': 'Se ha cessato di essere uomo non si esprima con le parole, ma con altri mezzi e altre attività, come i castori, come le formiche' (*SMAMS* 316).

14. Zanzotto, 'Da "Botta e risposta I" a *Satura*', 122. Elsewhere, in a characteristically pregnant formulation, Zanzotto describes the 'topo' as 'termine di coscienza-accettazione e insieme simbolo di un'abietta salvezza'. See Andrea Zanzotto, 'Sviluppo di una situazione montaliana', *Letteratura* 79–81 (1966), 97–101 at 100.

15. Croce, 'Due nuove poesie di Montale', 504.

16. Croce, 'Satura', 363.

17. Several early drafts are dated 'Versilia, 1968' (*OV* 1005). Elsewhere, references to the Tuscan resort range from its use in 'Proda di Versilia' as an image of a degraded world, to the indulgent irony with which its habitués are treated in

several prose pieces (e.g. 'Da una spiaggia mondana', *PR* 745–8), to its reappearance in later poems such as 'Sulla spiaggia' in *Diario* (*OV* 482) or 'Al mare (o quasi)' in *Quaderno* (*OV* 603).

18. See Carpi, *Montale dopo il fascismo*, 146–8. The article in question is now in *SMAMS* 1053–7.

19. Porphyry's paradise is derided, writes Franco Croce (see 'Satura', 365), as 'moralmente dubbio'.

20. Cambon, *Eugenio Montale's Poetry*, 218.

21. In a later interview, Montale reveals the identity of his correspondent here, who is quite distinct from the 'imaginary' figures of the first two 'botte': 'la Dalmati, una delle mie migliori traduttrici [...] Margherita Dalmati, [...] è anche concertista di clavicembalo'. 'Le reazioni di Montale', *Eugenio Montale: profilo di un autore*, ed. Cima and Segre, 197.

22. See 'Il sogno del prigioniero', 'Botta e risposta I'.

23. See Montale's explanatory note: 'In occasione delle nozze di Sofia di Grecia con Juan Carlos di Borbone un'infinità di principi del sangue traboccò dall'albergo King George (Atene 1962)', *OV* 1017.

24. See for example the references to the Danieli in Venice and the Saint James in Paris (XI 3, XII 3). See also 'Lettera' in *Satura*.

25. Forti, *Eugenio Montale*, 410.

26. Ramat, *L'acacia ferita*, 164–6.

27. Croce, 'Satura', 370.

28. Ramat, *L'acacia ferita*, 165.

29. Pasolini's review of *Satura* is in *Nuovi Argomenti* 21 (Jan.–Mar. 1971), 17–20. The identification of Malvolio with Pasolini is taken for granted by some critics (Becker, *Eugenio Montale*, 130–1; Cambon, *Eugenio Montale's Poetry*, 219). Forti seems less certain in 'Per *Diario del '71*', *La poesia di Eugenio Montale: atti del Convegno ... settembre 1982*, 161–9 at 166, while Franco Croce treats the matter with due circumspection in '*Satura*', 373. Ultimately, Mengaldo's attitude seems most sensible: while not ruling out the possibility that the poem may contain a personal polemic, he suggests that it clearly also addresses a 'category' of intellectuals, exponents of 'una falsa concezione dell'*engagement*', conluding that 'Ognuno di noi, poco o tanto, è un Malvolio' ('La "Lettera a Malvolio"', 148, 162). Pasolini himself replied in bitter terms in *Nuovi Argomenti* 27 (May–June 1972), 146–50. See also Enzo Siciliano, *Pasolini: A Biography*, trans. John Shepley (New York: Random House, 1982), 356–9.

30. Croce, '*Satura*', 375.

31. Mengaldo, 'La "Lettera a Malvolio"', 160, 150.

32. Pasolini, 'Satura', 17.

33. Elisabetta Graziosi, *Il tempo in Montale: storia di un tema* (Florence: La nuova Italia, 1978), 111–41.

34. 'Home' settings (23 poems): *Diario*: 'Rosso su rosso'; 'Nel cortile'; 'I nascondigli'; 'El Desdichado'; 'Il tuffatore'; 'Il fuoco'; 'A quella che legge i giornali'; 'Il rondone'; 'Le acque alte'; 'La Fama e il Fisco'; 'Il principe della festa'; 'Al mio grillo'. *Quaderno*: 'Il giorno dei morti'; 'La solitudine'; 'Leggendo Kavafis'; 'Sera di Pasqua'; 'Pasquetta'; 'Ho sparso di becchime il davanzale'; 'Siamo alla solitudine di gruppo'; 'Appunti'; 'Ribaltamento'; 'Fine di settembre'

(set at the poet's seaside retreat, but the situation and imagery belong clearly to the domestic group); 'Dormiveglia'. Other settings (13 poems): *Diario:* 'Il trionfo della spazzatura'; 'Senza sorpresa'; 'In un giardino "italiano"'; 'Sulla spiaggia'. *Quaderno:* 'Intermezzo'; 'Dopopioggia'; 'Soliloquio'; 'Sul lago d'Orta'; 'In una città del nord'; 'Nel disumano'; 'Sulla spiaggia'; 'Al mare (o quasi)'; 'Lungolago'.

35. Luperini, *Storia di Montale*, 236. See also Mark Grimshaw, 'Vertical and Horizontal Sightings on Montale's *Satura*', *Italian Studies* 29 (1974), 74–87, who speaks of 'a forced retreat from the mass-produced realities outside the window' (86). Montale lived at two different addresses in via Bigli: no. 11 from 1951 to 1967, and no. 15 from 1967 onwards. See *TP*, 'Cronologia', pp. lxxv, lxxviii.

36. See Pierluigi Pellini, 'L'ultimo Montale: donne miracoli treni telefoni sciopero generale', *Nuova corrente* 39 (1992), 289–324 at 314–21.

37. See West, *Eugenio Montale: Poet on the Edge*, 116–17; also Grimshaw, 'Vertical and Horizontal Sightings', 83.

38. 'Merlo' is used repeatedly in the Contini letters: see *Eusebio e Trabucco: carteggio di Eugenio Montale e Gianfranco Contini*, ed. Dante Isella (Milan: Adelphi, 1997). See also Contini's introduction to *Eugenio Montale: immagini di una vita*, ed. Contorbia, p. x; Grignani, *Prologhi ed epiloghi*, 31.

39. See Marchese, *Visiting angel*, 253.

40. On the hunting motif see Grignani, *Prologhi ed epiloghi*, 55–7; Luperini, *Montale o l'identità negata*, 94–6; and Laura Barile, introduction to *Lettere e poesie a Bianca e Francesco Messina, 1923–1925*, ed. Laura Barile (Milan: Scheiwiller, 1995), 23.

41. See Franco Fortini, 'I latrati di fedeltà', *Letture montaliane*, 379–85.

42. Ibid., 383.

43. See Nascimbeni, *Montale: biografia di un poeta*, 9.

44. One may assume that Montale's allusion to Nerval is ironic rather than an attempt to portray himself in a tragic light. Nevertheless it is worth quoting the opening lines of the French poem: 'Je suis le ténébreux, — le veuf, — l'inconsolé, / Le prince d'Aquitaine à la tour abolie; / Ma seule étoile est morte, — et mon luth constellé / Porte le soleil noir de la Mélancolie.'

45. See Cambon, *Eugenio Montale's Poetry*, 229–30.

46. Nascimbeni, *Montale: biografia di un poeta*, 10. Similar background or anecdotal material can be found in Marco Forti, 'Montale: ritratto milanese', *Nuovi saggi montaliani* (Milan: Mursia, 1990), 143–60. On the poet's increasingly domestic existence with Gina, see especially 154–6.

47. Macrì suggests that such ambivalence is characteristic of satirical discourse in general. See Oreste Macrì, 'Dante e la "Musa comica" dell'ultimo Montale', *La poesia di Eugenio Montale: atti del Convegno ... novembre 1982*, 493–510 at 507–8.

48. Zanzotto, 'La freccia dei diari', 52.

49. Cataldi, *Montale*, 60.

50. See Lonardi, *Il Vecchio e il Giovane*, 71.

51. For a detailed account of these 'assonanze-multisonanze', see Giorgio Orelli, 'Tra le ultime poesie', *Accertamenti montaliani* (Bologna: Il mulino, 1984), 95–135 at 101.

52. See Fortini, 'I latrati di fedeltà', 380: 'qui si parla *at home*'.

53. For Baudelairean elements, see Lonardi, *Il Vecchio e il Giovane*, 141–3.

54. For a similar view see Lorenzo Renzi, 'Effetti di sordina nell'ultimo Montale', *Studi novecenteschi* 19 (1980), 81–94 at 83–4.

55. On autocitation in Montale's later works, see Mario Martelli, 'L'autocitazione nel secondo Montale', *La poesia di Eugenio Montale: atti del Convegno ... settembre 1982*, 201–17; West, *Eugenio Montale: Poet on the Edge*, 104–9.

56. Gilberto Lonardi, 'L'altra Madre', *La poesia di Eugenio Montale: atti del Convegno ... settembre 1982*, 263–79 at 265.

CHAPTER 4

❖

L'Altro

The presence from *Satura* onwards of what can broadly be termed religious motifs or motifs of theological speculation represents in part an innovation and in part provides a degree of continuity with the earlier collections. Speculation on a possible 'oltrevita', a non-physical dimension lying just beyond the physical, historical world, is a thematic strand that can be discerned in Montale's poetry from the time of *Ossi*: from the search for the 'maglia rotta nella rete' of 'In limine', through Arsenio's pursuit of 'un'altra orbita', to the chorus of the dead, 'da noi divisi appena' in 'I morti'. In *Occasioni* the motif of communication with the dead appears again, for example in 'La casa dei doganieri' and in the closing poem 'Notizie dall'Amiata' with its 'lungo colloquio coi poveri morti'. This 'colloquio' with an 'other' world goes on to become one of the principal concerns of *Bufera* and, in particular, of that volume's central section 'Silvae'.[1] Such motifs appear again in *Satura* in parallel with the vein of direct commentary on contemporary reality already discussed, and their prominence tends to increase in the subsequent collections as the tone of the 'public' poems becomes ever more disenchanted and the poet's gaze turns increasingly away from the external world. In the absence of a dialogue with a significant *tu*, the use of quasi-religious or theological motifs is one way in which Montale can add a new figurative dimension to his deliberations on the historical world, a world now perceived to be in a state of irredeemable cultural collapse and ideological stalemate. It is a mechanism for the poet to posit a point of view beyond the confines of everyday space and time, to introduce a further ironic distance into his treatment of earthly reality, while simultaneously undermining any remaining traces of hope for some miraculous transcendence, debunking any aspirations to an understanding of the beyond, the *oltrevita*.[2]

Writing in 1972 shortly after the first appearance of *Satura*,

Mengaldo notes the 'continua emersione del motivo del Dio nascosto e perduto, sviluppo coerente della religiosità laica della *Bufera*'.[3] The pertinence of Mengaldo's observation is confirmed amply by Montale's widespread reuse of religious or pseudo-religious motifs in his subsequent collections. The critic's comments can also, however, give rise to a number of further preliminary considerations and questions. A formula such as 'religiosità laica' is just one possible way of defining a concept that has widespread currency in Montale criticism: Carpi writes of the poet's 'laicismo metafisico', Grignani of his sense of 'sacro laico'; Cambon speaks of Montale's 'lay religion', while Forti suggests 'una dimensione fra ereticamente cristiana e panteistica'.[4] One might, however, question the precise appropriateness of Mengaldo's formula as applied specifically to the poetry of *La bufera e altro*. If anything, in his third collection Montale introduces the language and imagery of an explicitly Christian religious mysticism, so that the religious element in *Bufera* is perhaps less *laico* than in any of his other works.[5] This is true especially of the poems of the Clizia cycle, whose powerful blend of Christian and erotic motifs draws directly on the central well-spring of the Italian poetic tradition. In these poems, as we have seen, the device of the stylized love-story is developed, along with the motif of broadly metaphysical speculation present from *Ossi* onwards, to culminate in Montale's own personal brand of *stilnovismo*, in what has been called his 'allegorismo cristologico'.[6] Clizia, who mediates between the poet's persona and a mystical *Altro*, is transformed, becoming (in Montale's own words) the 'inconsapevole Cristòfora' (*OV* 946). The implicit axis of dialogue (or of 'dramatic monologue'[7]) between *io* and *tu* found in *Ossi* and *Occasioni* is thus replaced in *Bufera* by a more complex, multi-dimensional relationship between the three poles *io–tu–l'Altro*, as the imagery and rhetoric of love, along with the language and symbolism of an explicitly Christian mysticism, are used by the poet to address contemporary historical reality and to express his ideological positions (as well as reflecting personal, private dramas).

Mengaldo goes on to note that in *Satura*, 'Dio si qualifica sempre più radicalmente come metafora dello smarrimento e della mancanza'.[8] A number of questions arise out of this statement. Firstly, what is meant by 'smarrimento' and 'mancanza' here? A sense of disorientation, loss and absence, but absence of what? A tentative answer, in the context of Mengaldo's essay, might be that the lost God represents the absence of positive, authentic values, the absence, broadly speaking, of truth from the world. It could, however, be argued that this is also the function of the equally absent *Altro* of *Bufera*, where the absence of a positive principle from contemporary reality is filtered through the unfolding drama of the woman's absence and the desperate wait for her return. What then is new in the use of the figure of a 'Dio nascosto' in *Satura*? First, the absence of narrative tension: while there was in *Bufera* an expectation, however slender, of salvation, an implicit aspiration to a positive dénouement in time, it is clear from *Satura* onwards that loss is not the prelude to any return. Any dealings with the hidden God are now conducted on the clear understanding that no further epiphanies are likely. Secondly, the manner of representation of God's absence has changed: it is no longer associated with or expressed through the obsessive and tragic 'assenza-presenza di una donna lontana' (*SMAMS* 1490), but perceived intellectually and described in comic and, as it were, theoretical terms. In short, the notion of 'mancanza', of an absence of positive, authentic values, is now, in *Satura* and especially in *Diario* and *Quaderno*, expressed through the use of what one might call theological discourse (though not in a technical sense) rather than through the language of religious mysticism and love.

After a transitional phase constituted by 'Xenia', where the figure of Mosca still represents a channel of communication with a world beyond, the poet's persona in the last collections is portrayed in a direct but impossible relationship with the unknown deity, 'l'Altro', a relationship no longer mediated by a female *tu*. Theological motifs are presented as part of an absurd *messa in scena*, the *dramatis personae* consisting on the one hand of an *io* open, or potentially open to dialogue, and on the other hand of the absent, silent divinity itself, indifferent or unable to respond.[9] So Montale's 'dramatic monologue' is reinvented, the principal voice being now that of the comic theologian, who aspires to participate in an impossible dialogue with an absent God. Meanwhile, in the absence of the *tu*, the only mediation between the two figures is that of language itself, as a series of new metaphorical devices in a minor key (images of hunting, theatrical performance, etc.) facilitate the poetic persona's posture of eschatological speculation.

To speak of such a speculative, theologizing posture on the part of the *io* is not, however, to suggest any serious theological or cosmo-logical intent on the part of the poet.[10] There have been attempts to find some (more or less hidden) orthodox religious vision in Montale's poetry. Carlo Bo, for example, writing on the centenary of the poet's birth, claims to find a Christian vision in his work, and other critics have discussed in depth religious or theological aspects of various texts.[11] Bo writes: 'c'è un abisso fra il Montale di certe sue improvvise fiammate di negazione assoluta e la sua storia segreta che parte dal cattolicesimo ingenuo della madre e da quello critico della sorella e termina con le preghiere sul letto di morte. [...] [In Montale] si vede che la visione della vita è pur sempre una visione cristiana, sia pure fra dubbi e riluttanze, si avverte che la sua morale non rifiutava mai l'eredità cristiana.'[12] Certainly, one may concur with Bo when he speaks of an 'eredità cristiana' in Montale. This is an ethical and cultural inheritance that emerges more than once in the essays of *Auto da fé*. In 'Soltanto inventariare' for example (1965), Montale, rejecting the notion of 'l'uomo concepito come fine', declares: 'Per quel che nega, più che per quello che afferma, il cristianesimo ha ancora molto da dire' (*SMAMS* 375–7). But this is no more than a negative acknowledgment of a problematic inheritance.

Similar views are expressed elsewhere in the prose writings (a 1971 interview, for example, gives full and explicit expression to Montale's basic scepticism—see *SMAMS* 1569–77). However, when Bo claims that the poet's reticence concerning religious belief serves to 'non tradire mai del tutto la sua verità', one must surely reply that Montale's deeply sceptical view of the world has been built, from the beginning, not on truth, but on doubt. In the many, sometimes enigmatic variations on theological themes in these later collections, Montale is not jealously guarding some private truth, but rehearsing some of the many forms of his constant unbelief. Just as he once used the device of the mystical and tragic love story as the vehicle for a complex blend of philosophical, ideological and personal themes, he now uses the scenario of an absurd theological monologue as a means of continuing to address the world in time. He uses language and attitudes pertaining to the sphere of religious belief (or unbelief, as the case may be), he constructs a representation of theological (or pseudo-theological) discourse, adopts a stance of potential religious openness as a vehicle for the ongoing discussion of ideas in a world of perceived ideological stasis.

Mosca and the *oltrevita*

Before examining the repertoire of imagery and situations used by

Montale in portraying the relationship with his 'Dio nascosto', we must consider briefly the pivotal role of 'Xenia' and the figure of Mosca in establishing the tone, the parameters and some of the possible meanings of that portrayal. Already in *Bufera* (in 'Ballata scritta in una clinica'), Mosca was depicted on the boundary between this world and the other, in a moment of critical illness, about to 'forzare la porta stretta', and it is she who offers the key to that gate in 'Xenia' by posthumously providing the *io* with a new paradigm of irony, contradiction and paradox with which to explore the *oltrevita*. In 'Xenia' the thematic motifs of death and the afterlife and the mysterious hidden ties between this world and a possible other take centre stage.

The establishment of communication between the living and the dead is a central concern especially of the first series of 'Xenia'. From the first appearance of Mosca's ghost in XI 1, where mutual recognition itself is in doubt ('non potevi vedermi / né potevo io senza quel luccichìo / riconoscere te nella foschia'), we witness repeated and at times problematic attempts to establish contact between the two realms. In XI 2 the question of the nature of the afterlife is raised, to be treated with black humour as the poet considers the ghost's silence: 'Ma è ridicolo / pensare che tu avessi ancora labbra'. The restless search for a sign of Mosca's presence continues with the introduction in XI 3 of the incongruous motif of the telephone as a possible channel of communication with the spirit world (the first of a series of images of such whimsical signalling devices), as the figure of the poet is portrayed with understated pathos in his attempt to find the ghost in her old haunt, the hotel switchboard.[13]

The fourth poem in the series brings together some recurring elements of these attempts by the *io* to contact the ghost:

> Avevamo studiato per l'aldilà
> un fischio, un segno di riconoscimento.
> Mi provo a modularlo nella speranza
> che tutti siamo già morti senza saperlo.

Here, using a typically quirky, unportentous mechanism for contacting the other world (one which will recur later in *Satura* in 'Pasqua senza week-end'), the poet brings together the motif of personal communication between the living and the dead (an area explored at length in the dialogue with his 'care ombre' in *Bufera*) with the related motif of speculation on a more abstract, universal level about the relationship between the *oltrevita* and this world. The poem raises a fundamental question concerning the very existence of life, of reality as we commonly perceive it, as a status distinct from death. This is a line of questioning and speculation whose presence and importance will increase throughout *Satura* and later. Here, characteristically, the invocation of Mosca is associated with a kind of paradoxical insight based on the subversion of conventional truths, the elimination of polarities, as the *io* tries to eliminate the gap between life and death. (We may also note, in the light of Chapter 3 above, that here, as elsewhere in 'Xenia', there is an active attempt by the *io* to move from within the privileged domestic space, the implicit setting for the entire series, to a dimension beyond the physical and the temporal).

However, the lyrical persona's aspiration to somehow contact the 'aldilà' is not without ambivalence, as can be seen in XI 7 :

> Pietà di sé, infinita pena e angoscia
> di chi adora il *quaggiù* e spera e dispera
> di un altro ... (chi osa dire un altro mondo?).
> 'Strana pietà ...' (Azucena, atto secondo).

The previous 'speranza / che tutti siamo già morti senza saperlo' is itself called into question here. Not only is the hope of an afterlife apparently cancelled out by an equivalent despair ('spera e dispera'), but the whole expectation is framed by a twofold qualification: first, this hope or despair is felt by someone who simultaneously expresses a love of this life, 'adora il *quaggiù*'; secondly, doubt is again cast on the very status of this 'world': the italicized, emphatically neutral '*quaggiù*' is the only acceptable way of naming it, and the doubts are intensified in line 3 with its accumulation of uncertainties, expressed formally in the interplay of ellipsis, parenthesis and interrogative. The object of the hope or despair then is an unspecified 'other': the speaker dare not call it another world, when the nature of the present existence is so uncertain. So, the attitude of the *io* towards an afterlife or other life is by no means straightforward. If the reality of the physical world is in doubt, so is the probability (and indeed the desirability) of an other world, and furthermore, as seen in XI 4, the relationship between the two realms, the very possibility of distinguishing one from the other, is clouded with uncertainty. (The allusion to *Il Trovatore* can perhaps best be understood as an ironic response by Mosca's ghost—by means of another mechanical device, a record player—to the speaker's 'angoscia'. The implicit identification of Mosca with Azucena would sit comfortably with her 'hellish' and clairvoyant character.[14])

The next two poems in the series return to the theme of communication and its difficulties: XI 8 reiterates the notion of a secret code, a search for the woman's 'parola' in some new cryptic form ('è mutato l'accento, altro il colore'). Here the *io*, in order to receive messages from beyond the grave, must be ready to decipher the signals of this new code: 'decifrarti / nel ticchettìo della telescrivente'. Montale never loses sight of the lightness of tone essential to these poems, as achieved here in part through this incongruous image of the telex as a medium of spiritual contact, rendered with playful onomatopoeic alliteration. This image also recalls the earlier allusion (in XI 3) to Mosca's predilection for the telephone, which is echoed again in the simple pathos of the brief XI 9:

> Ascoltare era il solo tuo modo di vedere.
> Il conto del telefono s'è ridotto a ben poco.

Though the attempts to communicate with the ghost of Mosca are played out against a background of general spiritual doubt, the question of another world, seen in more conventionally religious terms, is also touched upon in 'Xenia'. Mosca had, when alive, her own quirky forms of communication with the spiritual world: for example, her prayers for her own 'morti' would take second place to prayers for lost umbrellas and the like (XI 10). She had also given intimations of the existence of her own personal eschatology, with her laughter seeming 'l'anticipo di un tuo privato / Giudizio Universale' (XI 11). So the figure of Mosca is associated with a rather eclectic spiritual outlook, which embraces elements of a kind of mediumistic spiritualism (the attempts to communicate with the dead), along with an agnostic scepticism regarding the very existence of an afterlife and somewhat superstitious forms of Christian belief. These elements, as we shall see, will be subsumed in varying degrees into the poetic persona's own ironic deliberations on what lies beyond.

In the second series of 'Xenia', although the emphasis is on the re-evocation of a shared life together rather than on Mosca's absence in death, her figure continues to be associated with the themes of death and of the *oltrevita* in its relationship to the *quaggiù*. The first poem in the second series opens with an assertion of death's irrelevance for Mosca: 'La morte non ti riguardava'. Mosca's concerns ultimately transcended the divisions between life and death; life was as irrelevant to her as death: 'E neppure / t'importava la vita'. Her concerns lay elsewhere, in 'un punto [...] incomprensibile' beyond both life and death, a mysterious 'other' that implies the ultimate unimportance for her of the world as we perceive it (this 'punto' may be an echo of *Paradiso* XVII, 17–18).[15] This question of the possible unreality of the physical world arises repeatedly through memories of the existence shared by the *io* and Mosca. Thus in the fifth of the second series the figure of the poet, linked arm-in-arm in memory to that of the woman and so a party to her paradoxical insights, can dismiss the common belief 'che la realtà sia quella che si vede'. Later, in XII 7, the two figures are seen again to share a deep scepticism regarding the existence of the world, and in the eighth poem we find such scepticism extended by Mosca (albeit in jocular vein) to the question of an afterlife ('E il Paradiso? Esiste un paradiso?'). In the ninth the apparatus of formal religion is evoked once more (as in XI 10 and 11): Mosca's attitude is again a curious mixture of superstition and agnosticism, with widows and nuns feared as bearers of ill omen and God reduced to 'lui' (lower case), although seemingly never actually named by Mosca out of a judicious respect for religious taboos. This circumspect naming (or non-naming) of God will be echoed repeatedly by the poet's own persona in the later parts of *Satura* and beyond.

What emerges from 'Xenia', then, is an outlook in which distinctions between life and afterlife, between the physical and non-physical worlds, have been called into question (along with a vast range of other distinctions and apparent oppositions), and in which relationships between opposites in this context have often been inverted in keeping with Mosca's paradoxical 'agnizioni'. Thus when 'Celia la filippina', phoning for news of Mosca (XII 11), asks in surprise 'Non c'è più?', the *io* can reply 'Forse più di prima, ma ...', a response that encapsulates much of the uncertainty and openness that characterize the approach to the *oltrevita* throughout the two 'Xenia' series. These poems offer a basic repertoire of imagery, of ideas and models of relationships (including, for example, difficulties in communication, inversions of conventional values, problematic or antagonistic relationships, and the ubiquitous presence of paradox and contradiction) which will be employed widely in the poet's subsequent speculation on the nature of a possible Divinity and its relationship with humanity. Furthermore, the irony of tone, language

and imagery that pervades 'Xenia' also colours the portrayal of the
oltrevita, which even in its most abstract or rarefied aspects is thus, as
it were, domesticated and brought into the sphere of the comic, the
sphere of Mosca's ongoing influence.

The investigation of the afterlife on an essentially personal level
through the figure of Mosca is continued only intermittently in the
two subsequent sections of *Satura*. Her presence is evoked in 'La
morte di Dio' (*OV* 319), 'Cielo e terra' (*OV* 354) and 'Pasqua senza
week-end' (*OV* 375). Later, Mosca's last three appearances in *Satura*,
grouped together at the close of the book, contribute to the sense of
hidden thematic patterns in the collection by linking this last part of
'Satura II' to the highly personal opening poems of 'Xenia I'. 'Nel
silenzio' (*OV* 404) presents us again with the figure of the poet alone
at home in the silence of Mosca's absence, while 'Luci e colori' (*OV*
405) contains the last of her 'visite mute' to the setting of the poet's
apartment. Her rare appearances in the subsequent collections take the
form principally of memories, not of domestic epiphanies.[16] And
indeed the poem that brings to a close this short Mosca series at the
end of *Satura*, 'Il grillo di Strasburgo' (*OV* 406), is a particularly
significant memory, recalling the crucial moment of her passage from
this world into the other. Mosca is presented here again as a bearer of
memories, as exemplified in the catalogue of places, objects and
people, the 'nugae' that may have passed through her mind at the
moment of her ultimate leavetaking ('ti riappervero *allora*?'). The
dramatic nature of that event, and the poet's inability to frame a
coherent description of it, are encapsulated in the frank, helpless
intensity of the italicized '*allora*'. In focusing on that moment and the
unanswered questions it raises for him, Montale draws our attention
back to his and our ignorance surrounding the nature of the leap into
the void. We are left with the de-dramatizing banality of her last
earthly words to him, 'prendi il sonnifero', which focus our attention
back onto the figure of the solitary *io* in his ironic *dormiveglia*.

The Poet's 'commerci con l'Altro'

The portrayal of the relationship with Mosca as a possible key to a
radically 'other' reality, confined largely to 'Xenia', represents a
transitional moment in the treatment of the *oltrevita* and related
themes. The questions raised through the dialogue with the ghost
remain to be explored in her absence in the twilight world of *Satura*

and beyond, where the female *tu* fades almost completely from Montale's poetic repertoire, to be replaced in part by a new interlocutor, or potential interlocutor, namely the problematic, elusive figure of the unknown deity itself. The relationship, or putative relationship, between the *io* and *l'Altro* largely replaces the old *io–tu* axis and becomes a focus for figurations of the radical absence of meaning in the poet's world. This relationship, depicted in a number of different metaphorical guises, is characterized throughout by varying degrees of ignorance, absence, indifference and antagonism on both sides. Indeed, Montale's *Altro*, as Orelli points out, 'non pare piú vicino che non sia l'*altrui* per piú d'un abitante dell'*Inferno* dantesco'.[17] Representations of this Other are repeatedly constructed only to be mocked and undermined. The impossible relationship with the supreme, non-existent interlocutor is, in its absurd contradictions, constantly shifting connotations and repeated inversions of values, a central, enduring image of the later Montale's almost nihilistic outlook.

In referring to representations of *l'Altro*, I take my cue from the title of the final poem in *Satura*, which brings together and crystallizes in one concise formulation various elements of a vein of quasi-theological speculation present at intervals throughout the collection. Before examining this text, it may be useful to consider briefly some previous occurrences of such motifs. The word 'l'Altro' itself is the culmination of a series of non-committal 'namings' of the divinity encountered in *Satura*. Indeed, the use of the word to denote some kind of supernatural entity had previously occurred in *Bufera* in 'La primavera hitleriana', and can perhaps also be discerned in the phrase 'l'*altra* Emergenza' in 'Ballata scritta in una clinica' (given added intensity here by the use of italics and the upper case for 'Emergenza'). In this light one may even read into the title itself of *La bufera e altro* an understated reference to the 'other' dimension whose presence is felt so strongly in that collection. Similar reticent namings of a mysterious, ambiguous entity occur throughout *Satura*. Thus we find, for example: 'l'onniveggente, lui' ('Xenia' II 9), 'il sommo Emarginato' ('La morte di Dio'), 'il regista' ('Götterdämmerung'), 'l'Altro' ('Realismo non magico'), 'il Proto' ('Botta e risposta II'), 'il burattinaio' ('Sono venuto al mondo'), 'il creatore [...] / il fondatore' ('Divinità in incognito'). Although explicit namings of God, often in an ironic mode, do occur in these later collections, what these examples have in common (and share with others in *Diario* and

Quaderno) is an apparent reluctance to name God directly (an unwillingness shared with Mosca, as seen in XII 9). Some of the examples quoted represent the antonomastic elevation of an otherwise generic term ('l'altro', 'il fondatore'), which is thus invested with mock solemnity, while others resort to a kind of anthropomorphic figuration of the divinity as some kind of artist or artisan, whose attitude to the created work, however, is usually one of indifference, giving rise to comic effects of contrast and unfulfilled expectations. The most notable example of this, in the light of later recurrences, is that of 'il regista', a figure bound up with the image of the world as a meaningless spectacle. We find this, for example, in 'Götter-dämmerung', where the 'show' or performance has been postponed 'perché il regista è occupato, è malato, imbucato / chissà dove e nessuno può sostituirlo' (*OV* 322). This deity is fundamentally absent and unconcerned with his creation; elsewhere he is the distracted printer, 'il Proto', who does not deign to look at the proofs ('Botta e risposta II'), or the bored, indifferent puppeteer of 'Sono venuto al mondo':

> [...]
> Le infinite chiusure e aperture
> possono avere un senso per chi è dalla parte
> che sola conta, del burattinaio.
> Ma quello non domanda la collaborazione
> di chi ignora i suoi fini e la sua arte.
>
> E chi è da quella parte? Se c'è, credo
> che si annoi più di noi. [...] (*OV* 379)

Closely linked to this idea of an indifferent God is that of the improbability or randomness of creation, as found, for example, in 'Niente di grave':

> [...] Era improbabile
> anche l'uomo, si afferma. Per la consolazione
> di non so chi, lassù alla lotteria
> è stato estratto il numero che non usciva mai.
> [...] (*OV* 341)

The indifference of the deity is matched by the speaker's ignorance ('non so chi'). Associated with this gulf of ignorance and indifference separating the two sides is a radical absence of meaning touching even the realm of the divine, which, in an echo of the earlier '*quaggiù*' (XI 7), is devalued by the use of the distinctly non-committal 'lassù', a term further debased here by its alliterative juxtaposition with 'lotteria'. A similar image can be found in the 1962 prose piece 'L'uomo nel microsolco', where two hypotheses of creation are sketched: 'nella prima, l'Essere supremo ascolta, forse non senza sorpresa, l'opera da lui *gettata* in un solo *fiat* [...]; nella seconda, l'Essere gioca ai dadi, mescola le carte ed è curioso di vedere quel che accadrà' (*SMAMS* 283). Although both hypotheses are treated with due scepticism, the author goes on to signal clearly his preference for the latter (see also 'Lettera da Albenga', *SMAMS* 373–4). This absence of meaning in the absurdity of a cosmic lottery points clearly to a parallel on the (putative) spiritual or metaphysical level with the contemporary historical meaninglessness denounced elsewhere during these years.

The image of the world as aimless spectacle, as a show without a director, returns in 'Qui e là':

> Da tempo stiamo provando la rappresentazione
> [...]
> Da millenni attendiamo che qualcuno
> ci saluti al proscenio con battimani
> o anche con qualche fischio, non importa,
> purché ci riconforti un *nous sommes là*.
> Purtroppo non pensiamo in francese e così
> restiamo sempre al qui e mai al là. (*OV* 349)

The absurdity of such a performance evidently gives rise also to indifference on the part of the 'actors' as to its success or failure ('non importa'), just one example of the general disillusioned scepticism that permeates *Satura*, expressed here also in the tone of jaded irony of the closing lines, where the great divide between the physical and the spiritual is reduced to the banal alternative between 'qui' and 'là' (another variant of 'quaggiù'/'lassù'), and mocked by the whimsical bilingual word-play. Meanwhile the aimless rehearsal or performance continues in the absence of its audience, the deity, or indeed, in the uncomfortable suspicion of the latter's non-existence.

All of the above sheds light on the 'inghippo', the long *imbroglio* referred to in 'L'Altro' at the close of the collection. The poem begins as an act of debunking, of unmasking, what Cataldi describes as 'l'autodenuncia di un'illusione':[18]

> Non so chi se n'accorga
> ma i nostri commerci con l'Altro

> furono un lungo inghippo. Denunziarli
> sarà, più che un atto d'ossequio, un impetrare clemenza
> [...] (OV 407)

In this opening statement, the poet's general scepticism (directed elsewhere at the world of historical reality) is applied with equal vigour to relationships between the Godhead and humanity, relationships characterized as fraudulent or corrupt through the strong, rather incongruous lexical choices of 'commerci' and 'inghippo', which immediately undermine any possible sense of the sacred. The whole statement is framed in terms that emphasize the ignorance and indifference surrounding these relationships ('Non so chi'), as already seen elsewhere. The exposure of this 'inghippo', this fraud, is the primary theme of the poem, but in exposing it the speaker's purpose is not, apparently, to condemn humanity, but rather to plead (however ironically) its innocence in the affair. Indeed the poem is centred around a disclaimer of responsibility:

> [...]
> Non siamo responsabili di non essere lui
> né ha colpa lui, o merito, della nostra parvenza.
> [...]

Previous statements of the distance and indifference dividing us from any God are encapsulated in this comprehensive formula of disengagement: there is neither shared identity nor mutual responsibility between the two sides. The central tenet of the poem is the fundamental *otherness* of the deity and the spiritual dimension, the incommensurability of life in this world with the *oltrevita*, all of which justifies and explains the phenomena of indifference and ignorance contained in the various examples seen above. In this context, all mankind's astute calculations, all the niceties and intricacies of his pretended 'commerci con l'Altro' (and these must include the poet's own theologies), are reduced to absurdity. They are beliefs as flawed and naive as that of the flamingo:

> [...] Astuto il flamengo nasconde
> il capo sotto l'ala e crede che il cacciatore
> non lo veda.

This enigmatic image involves a motif, that of hunting, whose roots run deep in Montale's writings and in his childhood memories. Characterized by Barile as reflecting a hidden 'trauma originario', this motif is present in many poems of the Arletta cycle as well as in numerous prose pieces, not to mention a key poetic text such as 'Il gallo cedrone' in *Bufera*.[19] Meanwhile, however, this hunting motif also recalls quite clearly the opening poem in *Satura*, 'Il *tu*', where one reads:

> [...] Il male
> è che l'uccello preso nel paretaio
> non sa se lui sia lui o uno dei troppi
> suoi duplicati. [...] (*OV* 275)

Indeed, Cataldi sees the reiteration of this image at the close of the book as 'una ripresa e conferma dell'apertura'.[20] This is perhaps to oversimplify matters: while undoubtedly the imagery employed in both texts belongs to the same semantic area, it seems more significant that the two titles, at opposite ends of the book, 'Il *tu*' and 'L'Altro', reflect the change in the poet's main interlocutor during the collection. While the first text is concerned with problems of individual identity, the closing poem reflects a shift in the poet's concerns towards the great unanswerable questions. In this context, another notable difference is the presence in the latter text of the menacing figure of the hunter himself, an image we shall see taken up again in the subsequent collection as the poet concentrates increasingly, within this broad speculatory vein, on the possibly hostile character of the elusive Other.

The image of the unknown God as a sort of predatory or hostile figure comes to the fore in several texts in *Diario*, in a variety of tones ranging from the gently ironic to the openly antagonistic. 'Il Re pescatore' for example, while clearly playing on the Christian metaphor of the 'fisher of men' and toying with the English word 'kingfisher' (a literary allusion whose connotations have been pointed out by Grignani), can be linked directly to the close of 'L'Altro'.[21] Apart from the ornithological connection, the two images have in common the implied idea of God as hunter, in this case a hunter of souls (a motif which recurs later in 'Kingfisher'). So we have: 'Si ritiene / che il Re dei pescatori non cerchi altro / che anime' (*OV* 424). His realm, as usual, is radically 'other', and cannot be measured or recorded in human terms: 'Il suo regno è a misura di millimetro'. The poem concludes with the depiction of an uneasy relationship between a rapacious deity and his human prey (the latter characterized here as 'gli altri', a phrase with distinctly disdainful overtones for Montale, as seen in various other texts):

[...]
Solo il Re pescatore
ha una giusta misura,
gli altri hanno appena un'anima
e la paura
di perderla. (*OV* 424)

The prey (humanity), fearful of the unknown, clings to whatever tenuous status it has, recalling the earlier cowering, self-deluding gesture of the flamingo.

The idea that dealings with the spiritual world or afterlife are somehow dangerous or threatening is not new in Montale's work. It can be found in *Bufera*, for example in 'Ezekiel saw the wheel' (*OV* 247), where there is a troubled interaction between the *io*, the woman and the symbols of religion ('la scheggia, la fibra della tua croce / [...] la Ruota minacciosa'). Similarly, in 'La primavera hitleriana', the fate foreseen for Clizia is: 'che il cieco sole che in te porti / si abbàcini nell'Altro e si distrugga / in Lui, per tutti' (*OV* 249). The near-death of Mosca in 1944 (the episode that inspired 'Ballata scritta in una clinica') is referred to again in *Satura* in 'Gli ultimi spari', where the Other is depicted as an insidious predator: 'eri la preda / di chi non venne e ritardò l'agguato' (*OV* 339). In *Diario*, however, in the absence of a mediating *tu*, this dangerous relationship with *l'Altro* impinges more directly on the figure of the *io*.

A less explicit version of the hunter–hunted relationship occurs in 'Il tiro a volo'. This poem is noteworthy as it approaches the problems of the knowledge of life and death in an indirect way, using images and archetypes from Montale's existing repertoire in a manner reminiscent of an earlier, more emblematic style. It is addressed to an unspecified 'tu', and the poem's pretext of a question on the part of the interlocutor recalls the basic structure of the 'Botta e risposta' series. There is, more specifically, an echo of the exhortation of 'Botta e risposta I' ('penso [...] che sia tempo / di spiegare le vele') in the opening lines here:

Mi chiedi perché navigo
nell'insicurezza e non tento
un'altra rotta? [...] (*OV* 435)

This poem departs from the simple, at times facile, discursive mode of many of these later texts: by adopting the question-and-answer format, Montale constructs a miniature variant on the more complex model of the 'Botta e risposta' poems, where the *io* was similarly uncertain, indecisive. In that series, the 'risposta' was not so much an answer as a free-standing meditation, provoked by the 'botta' but not logically dependent on it. Similarly, here the 'answer' consists of another question, or at any rate, an exhortation to another question:

> [...] Domandalo
> all'uccello che vola illeso
> perché il tiro era lungo e troppo larga
> la rosa della botta.
> [...]

These lines provoke a further series of resonances within Montale's opus. They immediately call to mind the images of hunting and birds that we have just seen applied to questions concerning God and the *oltrevita*. Here the bird is again prey rather than predator, and so we are back in the line leading from 'Il *tu*' to 'L'Altro', where the deity became the hostile figure of the hunter. But in 'Il tiro a volo' the hunter is ineffectual and the prey escapes (we might even see an ironic lexical echo of the 'Botta e riposta' series in the re-use of 'botta': was the interlocutor's question wide of the mark?). So this poem presents another variation on the figure of the survivor, the individual who escapes the net, but who, like the escaped fish of 'La storia II', may not in fact be any better off than those inside: it is the ambiguous, contradictory figure of the poet himself, whose survival, whose biological persistence begins to seem increasingly incongruous.

Montale is also ironically subverting here the scenario of another text from an earlier period, 'Il gallo cedrone' (*Bufera*; *OV* 253).[22] The anguished intensity of that poem, with its images of violence and death preluding a rebirth from below, has vanished here: the hunter missed and the bird survived, but with what result? The problem, as we see in the second stanza, remains open, unresolved, and the ultimate outcome of the poet's journey 'nell'insicurezza' is expressed in highly ambivalent terms:

> [...]
> Se ci salva una perdita di peso
> è da vedersi.

As well as evoking the lightness of the bird flying free, this image recalls directly one of the Mosca poems at the close of *Satura*, 'Luci e colori'. There, loss of weight was one of the characteristics of the ghost, an indicator of her belonging to the *oltrevita*: 'Tu stessa non devi pesare di più' (*OV* 405). The return of the image here allows a clear reading of this poem's open-ended conclusion: death, even if inevitable, cannot be assigned an unambiguous value; it may or may not mean salvation.

The motif of humanity as the prey of the deity, along with a pedal-note of doubt as to whether the outcome of the encounter will be positive or negative, is taken up again in 'Il dottor Schweitzer':

> gettava pesci vivi a pellicani famelici.
> Sono vita anche i pesci fu rilevato, ma
> di gerarchia inferiore.
>
> A quale gerarchia apparteniamo noi
> e in quali fauci ...? Qui tacque il teologo
> e si asciugò il sudore. (*OV* 450)

Here the predatory bird is likened indirectly to the deity, and humanity to the fish, its prey. One may also perhaps discern here a passing reference to the iconographic representation of Christ as the pelican (although the image of the fish also occurs in Christian iconography—a further playful muddying of the waters perhaps?). In any case this poem with its lighter tone belongs more to the comic or grotesque vein established in the openly satirical parts of *Satura* than to the more introspective vein represented by 'Il tiro a volo'. The satirical sketch of a 'teologo' (presumably a reference to Albert Schweitzer himself, who kept a pet pelican), terrified at the prospect of the unknown afterlife, is typical of this more comic register, with its jaundiced view of the contemporary world and its inhabitants (one might compare, for example, the 'ceffo dei teologi' in 'Piove', or the listing of 'teologia' among less spiritual human pursuits in 'Fine del '68'). Nevertheless the relationship between mankind and *l'Altro* emerges from this poem fraught with still more tension and ambivalence: if the status of humanity vis-à-vis the deity is uncertain ('A quale gerarchia apparteniamo [...]?'), the doubt that causes the theologian most alarm concerns the very identity of the 'fauci', the nature and *bona fides* of the Other: is it ultimately good or evil?

The figure of the divine fisherman returns in 'Kingfisher'. The poem opens however with a disenchanted backward glance (whose connotations are analysed in detail by Martelli[23]):

> Praticammo con cura il carpe diem,
> tentammo di acciuffare chi avesse pelo o escrescenze,

gettammo l'amo senza che vi abboccasse
tinca o barbo (e di trote non si parli).
[...] (OV 476)

The casting of the hook here echoes 'Verso il fondo' earlier in *Diario*,
where, in a slightly different use of the fishing motif, the *io* was seen
casting the net of poetry and contemplating the 'pesci piccoli' of his
meagre catch in this late season: 'Ora che mi riprovo / con amo e
spago / l'esca rimane intatta' (OV 423). Similarly now in 'Kingfisher',
attempts to equal the catch of earlier halcyon days are futile, as we are
reminded by the the the aside 'e di trote non si parli', clearly an ironic
allusion to 'La trota nera' in *Bufera*. Now, in an upside-down world,
the *io*, reduced to the level of an impotent prey, can only wait for his
own uncertain end:

> [...]
> Ora siamo al rovescio e qui restiamo attenti
> se sia mai una lenza che ci agganci.
> Ma il Pescatore nicchia perché la nostra polpa
> anche al cartoccio o in carpione non trova più clienti.

With the fisher-god indifferent to the now-willing prey, the latter's
status is reduced even further, debased to that of an unwanted 'polpa'.
(The antecedents of such culinary imagery can be traced back to 'Il
sogno del prigioniero', where one fate feared by the prisoner was
'terminare nel *pâté* / destinato agli Iddii pestilenziali'.) Ultimately, the
figure of the deity that emerges from 'Kingfisher' is again that of an
absent, indifferent entity, accompanied by more than a hint of
potential menace.

   The figure of the poet is repeatedly portrayed in attempts to see
directly, to name or somehow to contact this elusive Other. The
matter is treated with a characteristically light self-deprecatory touch
in 'Come Zaccheo':

> Si tratta di arrampicarsi sul sicomoro
> per vedere il Signore se mai passi.
> Ahimè, non sono un rampicante ed anche
> stando in punta di piedi non l'ho mai visto. (OV 417)

The problem of making contact is a two-way one: if it is due in part
to the shortcomings of the *io* ('non sono un rampicante'), it also
involves the likely absence of the *Altro* ('se mai passi'). The explicit
naming of God, by no means unusual in these collections, occurs

again in 'La lingua di Dio', which also deals with the same problematic question of contacting the divinity:

> Se dio è il linguaggio, l'Uno che ne creò tanti altri
> per poi confonderli
> come faremo a interpellarlo [...] (OV 445)

The difficulty lies in the move from our 'balbuzie' to the divine 'linguaggio'. But even if this leap were achieved, it would, it seems, bring its own problems: 'E guai se un giorno / le voci si sciogliessero'. A meeting between two such profoundly different orders of existence would not necessarily be a happy one.[24]

The problem of naming God, of the apparent incommensurability of human and divine language, is a constant element in the problematic relationship between the io and the deity. This is reflected in the many further occurrences of indirectly named gods or god-surrogates in these collections. In Diario one finds, for example, 'l'Impronunciabile' (OV 430), 'l'Oggetto' (OV 444), 'il mio allenatore [...] l'idiota' (OV 448), 'Chi tiene i fili' (OV 468), 'il principe della Festa' (OV 486), 'Il mio Artefice' (OV 497), 'l'Unico' (OV 501); and in Quaderno di quattro anni, 'testa universale' (OV 511), 'chi può' (OV 549), 'la Mente' (OV 558), 'altri' (OV 562), 'Il Calafato' (OV 565), 'chi non può / fare a meno di noi [...] colui che ci ha posto in questa sede' (OV 580), 'Padre [...] artefice divino' (OV 584), 'il croupier' (OV 597), 'Il Creatore' (OV 604), 'gli dei' (OV 605).

So, the figure of the unknown and unknowable Deus absconditus that emerged in Satura has by now become a constant, an archetype in the repertoire of imagery deployed by Montale. As Marchese observes: 'Dio è sempre l'Alterità radicale, l'assente, il latente o latitante'.[25] The entity that ought to be in control has renounced its responsibilities and the io can only impotently denounce its negligence:

> Non mi stanco di dire al mio allenatore
> getta la spugna
> ma lui non sente nulla perché sul ring o anche fuori
> non s'è mai visto.
> Forse, a suo modo, cerca di salvarmi
> dal disonore. Che abbia tanta cura
> di me, l'idiota, o io sia il suo buffone
> tiene in bilico tra la gratitudine
> e il furore. (OV 448)

Despite the apparent anxiety to communicate on the part of the *io*, the Other is seemingly beyond the range of human sight and sound. In this complete absence of *l'Altro*, the attitude of the *io* is ambivalent: he is unable to formulate a coherent stance. Thus in this poem (within the clearly ironic overall posture of one who feels that it is time to 'throw in the towel'), there is on the one hand the communicative openness of line 1 and the willingness (lines 5–6) to accept the possibility of a benevolent God, while there is also the more negative tone of the impatient closing lines, just one example of what Zanzotto calls 'una specie di tracotanza' found throughout *Diario*, the truculent language and attitude of one who wishes to confront the gods, the language with which Montale denounces the 'non-paradiso' to which he is condemned.[26]

The idea of an encounter between the deity and some kind of diabolic opposite, or of their coexistence within one figure, occurs in a number of texts, where the hypothesis is advanced of an eternal, Manichaean co-presence of the positive and negative principles. Thus for example, in 'Il principe della Festa', while the 'prince' is announced (in the ironic Dantean pastiche of line 2) as an omnipotent ruler, his relationship with the *io* is again fraught with uncertainties, first with regard to his whereabouts and secondly with regard to the nature of the spectacle over which he presides:

> Ignoro dove sia il principe della Festa,
> Quegli che regge il mondo e le altre sfere.
> Ignoro se sia festa o macelleria
> quello che scorgo se mi affaccio alla finestra.
> [...] (*OV* 486)

The ambiguous nature of this 'festa o macelleria' raises once again the possibility that the godhead may represent a negative or potentially hostile force, a possibility that sits comfortably with Montale's sceptical relativism, as he casts doubt on the motives and mechanisms of the supposed moment of creation:

> [...]
> Forse un eterno buio si stancò, sprizzò fuori
> qualche scintilla. O un'eterea luce
> si maculò trovando se stessa insopportabile.
> [...]

Is the Other then a principle of darkness or of light? In either case, it is clear that the creation was an act concerned with the needs of the creator rather than those of the creatures, with whom indeed the 'prince' may be quite unconcerned. But equally, while the Other may indeed be absolute ruler of his ambiguous 'feast', his own position is seen to be fatally undermined, just as his identity is uncertain, and his place may be usurped by another 'Other' in a future turning of the tables, foreseen in grotesquely comical terms in the closing lines (the internal rhyme *omeopatiche : natiche* is a particularly good example of Montale's verbal inventiveness in the low or comic register):

> [...]
> Oppure il principe ignora le sue fatture
> o può vantarsene solo in dosi omeopatiche.
> Ma è sicuro che un giorno sul suo seggio
> peseranno altre natiche. È già l'ora.

An alternative hypothesis to that of a change of occupancy in the seat of celestial power is that of an eternal co-occupancy, as put forward towards the end of *Diario*: 'Non partita di boxe o di ramino / tra i due opposti Luciferi' (*OV* 501). With the deity indistinguishable from its opposite, there is no conflict possible: 'Non può darsi sconfitto o vincitore / senza conflitto e di ciò i gemelli / non hanno alcun sentore.' (A similar peaceful co-existence is described in 'Ipotesi', *OV* 578.) It is a duality in which each side is inextricably linked to its opposite, a mirror of the 'ossimoro permanente' which Montale decries in contemporary historical reality.

The portrayal of the deity in terms that are by turns whimsical, ironic and polemical continues in *Quaderno* and *Altri versi*. At times a more facile, almost derisory tone emerges, for example in 'Big bang o altro', where, in questioning various scientific views of the cosmos, the poetic voice mocks in passing the 'bacchetta magica / di un dio che abbia caratteri / spaventosamente antropomorfici' (*OV* 531). Such an openly satirical approach is found again in 'Sera di Pasqua', where religion is reduced to the status of one of the debased cultural artefacts purveyed by the television screen:

> Alla televisione
> Cristo in croce cantava come un tenore
> colto da un'improvvisa
> colica *pop*.
> [...] (*OV* 549)

This satire is directed principally however against humanity and contemporary culture: it is not religion as such but 'la religione del ventesimo secolo' that Montale derides here, and in fact the poem ultimately defends the realm of the spiritual, with its sublime 'Indifferenza', against the vulgarities and presumptions of humanity:

> [...] Intanto
> chiudiamo il video. Al resto
> provvederà chi può (se questo *chi*
> ha qualche senso). Noi non lo sapremo.

Nevertheless, the ultimate message, as elsewhere, is that of the deity's unknowability and possible or probable meaninglessness.

The figure of an indifferent God recurs frequently: for example as the *croupier* in the game of life in 'La vita oscilla', a text belonging to a straightforwardly comic register. In this poem opposing values are reversed or reduced to a common insignificance, underpinned by the use of a light rhythmic and phonic *cantilena*:

> · La vita oscilla
> tra il sublime e l'immondo
> con qualche propensione
> per il secondo.
> Ne sapremo di più
> dopo le ultime elezioni
> che si terranno lassù
> o laggiù o in nessun luogo
> perché siamo già eletti
> tutti quanti e chi non lo fu
> sta assai meglio quaggiù
> [...] (*OV* 597)

In the afterlife 'lassù' and 'laggiù' are apparently interchangeable, both being of equal value with 'nessun luogo' (and in any case the 'quaggiù' seems preferable to both). The whole question of life and *oltrevita* is reduced to the status of an absurd game of chance presided over by a detached, indifferent divinity, an echo of the 'lotteria lassù' seen in an earlier text, now couched in the jargon of the international cosmopolitan ambience that has lurked in the background of Montale's verse since *Satura*:

> [...]
> les jeux sont faits
> dice il croupier per l'ultima volta
> e il suo cucchiaione
> spazza le carte.

In the final collection, *Altri versi*, the question of the *oltrevita* continues
to be a key theme in the more broadly meditative or speculative texts
(largely confined to the first section of the volume). There are few
significant innovations in the imagery, tone or register of language used
in dealing with the figure of the deity, but rather we find repeated
variants on now-familiar themes. The motifs of uncertain identity,
inversion of values and reversal of roles (between humanity and deity,
creator and creatures, living and dead) recur in several texts. In 'L'inverno
si prolunga' the gods are again characterized by their absence: 'chiaro
che Dei o semidei / si siano a loro volta licenziati / dei loro padroni,
se mai n'ebbero. / Ma ...' (*OV* 633). The tone is one of disillusionment
and resignation to a state of ignorance and separation from the realm
of the divine. Those who would claim knowledge of *l'Altro* are mocked
as 'ciarlatani e aruspici'. There is a sense here, as elsewhere in these last
collections, that the poet's weary scepticism runs the risk of descending
into tired repetition of empty formulae, that the potential openness and
disponibilità of the inconclusive ending, 'Ma ...', may merely reflect an
unwillingness even to attempt any more a resolution of the problems
raised, or their distillation into coherent, unequivocal images. (A similar
inconclusiveness marks the end of the collection as a whole, with the
final poem closing on an equally open 'Mah?'.) In 'Vinca il peggiore'
(*OV* 653), where the divinity is named with ironic circumspection as
'Colui del quale non può dirsi il nome', distinctions are annulled
between 'Il vincitore il vinto / il vivo il morto l'asino il sapiente', all
strung together in an unpunctuated continuum. Not only is their status
relative to one another questioned, but also their very existence as
phenomena belonging to an order of being expressible in human terms:
'anzi non stanno affatto / o sono in altro luogo / che la parola rifiuta'.

The images of hunter and prey are also present in *Altri versi*: in the
gnomic irony of 'A caccia' (*OV* 640), and indirectly in 'Reti per
uccelli' (*OV* 562), where to some extent the imagery itself is mocked
and satirized. The familiar trapped bird returns in 'La buccia della
Terra è più sottile' (*OV* 651). Here the all-embracing pessimism of a
world viewed as 'questo nulla' (in which we are all, including perhaps
the gods or their surrogates, 'incastrati fino al collo') leads to a
conclusion whose echoes reach back to the early part of *Satura*:

> [...]
> questo è il guaio
> che ci fa più infelici dell'uccello
> nel paretaio.

So the poet has returned once again to the uncertainties regarding identity and status posed in 'Il *tu*' and 'La storia II': it is unclear whether the escapee/survivor is saved or damned. Moreover, it no longer seems to matter very much.

There is now an ever more widespread sense of absurdity, of meaninglessness, and here as before a favourite image of the absurdity of our dealings with the deity is that of the futile performance or spectacle, which recurs frequently in this last collection. Thus we find, for example: 'lo spettacolo / annoiava gli attori più che il pubblico' ('Rimuginando', *OV* 645), 'Non siamo che comparse, in gergo teatrale / utilités' ('Oggi', *OV* 646), 'Noi siamo i comprimari, i souffleurs nelle buche' ('L'allegoria', *OV* 652), 'colui che di tutto tiene i fili' (an implicit reference to puppet theatre, in 'Una zuffa di galli inferociti', *OV* 655), 'qualche replica [...] le prenotazioni [...] gli abbonati alle prime' ('L'avvenire è già passato da un pezzo', *OV* 657). The image comes to the fore in 'Lo spettacolo':

> Il suggeritore giù nella sua nicchia
> s'impappinò di certo in qualche battuta
> e l'Autore era in viaggio e non si curava
> dell'ultimo copione contestato
> sin da allora e da chi? Resta un problema.
> [...] (*OV* 662)

The Author-God is both absent and indifferent, his creation flawed from the beginning (the script is disputed) and the question of just who is concerned with the whole shaky performance and whether it is a success or a failure remains to be resolved: 'è ancora aperta e tale resterà'.

There immediately follows another (untitled) text, which can be read as a final compendium of the tone, attitudes and some of the key images associated with this thematic strand throughout these collections:

> Colui che allestì alla meno peggio
> il cabaret
> tutto aveva previsto gloria e infamia
> o cadde in una trappola
> di cui fu prima vittima se stesso?
> Che possa uscirne presto o tardi è dubbio.
> È la domanda che dobbiamo porci
> uomini e porci, con desideri opposti. (*OV* 663)

With wry scepticism, the potentially sacred is rendered in terms of the thoroughly profane. The theatrical image is reduced to its most banal manifestation, the cabaret (itself devalued further by 'alla meno peggio' in line 1). The whole text is framed in terms of questioning, doubt and ultimate indifference regarding the status and fate of the nameless 'Colui': he was apparently a setter of traps but, in a well-established procedure, roles have been reversed and hunter has become victim. The deity becomes, potentially, an object of derision or of pity, a trapped and helpless animal. The closing lines remain within the sphere of animal imagery, but represent a further debasement of this type of motif. The use of the comic or grotesque image of 'porci', placed on the same level as humanity, while it may echo the kind of absurdity portrayed with an earlier image such as that of the flamingo of 'L'Altro', seems motivated here by a mere pun, by the poet's playful instinct, a clear testimony to the marked lessening of poetic and communicative tension in these final years and to the increasing prominence in Montale's work of a vein of blithe nihilism, in which all possible outcomes, in this world or another, are seen as equally meaningless.

In retrospect, the placing of 'L'Altro' at the close of *Satura* must appear highly significant. It functions both as a summing-up and as an indicator of a new direction, a new orientation towards the attitudes and discourse of direct theological (or pseudo-theological) speculation, as well as establishing decisively the ironic tone of this speculatory vein, in which essentially comic representations of the deity and of the spiritual dimension become useful new correlatives for the poet's continuing earthly scepticism. Thus, while Mengaldo writes that in *Satura* 'solo parlando d'*altro* [Montale] può parlare dell'*Altro*', it might equally be observed that in these later works as a whole, Montale, *parlando dell'Altro, parla anche d'altro*.[27]

Describing the overall shift in Montale's work from 'allegoria piena' to the 'allegoria vuota' of the last collections, Luperini writes: 'L'allegoria vuota tende, alla fine, a negare anche se stessa: cioè qualsiasi possibilità di discorso. Sulla soglia del silenzio, non resta allora che l'estremo *divertissement* del Vecchio scettico e melanconico che gioca con i frantumi delle parole e con le interiezioni.'[28] Modifying this approach slightly, one might say that the situation portrayed in the texts examined here consitutes a practically moribund allegory, drastically limited in vitality and in its events, and almost devoid of the 'aspiration to narrative' cited by Luperini as characteristic of allegorical discourse.[29]

It is an increasingly static scenario, that of an old man waiting for death, a scenario, in Barile's words, of 'progressiva paralisi e chiusura claustrofobica'.[30] And yet the representation of the relationship or standoff between the *io* and *l'Altro*, while it may not constitute an 'allegoria piena', can perhaps be seen as the staging of a last allegorical *tableau*, requiring, in order to be fully understood, an 'intellectual complicity' on the part of the reader, a knowledge of and engagement with the macro-text of Montale's work as a whole and its cultural and ideological terms of reference.[31] And it does contain an irreducible potential for narrative development: the potential implicit in the inevitable, awaited dénouement of death .

Meanwhile the *io*, condemned to wait for his unknown interlocutor, can only engage in a Beckettian monologue, a monologue that, as Barile points out, no longer implies the presence of a listening *tu*, but involves the 'disintegrazione del linguaggio come possibilità di comunicazione'.[32] The presentation of this monologue of the elderly sceptic railing against a God in whom he does not believe constitutes the last allegorical figuration of the absurdity of the contemporary world, of its surrender to non-meaning. Meanwhile, the old man's impossible dialogue with God also encapsulates the ageing Montale's own increasingly absurd ideological position of denying all positive values while lamenting their absence, of deriding poetic discourse while engaging in it ever more assiduously.

Notes to Chapter 4

1. On this theme, see Luperini, *Montale o l'identità negata*, 86–125; Lonardi, *Il Vecchio e il Giovane*, 139–43.
2. For the term 'oltrevita', see 'Sono pronto ripeto' (*OV* 452) and 'Vivere' (*OV* 564). I have used it here as a shorthand term to refer to the 'beyond' in the widest sense possible.
3. Mengaldo, 'Primi appunti su *Satura*', 341.
4. See Carpi, *Montale dopo il fascismo*, 175; Grignani, *Prologhi ed epiloghi*, 34–5; Cambon, *Eugenio Montale's Poetry*, 209; Forti, *Eugenio Montale*, 481.
5. See Jacomuzzi, *La poesia di Montale*, 35–7.
6. Pipa, 'L'ultimo Montale', 257.
7. See Laura Barile, *Adorate mie larve: Montale e la poesia anglosassone* (Bologna: Il Mulino, 1990), 12, 116.
8. Mengaldo, 'Primi appunti su *Satura*', 341.
9. Forti (*Eugenio Montale*, 387) speaks of 'una finzione scenica' .
10. Montale does not propose 'una qualsivoglia teologia o, peggio ancora, una mistica dell'ineffabilità' (Grignani, *Prologhi ed epiloghi*, 39); see also Forti, *Eugenio Montale*, 450.

11. See Sergio Antonielli, 'Clizia e Altro', *Letteratura* 79–81 (1966), 102–7 ; Rocco Montano, 'Note per un'interpretazione di Montale', esp. 241–5; Cinzia Lonati, 'Montale e Clizia', *Cultura* 8 (1990), 17–24; Rina Virgillito, *La luce di Montale: per una rilettura della poesia montaliana* (Milan: Edizioni Paoline, 1990), esp. chap. 4.

12. Carlo Bo, 'Montale, un gioco a nascondino nel mare inquieto della poesia', *Corriere della sera* (12 Oct. 1996), 35.

13. On the image of the telephone, see Pellini, 'L'ultimo Montale', 303–4.

14. See Mario Aversano, *Montale e il libretto d'opera* (Naples: Editrice Ferraro, 1984), 16–19; also Lonardi, 'L'altra madre', 275–6.

15. 'il punto / a cui tutti li tempi son presenti'. See Virgillito, *La luce di Montale*, 128.

16. These few subsequent appearances are as follows: in *Diario*, 'I nascondigli' (*OV* 426), 'Il pirla' (*OV* 432), 'Sorapis, 40 anni fa' (*OV* 502), 'Al mio grillo' (*OV* 507); in *Quaderno*, 'Quando cominciai' (*OV* 520), 'Nel disumano' (*OV* 583); Mosca then reappears along with other ghosts of the past in the closing texts of *Altri versi*.

17. Orelli, *Accertamenti montaliani*, 96.

18. Cataldi, *Montale*, 54.

19. See Barile's introduction to *Lettere e poesie a Bianca e Francesco Messina*, 23.

20. Cataldi, *Montale*, 56.

21. As well as a reference to Matthew 13, 47–8, Grignani (*Prologhi ed epiloghi*, 38–42) sees here an allusion to Eliot's 'Burnt Norton'.

22. On this poem, see especially Lonardi, 'Con il gallo cedrone', *Il Vecchio e il Giovane*, 171–89.

23. Martelli, *Eugenio Montale: introduzione e guida*, 145–51.

24. On this poem, see Cambon, *Eugenio Montale's Poetry*, 248–51.

25. Marchese, *Visiting angel*, 260.

26. 'è una requisitoria pronunciata [...] da uno che persiste ad argomentare contro il padrone stando sotto la sferza del padrone'. Zanzotto, 'La freccia dei diari', 51.

27. Mengaldo, 'Primi appunti su *Satura*', 341.

28. Luperini, 'Note sull'allegorismo novecentesco', 73.

29. Ibid., 55.

30. Barile, *Adorate mie larve*, 113.

31. Jacomuzzi (*La poesia di Montale*, 72–3) suggests that allegory requires of the reader 'una complicità di natura schiettamente intellettuale' .

32. Barile, *Adorate mie larve*, 114.

CHAPTER 5

Memories:
'Fummo felici un giorno ...'

From *Diario* onwards there is a sense in Montale's work that time, the
old enemy, is finally catching up to the poet. The closing poems in
both *Diario del '71* and *Diario del '72*, for example, are clearly intended
as potentially valedictory texts. In this context, questions surrounding
the existence and possible nature of an afterlife are given a more
earnest and at times a more anguished treatment in a number of
poems in which the *io* contemplates his own immediate future, now
increasingly reduced to the prospect of his impending leap into the
unknown. Meanwhile, in the face of a present that is debased and
absurd, the past—the dimension of memory—becomes increasingly
important as the only remaining source of potentially positive themes
and imagery, the only remaining space in which individual integrity
can be maintained intact.

The Death of the Future

Already in *Satura* the *io* is seen openly pondering his own passage into
the *oltrevita* in at least two poems, 'Nell'attesa' (*OV* 345) and 'Prima
del viaggio', where after an extended sequence of images of travel
(associated elsewhere with Mosca and typical of the ironic, *mondano*
register of the collection), he concludes:

> [...] E ora che ne sarà
> del *mio* viaggio?
> Troppo accuratamente l'ho studiato
> senza saperne nulla. Un imprevisto
> è la sola speranza. Ma mi dicono
> ch'è una stoltezza dirselo. (*OV* 380)

Clearly poems such as this are broadly related to the thematic strand explored in Chapter 4 above, in so far as they are concerned with the Other dimension, the invisible world. And as in those discussions of the relationship with the deity, ignorance is the keynote, certainties are impossible. However, whereas that thematic strand was centred principally on comic or fictive representations of the deity and its relationship with the *io*, these texts, in which the poet's own impending death is contemplated with perplexed anxiety, can be seen to constitute a separate, more meditative and ultimately much more problematic vein.

In *Diario* the theme is taken up in 'Sono pronto ripeto', where the *io* prepares to face the unknowable:

> Sono pronto ripeto, ma pronto a che?
> Non alla morte cui non credo né
> al brulichio d'automi che si chiama la vita.
> L'altravita è un assurdo, ripeterebbe
> la sua progenitrice con tutte le sue tare.
> L'oltrevita è nell'etere, quell'aria da ospedale
> che i felici respirano quando cadono in trappola.
> [...] (*OV* 452)

Marchese sees a 'tragico problematicismo' in this text: far from any religious acceptance of death's inevitability, the poet's attitude is one of absolute scepticism as he meditates on the absurdity of life and the absence of any possible consolation in the approach of death.[1] The *oltrevita* is treated with characteristically dark humour as any 'ethereal' connotations are immediately undermined through the word-play on 'etere' and through the wry irony with which the 'felici' are depicted as they fall, unwittingly, into the trap of death. In the remaining lines, however, the comic elements disappear and the tone becomes more straightforwardly meditative as the poet denies the validity of any attempt to tear the 'veil':

> [...]
> L'oltrevita è nel tempo che se ne ciba
> per durare più a lungo nel suo inganno.
> Essere pronti non vuol dire scegliere
> tra due sventure o due venture oppure
> tra il tutto e il nulla. È dire io l'ho provato,
> ecco il Velo, se inganna non si lacera.

Any notion we may have of an *oltrevita* is inseparable from our flawed perception of the world in time, which, in a self-perpetuating circle, is given definition by the hypothesis of a non-temporal dimension.[2] In this context the *io* (like the rest of humanity) is helpless, incapable of any meaningful choice apart from the choice of acknowledging the barrier, the veil, which cannot, by definition, be breached. He can no longer blithely believe, as he did in *Ossi*, that 'svanire è la ventura delle venture' (*OV* 32). Temporal existence, for as long as it persists, is inseparable from the impenetrable veil.

The sense of touching the 'veil' at close quarters, the sense that death is now at hand and that the future (within human time) is a shrinking space, can be felt in many texts in *Diario* and *Quaderno*. The image of the impending 'viaggio' with its associated preparations and uncertain outcome returns in 'Quel che più conta' (*OV* 475). In 'Testimoni di Geova' (*Quaderno*), the poet pokes fun once again at a form of organized religion, but concludes on a more pensive note: 'Se fu triste il pensiero della morte / quello che il Tutto dura / è il più pauroso' (*OV* 537). Similar musings on the impending 'Evento', where the anguish of uncertainty is in part tempered by elements of dark humour, occur elsewhere in *Quaderno*, in 'Appunti' (*OV* 570), 'Ai tuoi piedi' (*OV* 579), 'Le prove generali' (*OV* 592), 'Ci si rivede' (*OV* 602), as well as in several texts in *Altri versi*: 'Motivi' (*OV* 638–9), 'Rimuginando' (*OV* 645), 'Nell'attesa' (*OV* 647), and notably in one of Montale's last poems, '*Poiché la vita fugge ...*' (*OV* 701).

Underlying texts such as these, there is, as Marchese observes, 'una condizione disperatamente angosciosa (anche se non esibita e anzi occultata con getti di desublimante ironia o di polemica ideologica)'.[3] On rare occasions, the ironic or comic element provides the dominant tone, as for example in 'In hoc signo ...' (*Diario*):

> A Roma un'agenzia di pompe funebri
> si chiama L'AVVENIRE. E poi si dice
> che l'umor nero è morto con Jean Paul,
> Gionata Swift e Achille Campanile. (*OV* 504)

Even this overtly comical piece, however, goes right to the heart of the problem: the realization that the future, if it exists at all, will soon mean death. In 'Le prove generali', the figure of a poet who, through practising some ancient oriental rite, procures 'uno stato di vitamorte / che parrebbe la prova generale / di ciò che sarebbe di noi quando cadrà la tela', can be easily seen as an ironic self-portrait by the eighty-year-old Montale, whose continued survival seems increasingly incongruous. But there is still, not far below the surface, the genuine anxiety associated with the unknown, with the awareness of the void, whose proximity provokes, as it did fifty years earlier in 'Forse un mattino andando', an ambivalent response:

> [...]
> Pure rendiamo omaggio ai nuovi Guru
> anche se dal futuro ci divide
> un filo ch'è un abisso e non vogliamo
> che la conocchia si assottigli troppo ... (*OV* 592)

In this late phase, the prospect of the miracle, the breakthrough into the void, is treated (just like the deity itself) with open suspicion. The only future, the only miracle remaining, is that of death.

Riccardo Scrivano writes of the 'improbability' of the future for Montale in the scenario presented in *Quaderno*.[4] It is perhaps more accurate, however, to speak of the *impossibility* of the future, of the end of any meaningful idea of a future whether on a personal or hence on a collective level. In a sense, it can be argued that the future, as a dimension with a strong symbolic or allegorical meaning, ceased to have a function in Montale's poetry from *Satura* onwards. Luperini, for example, sees *Satura* as dominated by 'un presente totalitario e assoluto' from which any positive vision of historical renewal or change has been removed and where the future 'non esiste più, neppure come attesa'.[5] This is part of the wider process by which time itself is problematized, as Montale calls into the question the validity of any model of history based on sequential temporal progression, and derides the concept of historical progress. This process is taken to its most radical conclusions in *Diario* and *Quaderno*, where the death of the future is given tangible expression in the image of the poet's own impending, ineluctable death. Since *Satura*, as we have seen, any residual positive values in Montale's world have existed only within a restricted, jealously guarded private sphere, represented spatially by images of withdrawal and enclosure. Now even that private haven, inhabited only by the *io* and his ghosts, is threatened with annihilation, and all values, all forms of meaning within conventional time, face the prospect of imminent death.

Only by subverting time, by disregarding the temporal dimension, can Montale now posit any possible meaning at the end of his world. The very structure of *Diario* and *Quaderno* reflects paradoxically the poet's wilful disregard for time. (*Altri versi* is a somewhat different case, as discussed below.) For the first time, Montale presents collections of poetry with no significant subdivisions, no apparent structure except ostensibly that of the 'diary' (as underlined by the choice of titles). Even though chronological order is not in fact strictly followed (as noted by Luperini), there is clearly an attempt to convey the impression of 'un'asistematicità totale' in the diaristic recording of thoughts and events. However, by apparently accepting the arbitrary order imposed by time, Montale is subtly refuting time's importance, demonstrating the irrelevance of any further portrayal of deliberate temporal progression in his work. Chronological order becomes, paradoxically, a structural figuration of the poet's rejection of time as a significant factor in the construction of meaning.[6]

In a number of texts the theme of imminent death is linked closely to that of the subversion of temporal order, as for example in 'Rimuginando' (*Altri versi*).[7] This poem opens with yet another image of approaching darkness: 'Probabilmente / sta calando la sera'. After a passing reference to the memory of Clizia and her mystical concerns, the poet declares a paradoxical reversal of time:

> [...]
> Non si tarda ad apprendere che gli anni
> sono battibaleni e che il passato
> è già il futuro. [...] (*OV* 645)

With time abolished and the future annihilated (the poem ends with the words 'l'avvenire è già passato da un pezzo') the only thing to which the poet can look 'forward' now is the past. In the timeless private zone of the home, the poet's retreat from history, he now inhabits his own 'fuordeltempo' in which, as Lorenzo Greco observes, 'l'altra dimensione è qui, è ora', and where, in dreams and distant memories, 'il ricordo si confonde con la proiezione nel futuro; il ricordo è attesa, è futuro'.[8]

Memories

The poet explicitly declares his intention to explore the timeless world of memories in 'Ai tuoi piedi' (*Quaderno*), the only text where, possibly, the divinity itself appears in the second person singular. The poem opens with the description of an imagined judgement scene, where the *io*, for once 'quassù' rather than 'quaggiù', regards his predicament with the now familiar mixture of anxiety and levity. While awaiting the verdict, he gives what amounts to a manifesto of the last major thematic strand to emerge in these collections, that of memory:

> [...]
> ricorderò gli oggetti che ho lasciati
> al loro posto, un posto tanto studiato,
> agli uccelli impagliati, a qualche ritaglio
> di giornale, alle tre o quattro medaglie
> di cui sarò derubato e forse anche
> alle fotografie di qualche mia Musa
> che mai seppe di esserlo,
> rifarò il censimento di quel nulla
> che fu vivente perchè fu tangibile
> e mi dirò se non fossero
> queste solo e non altro la mia consistenza
> e non questo corpo ormai incorporeo
> che sta in attesa e quasi si addormenta. (*OV* 579)

As occurred in 'I nascondigli' in *Diario*, domestic and personal objects are the key to the memorial dimension. The objects listed here imply a heightened degree of cultural mediation of memory (as underlined by the words 'tanto studiato'). This is part of a widespread phenomenon in these later works, whereby memories acquire their special significance through the mediation of Montale's poetic past. Thus 'uccelli impagliati' here almost certainly refers to the poet's stuffed hoopoe (present in a well-known photograph[9]), which in turn represents the distant poetic past of *Ossi* (see *OV* 47); 'ritaglio di giornale' underlines the importance of the written (journalistic) word in the scenario of the poet's memories, and the 'medaglie' point to his public presence, the official image which he repeatedly ridicules in these later poems. Even the presence of his muses is mediated by photographs, an image that recurs in 'I ripostigli' (*OV* 616), and in 'Nel '38' and 'Quartetto' (*OV* 699–700.). All of these memory-objects, even if they are reduced to an ironic 'nulla', are invested with a peculiar privilege, a peculiar vitality ('fu vivente') as tangible proofs of an individual identity, a unique experience of existence that now seems more real and more important than present reality, represented here by the poet's own declining body.

With the present reduced, since *Satura*, to a meaningless 'palta', and with the disappearance of a future dimension, only the past remains as a place in which to explore the possibility of some tangible meaning. Thus, the thematic area of memory is given increasing prominence between *Diario* and *Altri versi*. In *Satura* the theme of memory was associated predominantly with the figure of Mosca, and apart from her appearances in 'Xenia', only a handful of memorial texts occurred in 'Satura' I and II ('Due prose veneziane', 'Senza salvacondotto', 'Lettera' and 'Il repertorio'). In *Diario*, memorial texts begin to assume a more highly visible position, with a notably greater number of occurrences (at least twelve poems).[10] Significantly, these include two types that will come to the fore in *Altri versi*: those dealing with early childhood recollections of Genoa, such as 'Corso Dogali', and those concerned with female figures, notably three poems marking the return of Arletta: 'Il lago di Annecy', 'Ancora ad Annecy' and 'Annetta'.

It is in *Quaderno* however that the theme of memory begins to become more dominant and all-pervading (it is present in some twenty-four texts).[11] From the opening poem, 'L'educazione intellettuale', the musings of the *io* range freely over time as ghosts of the distant past reappear at regular intervals. Again, recurring motifs are those of early childhood ('Nei miei primi anni abitavo', *OV* 517; 'Ribaltamento', 586) and of female figures, especially Arletta ('Per un fiore reciso', *OV* 542; 'La capinera non fu uccisa'; 555; 'Se al più si oppone il meno', 561), along with considerations of the idiosyncratic operations of memory itself ('I pressepapiers', *OV* 566; 'Ai tuoi piedi', 579; 'I ripostigli', 616).

With *Altri versi*, the special position of memory is sealed and explicitly highlighted by the structure of the work. This collection, the last to be published in the poet's lifetime (and consisting, for the most part, of texts written between 1977 and 1980), differs in a number of notable respects from the preceding volumes: not only is there a clear structural and thematic subdivision, but the definitive form, and indeed the title itself, are due in large part to Bettarini and Contini, the editors of *L'opera in versi*, in which *Altri versi* first appeared in 1980. The 'Nota dei curatori' explains the thematic and stylistic basis of the book's bipartite structure:

La sua divisione in due sezioni vuol rispecchiare la duplice organizzazione assunta dall'ultimissima poesia di Montale, per un verso stabilendo la prevedibile continuità col linguaggio e la tematica inaugurati da *Satura* nell'ostentata intenzione di 'non-poesia' e comunque di non-lirica, ma per altro verso ripensando, sobriamente quanto elegiacamente, la propria vita [...] con la saggezza a suo modo retrospettiva di chi è vissuto col ritmo lento di cui parlano i *Diari*. (*OV* 835)

It is made clear in the editors' note that the poet maintained an active interest in the collection's structure, which reflects 'alcuni punti ben fissi dell'autore', but nevertheless the exact proportions of editorial and authorial input will never be satisfactorily quantified, and thus one must be careful not to place too great an interpretative burden on this question of structural organization.[12] However, it is indisputable that Montale's imprimatur was given to a finished product whose division into two parts, reflecting the thematic 'duplice organizzazione' referred to above, departs radically from the practice of the preceding collections. While there are few major thematic or stylistic innovations on the level of individual texts, the new structure underlines the gradual shift in the balance of Montale's work since *Satura*. So Part I gathers together poems belonging to the 'anti-lyrical' vein of philosophical and cosmological speculation, as well as those belonging to the more strictly diaristic genre of everyday chronicle, whereas Part II, with its 'testi affabili' (as characterized by the editors, *OV* 835) creates an unprecedented focus on the theme of memory.

The last three books are frequently regarded as a single undifferentiated block, the 'quinto' or 'ultimo' Montale.[13] But the structural division of *Altri versi*, by crystallizing into a clear duality the broad variety of themes and approaches found throughout *Diario* and *Quaderno*, also helps to clarify an underlying trend, away from the dominance of public poetry established in *Satura*, towards the emergence of a more intimate poetry of memory. Francesco De Rosa, in a recently published study, makes a convincing case for a thematic and formal division between the two poles of a 'quarto Montale' (*Satura* and *Diari*) and a 'quinto' (*Altri versi*), with *Quaderno* marking a transitional phase.[14] One of the key elements cited in putting forward this division is the emergence of a new kind of memorial 'canzoniere' in the final collection. It is undoubtedly the case that the concentrated grouping of memorial poems (especially poems addressed to a female *tu*) in the closing stages of *Altri versi* gives these texts a unique status within Montale's later work as a whole and highlights the importance of the thematic strand revolving around memory as the vehicle for some of the poet's last messages.

The Return of the Woman in Memory

The memories that play a key role in the thematic economy of the last three collections are not mere nostalgic reminiscences. They are almost always poetic memories mediated by earlier textual experiences (which are thus frequently the object of ironic revision), recurrences of figures whose meanings are inseparable from the cultural and historical meaning of Montale's work as a whole.[15] They are now invested with a life of their own, as they overturn the laws of space and time, in which the poet no longer believes, and engage in a game of disguise, of shifting identity and mutual contamination. In 'I pressepapiers' (*Quaderno*) memories are 'lampi che s'accendono / e si spengono', but they are the only light left:

> [...]
> Il guaio è che il ricordo non è gerarchico,
> ignora le precedenze e le susseguenze
> e abbuia l'importante, ciò che ci parve tale.
> Il ricordo è un lucignolo, il solo che ci resta.
> C'è il caso che si stacchi e viva per conto suo.
> [...] (*OV* 566)

The dialogue between the *io* and these memories in the *fuordeltempo* consitutes the last major thematic and figurative device employed in Montale's poetry.

The figures of Mosca, Arletta and Clizia all return in the last collections, especially in *Altri versi*. Mosca's presence is perhaps the least notable: she had never entirely disappeared from the scene and in any case the language and imagery used in poems such as 'Non più notizie' or 'Tergi gli occhiali' (*OV* 690–1) are broadly analogous to those found in 'Xenia'. More significant are the returns of Arletta and Clizia. The reappearance of Arletta, the shadowy figure of 'La casa dei doganieri', is accompanied by a reprise of themes of memory and absence which ran through that poem ('Tu non ricordi la casa', *OV* 161). Arletta returns in *Diario* in 'Il lago di Annecy', 'Ancora ad Annecy' and 'Annetta', where she is named explicitly for the first time (see also Chapter 1 above):

> Perdona Annetta se dove tu sei
> (non certo tra di noi, i sedicenti
> vivi) poco ti giunge il mio ricordo.
> Le tue apparizioni furono per molti anni
> rare e impreviste, non certo da te volute.
> Anche i luoghi (la rupe dei doganieri,
> la foce del Bisagno dove ti trasformasti in Dafne)
> non avevano senso senza di te.
> [...] (*OV* 490)

The complex web of recall and forgetfulness echos and elaborates on that of 'La casa dei doganieri': there, the *io* had remembered for both parties, holding one end of the thread, whereas here his role in the process seems more passive, while her sporadic reappearances, 'non certo da te volute', are mysteriously spontaneous events, in keeping with the unpredictable nature of memory itself. What is clear, however, is that her presence through memory can provide some kind of meaning where it is otherwise absent. The youthful game of charades, described at length in the following lines, has the extraordinary privilege of 'certainty' (in the present tense) in this late season of doubt and scepticism: 'Di certo resta il gioco delle sciarade incatenate / o incastrate che fossero di cui eri maestra'. So the figure of Annetta/Arletta opens up a world of distant memories, which, even if it is now seen with ironic detachment as 'la stagione più ridicola / della vita', has within it a kernel of almost ineffable truth and wonder:

> [...]
> Oggi penso che tu sei stata un genio
> di pura inesistenza, un'agnizione
> reale perché assurda. Lo stupore
> quando s'incarna è lampo che ti abbaglia
> e si spenge. [...]

The motif of intermittent light has already been seen as a recurring attribute of Arletta (e.g. in 'Vecchi versi' and 'La casa dei doganieri') and the re-use of the image underlines her crepuscular legacy. But something more is added here: 'stupore', 's'incarna', 'lampo', 'abbaglia'. These surely are the powerful attributes, the emblems of Clizia, she who was gazed upon by the 'stupefied' chessmen in 'Nuove stanze', who was the incarnation of the Other in 'Iride', and who is repeatedly associated with blinding flashes of light ('se poco è il lampo del tuo sguardo': 'Nuove stanze', *OV* 177).[16] Are we to believe, then, that the crepuscular Arletta, the evanescent young girl, has undergone a Clizia-like transformation in the Other world? In part, perhaps, yes: there were already instances of a superimposing of the two figures in *Occasioni* and *Bufera* (see for example 'Eastbourne' and 'L'orto'). But this is also part of a more widespread phenomenon that emerges in the subsequent collections: the gradual blurring of lines between the fields of imagery associated with the main female figures.[17]

This notable innovation, seen in particular in the treatment of Arletta and Clizia, reflects the changed function of the *tu*: the remembered women no longer carry clearly delineated or sharply contrasting ideological connotations, to be deployed in quasi-narrative structures. Their respective meanings now complement each other, and are bound up with the meaning of memory itself for the besieged *io*. (Already, memory's unpredictable tricks provided the basis for the 1946 prose piece 'Sulla spiaggia', where the dimly remembered name of a female acquaintance—'Annalena o Annagilda o Annalia'—suggested a link with the Arletta cycle, while other elements pointed towards the figure of Clizia. Ultimately, that piece too was concerned not so much with specific women as with 'scherzi della memoria', and the process by which a figure, having emerged from 'il pozzo di San Patrizio della memoria' could be re-shaped and transformed in the creative act—see *PR* 193–8.)

The interplay of memory and oblivion is the focus of the two 'Annecy' poems in *Diario*, whose inspiration derives, apparently, from the girl's education in a 'collège' on the Alpine lake (as emerges more clearly in 'Ah!', *OV* 708). In 'Il lago di Annecy' in particular, the poet investigates the curious mechanisms of memory. The poem contains a string of negations:

> Non so perché il mio ricordo ti lega
> al lago di Annecy
> [...]
> Ma allora non ti ricordai [...]
> Perché può scattar fuori una memoria
> così insabbiata non lo so; tu stessa
> m'hai certo seppellito e non l'hai saputo.
> Ora risorgi viva e non ci sei. [...] (*OV* 438)

It seems as if the *io* seeks to deny the autonomous power of memory, even to the extent (in the last line quoted) of an oxymoronic insistence on the woman's absence. But in the twilight world of this poetry, a simple object, in this case a photograph of the lake, can suffice to spark off the powerful and arbitrary mechanisms of memory.

The ghost of Arletta becomes an even more elusive and multi-faceted figure in *Quaderno*, where she appears in a scattered series of texts dedicated to 'la capinera': 'Per un fiore reciso', 'La capinera non fu uccisa', 'Se al più si oppone il meno', 'Quella del faro' (the series continues in *Altri versi* with 'Il big bang dovette produrre' and

'Quando la capinera'). That this figure is another manifestation of Arletta is established by the use of several of her characteristic motifs, such as those of hunting, premature death and lost memories:

> La capinera non fu uccisa
> da un cacciatore ch'io sappia.
> Morì forse nel mezzo del mattino. E non n'ebbi
> mai notizia. Suppongo che di me
> abbia perduto anche il ricordo. [...] (*OV* 555)

In 'Se al più si oppone il meno', the familiar twilight coastal setting is recreated:

> [...]
> brillò, si spense, ribrillò una luce
> sull'opposta costiera. Già imbruniva.
> 'Anche il faro, lo vedi, è intermittente,
> [...].' (*OV* 561)

However, while the identification of this figure with Arletta seems clear enough at first sight, other elements are introduced which give the 'capinera' some further unexpected attributes. Up to now she has been a silent figure: this is emphasised from *Ossi* (see her 'messaggio muto' in 'Delta', *OV* 95) to *Bufera* (the silent 'labbro di sangue' in 'Da una torre', *OV* 208). But now she speaks, and both the tone and content of her speech are somewhat surprising. The poem opens with her words:

> Se al più si oppone il meno il risultato
> sarà destruente. Così dicevi un giorno
> mostrando rudimenti di latino
> e altre nozioni. [...] (*OV* 561)

In the context of *Quaderno*, the reader is here faced with what initially appears to be another piece of abstract, sententious philosophizing by the poetic *io* ('destruente', an Italianization of the Latin *destruens*, meaning 'destroying' or 'destructive', recalls the extravagant lexical register of some of the more comical or satirical texts). Only in line 2 are the words attributed to a *tu*, subsequently identifiable as Arletta. The scope of this poem thus goes beyond the theme of memory to include elements of the cosmological problems so often discussed ironically since *Satura*. Similarly, in 'La capinera non fu uccisa', the evocation of Arletta's 'fantasma' leads the *io* to question his own status within the shaky 'messa in scena di cartone che mi circonda', with the conclusion that 'Non c'è scienza / filosofia teologia che se ne occupi' (*OV* 555). This is the kind of prosaic, speculative language that up until now was far more likely to have been associated with the figure of Mosca. Meanwhile, with her new-found loquacity, Arletta-Capinera also becomes a more dramatically active character, whose utterances, as for example in 'Per un fiore reciso', can even recall the peculiar energy of Mosca's interventions in 'Xenia':

> [...]
> Una traccia invisibile non è per questo
> meno segnata? Te lo dissi un giorno
> e tu: è un fatto che non mi riguarda.
> [...] (*OV* 542)

Arletta's reply is concise and almost peremptory, dismissive (recalling elements of 'Xenia' II 1 and 7): it is as though her own remembered figure has been, as it were, contaminated by Montale's poetic memory of the intervening years, during which time the dialogue with Mosca in 'Xenia' has had a decisive effect on the development of his themes, tone and diction. Arletta has grown up to become the enigmatic 'capinera', one of whose attributes is precisely that of uncertain identity, as seen in the lines directly following those quoted above:

> [...]
> Sono la capinera che dà un trillo
> e a volte lo ripete ma non si sa
> se è quella o un'altra. E non potresti farlo
> neanche te che hai orecchio.

With the blurring of her identity, its contamination by elements of both the Clizia and Mosca cycles, her voice becomes a voice of memory itself, she becomes an embodiment of its unpredictable, shifting character in these late works, its independence from conventional laws of space, time and logic.

It is also likely that here Montale is gently chiding those who would seek to catalogue unequivocally the women in his poetry. This is undoubtedly the case in 'Domande senza risposta' (*Quaderno*), where he replies with unconcealed irony to questions regarding his 'onlie begetter':[18]

> [...]
> Ahimè,
> la mia testa è confusa, molte figure

> vi si addizionano,
> ne formano una sola che discerno
> a malapena nel mio crepuscolo.
> [...] (*OV* 563)

While mocking the critics' curiosity and reinforcing the image of a senile *dormiveglia* on the part of the *io*, Montale points again to the genuinely problematic identity of his female figures, who, as poetic creations, have emerged from memory changed and enriched, fixed in poetic form:

> [...]
> Non ho avuto purtroppo che la parola,
> qualche cosa che approssima ma non tocca;
> e così
> non c'è depositaria del mio cuore
> che non sia nella bara. [...]

Montale's women, once vital presences, now living in memory through the mediation of poetry, are all (regardless of the status of their flesh-and-blood counterparts) 'nella bara': transfigured in the frozen life of art.

While Arletta is a constant presence just below the surface of Montale's poetry, the figure of Clizia passes from one extreme to another: from her dominance of *Bufera*, she practically disappears in *Satura*, *Diario* and *Quaderno*, only to return in the closing stages of *Altri versi*, where she, like Arletta, acquires new connotations and attributes. In *Satura* she is present or addressed in four poems: 'L'Eufrate', 'Gli uomini che si voltano', 'Due prose veneziane', 'Senza salvacondotto'.[19] 'Gli uomini che si voltano' opens with the realization that she too may have changed: 'Probabilmente / non sei più chi sei stata' (*OV* 376). One can perhaps recognize the motifs of uncertainty and loss of identity associated elsewhere with Arletta. Nevertheless, though her power has faded and she is now seen disappearing into the underworld, 'tra cadaveri in maschera', she is still essentially a mythic, non-realistic figure here. In 'Due prose veneziane', however, she has lost her other-worldly connotations and appears for the first time as part of a prosaic, autobiographical reminiscence, 'comprando keepsakes cartoline e occhiali scuri sulle bancarelle' (*OV* 391). The portrayal of realistic details here prefigures an important element of her eventual return in *Altri versi*.

In *Diario* there is only one clear reference to Clizia, in the minimal form of the abbreviated title 'A C.' (*OV* 420), and in *Quaderno* her appearances are rare and intermittent: she is referred to explicitly in 'Due destini' (*OV* 515) and 'L'eroismo' (*OV* 535) and, while signs of her presence can be discerned in some other texts, her role is extremely limited. In 'L'eroismo', for example, she is referred to only in the third person (and in the past tense) rather than addressed directly as an active interlocutor. However, two poems near the end of *Quaderno* can be seen as the first tentative steps towards the return of Clizia as a significant presence, foreshadowing her reappearance at the end of *Altri versi*. The title of 'Una lettera che non fu spedita' clearly recalls a poem in the Clizia cycle in *Bufera*, 'Su una lettera non scritta', thus establishing a textual bridge to that earlier period. This new letter, though never posted, reintroduces the second person singular for Clizia and, as he had not in her more recent appearances, the *io* addresses her again in the present tense:

> Consenti mia dilettissima che si commendi
> seppure con un lasso di più lustri
> il mirifico lauro da te raccolto,
> uno scavo di talpa neppure sospettabile
> in chi era e sarà folgorata dal sole. Non importa
> né a te né a me se accada che il tuo nome
> resti nell ombra. [...] (*OV* 607)

There appears to be a new spiritual intimacy here between the *io* and his *ispiratrice* (the 'lauro' refers to Clizia's 'scholarly achievements').[20] Furthermore, what was previously a closed book, a relationship described in the *passato remoto* ('A C.'), is here opened up not only to the present but also to the future, projecting the poem into the atemporal dimension of the *oltrevita* as past and future merge ('chi era e sarà [...]'). 'I ripostigli', on the other hand, introduces the recurring image of Clizia's photograph (here remembered, later physically 'ripescata'): 'Non so dove io abbia nascosto la tua fotografia. / Fosse saltata fuori sarebbe stato un guaio' (*OV* 616). Even here, Mosca's presence continues to be felt in the problematic set of relationships alluded to in the second line. But what is more interesting is that this poem also recovers some of Clizia's unmistakable characteristics from the time of Finisterre: her hair, 'una nube, quella dei tuoi capelli' and her eyes 'che contenevano tutto / e anche di più'. And yet, even here there are other notes, more reminiscent perhaps of the tone and imagery of the Arletta cycle, such as the statement of ignorance and loss: 'Non si è saputo più nulla di te'. Clizia's eyes, once the 'occhi d'acciaio' of the sublime angel-woman, have here, despite the omniscience, become the infinitely more human and perhaps vulnerable 'occhi innocenti'.

The counterpoint of past, present, future and *oltretempo* will be an important element in the Clizia texts in part II of *Altri versi*. Some eleven poems, written between 1976 and 1980 form a clearly identifiable block just before the end of the collection, beginning with 'Il mio cronometro svizzero' and ending with 'Credo'.[21] In this final phase, Clizia appears at her most human, as her figure is treated with the kind of memorial intimacy previously seen only in the poems for Mosca and Arletta. The *io* recalls the places and events of a distant shared past, as he sketches fragments of a relationship that provided the background for the great poems of the 1930s and '40s. We now see Clizia in a quasi-domestic setting (much as we have already seen the figures of the *io* and Mosca since *Satura*), in the garden or veranda of her Florentine *pensione* (the 'Annalena'[22]), where the topics of discussion ranged from 'patrologia' to the poetry of Donne (*OV* 695). This is a very flesh-and-blood figure, as described in 'Clizia nel '34':

> Sempre allungata
> sulla chaise longue
> della veranda
> che dava sul giardino,
> un libro in mano forse già da allora
> vite di santi semisconosciuti
> e poeti barocchi di scarsa reputazione
> non era amore quello
> era come oggi e sempre
> venerazione. (*OV* 696)

It is a glimpse of the woman behind the myth of the winged messenger, and even if the emphasis here is still ostensibly on the more spiritual aspect of the relationship (which transcends time—'era come oggi e sempre / venerazione'), the opening lines introduce a certain voluptuousness, a note of erotic tension of a type seen previously only in the cycle of Volpe. Indeed the term 'erotic' occurs twice in these late poems: in 'Il mio cronometro svizzero' ('manuale di Erotica') and again in 'Previsioni':

> Ci rifugiammo nel giardino (pensile se non sbaglio)
> per metterci al riparo dalle fanfaluche

erotiche di un pensionante di fresco arrivo
e tu parlavi delle donne dei poeti
fatte per imbottire illeggibili carmi.
Così sarà di me aggiungesti di sottecchi.
Restai di sasso. [...] (*OV* 697)

Something else rather surprising happens here: as occurred in the case
of Arletta, Clizia now speaks for the first time, but it is with a
disarming combination of simplicity and coquettishness ('di
sottecchi') which could never have been expected of the steel-eyed
sibyl of *Occasioni*. Perhaps even more striking, however, is the sharply
ironic twist in her subsequent reply:

[...] Poi dissi dimentichi
che la pallottola ignora chi la spara
e ignora il suo bersaglio.
                    Ma non siamo
disse C. ai baracconi. E poi non credo
che tu abbia armi da fuoco nel tuo bagaglio.

Here Clizia takes on a function of pungent demystification with regard
to the poet's own persona, undermining any authority inherent in his
figure. The only model in the previous poetry is, once again, to be
found in the various deflating interventions of Mosca in 'Xenia'.
Montale once expressed his wish to reveal 'l'envers du décor' in his
post-*Satura* work (*SMAMS* 1702), and here he finally applies this to the
figure of Clizia, showing the human occasions behind the poetic ones.

Two poems, 'Nel '38' and 'Quartetto', present the *occasione* behind
the intense, complex 'Palio' of 1939, now reduced to the squalid
spectacle of 'quattro ronzini frustati a sangue / in una piazza-
conchiglia / davanti a una folla inferocita' (*OV* 700). Here, in a
procedure seen before in the Mosca cycle ('Xenia' I 13), memory is
activated by a photograph, an 'istantanea ingiallita' found in a
drawer.[23] Clizia is still recognizable by her exceptional qualities, by the
note of 'veneration' that is reserved only for her: 'c'è il tuo volto
incredibile' (*OV* 699). But the memory of distant events soon merges
in 'Quartetto' into a disenchanted meditation on time, in the abstract,
philosophizing manner of the later Montale's solitary *io*: 'Non credo
al tempo, al big bang, a nulla / che misuri gli eventi in un prima e in
un dopo'. Just like Arletta, Clizia now becomes a voice in the chorus
of memories, a chorus whose message, learned in part from Mosca,
revolves around the meaninglessness of time and history.

These last Clizia texts are built on the juxtaposition and interweaving of several temporal dimensions: the distant past of the 1930s, the present of the poet's old age (a kind of *oltretempo*) and the future (which is also the *oltrevita*):

> Ho tanta fede in te
> che durerà
> (è la sciocchezza che ti dissi un giorno)
> finché un lampo d'oltremondo distrugga
> quell'immenso cascame in cui viviamo.
> Ci troveremo allora in non so che punto
> se ha senso dire punto dove non è spazio
> a discutere qualche verso controverso
> del divino poema.
> [...] (*OV* 694)

Here another specific, distant reminiscence ('ti dissi un giorno') opens up a future beyond space and time. Again it is a poetically mediated reminiscence, as the solemn, apocalyptic tone of line 4 recalls for a moment the mystical language of an earlier time (that of 'La primavera hitleriana'), but this is attenuated by the very different tone of the preceding and following lines (the self-directed irony of line 3 is again reminiscent of the Mosca cycle). Now the only prospect of recreating shared past experiences lies in a conjectural future ('ci troveremo'), evoked in an ironic, self-deprecating comparison with the scenario of *Paradiso*.[24] The angel-woman, Montale's Beatrice, is now the erudite but human Dante scholar. (The reappearance of Clizia may also recall the intimacy of some of Petrarch's visions of Laura after her death, in which, 'più bella e meno altera', she comforts and advises him: see for example sonnet CCCII, 'Levommi il mio pensier'.)

There is a strong sense that some contamination or cross-fertilization has occurred between the figures of Clizia and Mosca: in both cases the dialogue between the *io* and the woman is initially located in the sphere of distant memories, but it is also projected into the Other dimension, and feeds into speculative discussions of the *oltrevita* itself and its relationship to the *quaggiù*. Contamination on the level of imagery and language is most clearly visible in 'Interno/esterno' (*OV* 698) as demonstrated by Pellini.[25] The notion that reality is mere illusion, as well as the use of motifs such as 'etere' and 'clinica', are unmistakably part of Mosca's inheritance. Similarly, the arrival of an unexpected telephone call from Clizia's friend

Giovanna immediately recalls the situation of 'Xenia' II 11, with its call from 'Celia la filippina'. Underlying this intermingling of imagery is the fact that temporal considerations are now definitively superseded in the *oltretempo* that is the poetic present of these last years. Different periods of the poet's life, along with their respective muses, are co-present in memory. As he delves into the past of forty years earlier, Clizia's departure for America is perceived in a timeless present ('ti vedo [...]'), as alive as the voice of Giovanna now on the telephone, which carries with it the poetic past of Mosca. However, all of these figures and their stories have in common the absence of a meaningful future, as the poet concludes: 'Non aggiungo altro / né dico arrivederci che sarebbe ridicolo / per tutti e due' (*OV* 698).

'*Poiché la vita fugge* ...' (dated '20/1/80') was the last poem to be composed in this series, and so, chronologically, is the last in the entire Clizia cycle (and indeed may have been originally intended by the poet to close the volume).[26] It deals with some of the same themes as the distant Petrarchan precursor alluded to in the title: the ineluctable passing of all things, and the doubts and fears provoked by thoughts of what the future beyond time may hold. As the *io* wonders how to preserve the objects in which memory and identity are invested ('gli oggetti che ci parvero / non peritura parte di noi stessi'), the figure of Clizia can still provide a hypothesis of survival, of endurance beyond the oblivion of death:

> [...]
> C'era una volta un piccolo scaffale
> che viaggiava con Clizia, un ricettacolo
> di Santi Padri e di poeti equivoci che forse
> avesse la virtù di galleggiare
> sulla cresta delle onde
> quando il diluvio avrà sommerso tutto.
> Se non di me almeno qualche briciola
> di te dovrebbe vincere l'oblio.
> [...] (*OV* 701)

She is represented by her 'scaffale', an eclectic collection of cultural and literary fragments riding out the storm (unlike the poet's own submerged cultural artefacts in 'Xenia' II 14), and so the Clizia who survives will perhaps be some fragment of her literary persona, living on in the timeless world of poetry.

The second part of the poem, however, goes on to consider the more pressing problem of the great leap into the unknown, to be faced by both the *io* and the woman:

> E di me? La speranza è che sia disperso
> il visibile e il tempo che gli ha dato
> la dubbia prova che questa voce È
> (Una E maiuscola, la sola lettera
> dell'alfabeto che rende possibile
> o almeno ipotizzabile l'esistenza).
> Poi (sovente hai portato
> occhiali affumicati e li hai dimessi
> del tutto con le pulci di John Donne)
> preparati al gran tuffo.
> [...]

Here, in part, is another variant on the theme of the anxious wait for the unknowable, which runs throughout these last collections. The hope of oblivion is combined with deep scepticism about the reality of our existence. Meanwhile, the *io* looks ahead to the 'gran tuffo' in an attitude of openness and *disponibilità*. However, while recommending this stance also to the woman, he simultaneously reminds her of the minutiae of their shared past, as the parenthesis introduces a complex interplay of temporal dimensions. It is in the memory of this past that he indicates a last possibility of happiness:

> [...]
> Fummo felici un giorno, un'ora un attimo
> e questo potrà essere distrutto?
> [...]

This is perhaps the most frank expression given in these last years to a recurring theme in the poet's treatment of memory. Just as he found 'certezza' in object-memories in 'I nascondigli' (*OV* 426) and affirmed the 'certainty' of Arletta's remembered game of charades, he now posits the existence in memory of an intact knowledge of the positive, an experience of irreducible vitality, whose brief duration is irrelevant as it transcends time and lives in the eternal present of poetry. Set against this momentary certainty from the past, the impenetrable veil of the future is perhaps a less pressing concern:

> [...]
> C'è chi dice che tutto ricomincia
> eguale come copia ma non lo credo
> neppure come augurio. L'hai creduto

anche tu? Non esiste a Cuma una sibilla
che lo sappia. E se fosse, nessuno
sarebbe così sciocco da darle ascolto.

Given the poem's portentous title, one might have expected a last testamentary or prophetic utterance, but instead the very notion is derided in an ending whose falling tone and wry scepticism typify Montale's later manner.

Meanwhile, he has demystified and humanized his own sibyl. In these last pages, as the culmination of a long process, he has sketched an intimate, at times tender portrait of the woman behind his central poetic myth. But this could only happen when that myth had long ceased to function. In *Occasioni* and *Bufera*, where Clizia was the bearer of salvation who embodied the poet's political aspirations, she was necessarily *in*human, she belonged to an Other reality. Her return as a character in the post-*Satura* world involves profound changes in her role, attributes and connotations. Here I would disagree with De Rosa's contention that Clizia's return includes the return of her 'significato salvifico'. Rather, it is limited to a more modest 'recupero [...] di certezze' on an individual, human level.[27] The intervention of the Mosca cycle (and, to some extent, that of Arletta) has provided new paradigms of language, tone and imagery, as well as the necessary scenario of an intimate dialogue through memory. Clizia can now return as a remembered individual, but an individual also projected forward and beyond, into the *oltretempo*, the realm of Mosca and, increasingly, of the poetic *io* himself since *Satura*.

Conclusion

It is almost axiomatic in Montale criticism that the poetry of the first three books takes precedence in terms of its quality and its broader cultural importance over the work of the 1960s and '70s. As Guido Mazzoni writes (outlining Montale's place in the modern canon), 'la parte dell'opera montaliana che occupa, nella letteratura di questo secolo, una posizione eminente è quella compresa fra le poesie aggiunte alla seconda edizione degli *Ossi di seppia* e *La bufera*'.[28] The present study does not seek ultimately to challenge such a view, based as it is on a large and solid corpus of critical work, on the reactions of generations of readers and often on the undeniable evidence of the texts themselves. I would hope, however, to have helped somewhat to redress the balance, lest the later work be dismissed out of hand as uniformly inferior or insignificant, a mere curiosity or simply an exegetic resource to be used in the interpretation of the first three collections. The poetry of the later years consititutes an essential part of Montale's overall poetic vision (as the poet himself declared in 1975, 'ho scritto un solo libro'— *SMAMS* 1724). The content and style of the later work, indeed its very existence, change the way we must read the 'classic' Montale of the 1930s and '40s.

As Luperini declared on the occasion of Montale's centenary in 1996, the later poetry can be seen to have modified the very idea of the twentieth-century Italian poetic canon. From a pre-*Satura* orthodoxy which posited a more or less unitary line of 'lirici nuovi' with Montale and Ungaretti at the forefront, post-*Satura* overviews have moved towards a more complex picture, 'variegato e frastagliato, policentrico e multidirezionale'.[29] The perception of Montale's position in this canon (if such a term can be used with reference to such a diverse and multi-faceted period) is also irreversibly altered by the poetry of the later collections. From being a veritable icon of literary modernism, Montale finally comes to span both the modern and postmodern eras. He becomes not merely, as Rebecca West has it, a 'prophet' of postmodernity (a cultural phenomenon that she sees foreshadowed in many of his prose writings[30]), but a participant in the practice of postmodernism itself. Thus he continues to innovate in his poetry, though in subtle, individual ways that tend often to emphasize his isolation rather than his belonging to his time.

As well as giving due importance to the later collections for their impact on our overall perception and interpretation of Montale's work, this study has aimed to highlight and elucidate certain key texts within these collections. While the later books do demand to be read as a whole and interpreted as a composite figuration of contemporary inauthenticity and meaninglessness, individual texts repeatedly stand out as worthy of inclusion within the specific canon of Montale's greatness. The understated memorial texts at the close of *Altri versi* are a case in point. Luperini tends to limit radically the possible significance of this vein of 'aneddotica memorialistica': 'il ricordo è spogliato del suo valore epifanico e simbolico ed è ridotto a una nuda datità empirica e cronachistica'.[31] This interpretation, part of a reading that denies the post-*Satura* work as a whole any 'strong' (allegorical or historical) meaning, must be seen in the context of Luperini's extensive work on Montale's earlier use of memorial motifs (especially in *Bufera*). There, the critic revealed a clear link between the theme of memory ('recupero del mondo perduto, ricerca nel passato di una zona d'autenticità da contrapporre al presente') and the poet's firm ideological opposition to contemporary historical and cultural developments.[32] Such a function for memory is no longer feasible in the 1970s: the sense of a meaningful temporal continuum, leading from the past to a possible future, has been destroyed, and the notion of meaning itself has been undermined. Similarly, Cataldi's reading emphasizes the limitations of Montale's work from *Diario* onwards, with its 'sperpero postmoderno di significanti', which, however, can serve only to highlight 'l'unico significato, quello dello *status quo*'.[33] Thus the poet can apparently put forward no positive vision of the future or of the past in opposition to the degraded and degrading reality of the contemporary world. No aspiration to ideological renewal can exist in a context where the future itself no longer exists, and memories have been removed to a dimension outside of historical time.

Historical or ideological readings such as these provide an invaluable framework for any concrete discussion of Montale's work, and indeed such readings have supplied some of the key interpretative premises on which this study has been based. Thus, having initially outlined some of the principal elements of Montale's ideological beliefs, we have explored the ways in which the poet has expressed his relationship with history from *Satura* onwards, after the exhaustion of the device of the allegorical love-story in *Bufera*. These have included direct polemical engagement with public themes as well as the development of new images of detachment and withdrawal from the contemporary world and its collective concerns. We have seen that the poet has withdrawn progressively from any perspective involving faith in history. Montale has rejected the notion of time itself, of a linear chronological continuum, along with ideas of political or historical progress. He has satirized and mocked belief in such notions, and has reflected their absurdity in his own absurd dialogue with his non-existent God.

There has been throughout, however, an implicit opposition to and rejection of the historical status quo. Montale's liberal ideology, though perhaps more sceptical and idiosyncratic in the political context of his later years, is ultimately no less robust. In conclusion I would argue that this stance of opposition continues to play a role in the late poetry of memory, even if it can no longer be expressed through images and figures of active engagement with history bearing clear ideological messages. Formerly, Montale's forays into memory were inseparable from a desire for historical change: they had a meaning that transcended individual experience and addressed collective concerns of history and society. Now even the appearance of the remembered woman seems to lead nowhere, 'è lampo che ti abbaglia / e si spenge' (*OV* 491), and memories of the people, places and events connected with childhood and youth are closed within a personal sphere. A remembered figure such as 'Schiappino' (*OV* 681), son of the Montale family's 'fattore', cannot impinge on the poet's relationship with present reality nor can the distant light in the darkness at the close of this text point to any salvation: it is revealed as merely the banal glow of someone trying to light a pipe. The enclosure of memories within a strictly individual, personal sphere is underlined strongly by the bipartition of *Altri versi*: figures and events from the past no longer even rub shoulders with the present world.

Nevertheless, there is still a special significance attached to the area of memory in the last collections. It is a thematic area which comes to dominate the poetry of these years, as highlighted structurally by the final concentration of memorial texts in part II of *Altri versi*. Its significance is underlined by Franco Croce, even as he pronounces a generally negative judgement on the poetry of *Diario* and the later volumes (which, he notes, have a 'modest' cultural weight, lacking the 'forza originale' of Montale's previous work).[34] Croce goes on, in fact, to salvage a small number of the late poems which he sees (rightly, I believe) as containing the germ of a genuinely innovative approach. These are, specifically, texts in *Diario* and *Quaderno* that deal with personal memories, that explore the special, 'miraculous' value of individual experiences as viewed through the intimate lens of memory, where the terms 'miracolo' and 'prodigio' no longer have an authentically metaphysical meaning, but rather are merely metaphors, 'per indicare fatti insoliti sì, ma tutti umani'. Thus, in 'Annetta', Croce sees the remembered 'prodigio' of the young girl's presence in the game of charades as simply a metaphor for the emotion she provoked. It is precisely this emotional dimension that gives the poetry a new vitality, 'una passionalità sorridente', introduces 'una meditazione pacata e straziante'. Similarly, in another memory poem, 'Sorapis, 40 anni fa', the 'miracle' ('qualcosa che dice / che ci fa dire siamo qui, è un miracolo / che non si può ripetere', *OV* 502) is recalled with the greatest simplicity, as the poet evokes a unique moment of private happiness. Thus, though Montale insists on ostentatiously declaring the deliberate 'weakness' of his late poetry (whose limitations are repeatedly flaunted, to the point perhaps of self-indulgence), he can also transcend that weakness while maintaining a problematic awareness of it, and without reverting to 'sentimentalismo ottocentesco' he opens up 'uno spazio per più umane — e più libere — emozioni'.[35]

This description can be applied equally to the space explored in part II of *Altri versi*. In these poems, as in others in *Diario* and *Quaderno* that re-evoke the distant past, themes and motifs associated with memory acquire a new meaning, independent of historical or ideological allegories: they represent an assertion of individual identity and integrity. The return of the figure of Clizia epitomizes this process. Stripped of her metaphysical or spiritual attributes (which are nevertheless recalled, with intertextual irony), she no longer has an ideological function. There has been an apparent blurring of her identity, as she acquires characteristics previously associated with other female figures in the poetry. But this process leads to the loss only of her former, allegorical identity. As she sheds the apparatus of a poetic myth (the angel's wings, the blinding light, the sunflower imagery) and acquires corporeal, sentimental and psychological attributes more immediately associated with Mosca or Arletta, she assumes a truly personal human identity for the first time. This is the last miracle in Montale's work: the dogged persistence of individuality amidst the flood-tide of collective existence, the knowledge that the individual's experience of reality has a meaning that cannot be reduced to that of a mere ideological cypher, a value that cannot be touched by the storms of history: 'Fummo felici un giorno, un'ora un attimo / e questo potrà essere distrutto?'

Altri versi marks the culmination of the retreat from history discernible in Montale's work from the end of *Bufera* onwards. However, to view such a retreat necessarily as a negative development (the inevitable conclusion of a merely ideological critique of the work) is to miss the point of Montale's art. While his poetry has always been firmly rooted in a specific historical and cultural context, the quest for positive values has been constantly focused on the individual. The meaning of Montale's later work emerges from the shifting interplay of private, personal concerns and long-standing public passions. His perennial refusal to seek 'la parola che squadri da ogni lato / l'animo nostro informe', his insistence on the complex integrity of the individual, lead him back in this late season to a poetry of deceptive simplicity, where, though his quarrel with history persists, one of the ways he can choose to pursue that quarrel is to reiterate his fidelity to an individual vision, to focus (albeit with due ironic distance[36]) on the timeless miracle of individual human experience.

Notes to Chapter 5

1. Marchese, *Visiting angel*, 263–4.
2. See Cambon, *Eugenio Montale's Poetry*, 247.
3. Angelo Marchese, *Amico dell'invisibile: la personalità e la poesia di Eugenio Montale* (Turin: SEI, 1996), 28.
4. Riccardo Scrivano, 'Eugenio Montale: *Quaderno di quattro anni* o i modi della ragione', *Critica letteraria* 6 (1978), 466–94 at 479.
5. Luperini, *Storia di Montale*, 197, 231.
6. Ibid., 234–5; Scrivano, 'Eugenio Montale: *Quaderno di quattro anni*', 467.
7. For a detailed reading of this text, see Orelli, *Accertamenti montaliani*, 130–6.
8. Lorenzo Greco, 'Tempo e "fuor del tempo" nell'ultimo Montale', *La poesia di Eugenio Montale: atti del Convegno ... settembre 1982*, 487–94 at 491–3.
9. See the front cover of *Eugenio Montale: immagini di una vita*, ed. Contorbia.
10. The following poems in *Diario* contain significant thematic elements concerned with memories of one sort or another: 'Trascolorando', 'A C.', 'Corso Dogali', 'I nascondigli', 'Il lago di Annecy', 'Lettera a Bobi', 'Visitatori', 'L'odore dell'eresia', 'La pendola a carillon', 'Ancora ad Annecy', 'Annetta', 'Sorapis, 40 anni fa'.
11. The following texts in *Quaderno* can be identified as belonging to a 'memorial' vein: 'L'educazione intellettuale', 'Nei miei primi anni', 'A Pio Rajna', 'Quando cominciai a dipingere', 'Il giorno dei morti', 'L'eroismo', 'Per un fiore reciso', 'Sotto la pergola', 'Ho sparso di becchime', 'La capinera non fu uccisa', 'Se al più si oppone il meno', 'Domande senza risposta', 'I pressepapiers', 'Ai tuoi piedi'; 'Ribaltamento', 'Quel che resta (se resta)', 'Scomparsa delle strigi', 'Quella del faro', 'Dall'altra sponda', 'Aspasia', 'Una lettera che non fu spedita', 'I ripostigli', 'Oltre il breve recinto', 'Morgana'.
12. An insight into the collaboration between Montale and his editors can be gained from Rosanna Bettarini et al., 'Dedicato a Montale', *Antologia Vieusseux* 64 (Oct.–Dec. 1981), 13–25.
13. See Croce, 'Satura', 353. Martelli (*Eugenio Montale: introduzione e guida*, 140) sees the last three collections as 'un solo libro'.
14. Francesco De Rosa, 'Scansioni dell'ultimo Montale', *Montale e il canone poetico del Novecento*, ed. Grignani and Luperini, 47–72.
15. See Grignani, *Prologhi ed epiloghi*, chap. 6.
16. Other occurrences of this image can be found in *Occasioni* in 'Il ramarro, se scocca' (*OV* 141), 'Elegia di Pico Farnese' (*OV* 175); and in *Bufera* in 'La bufera' (*OV* 189), 'Su una lettera non scritta' (*OV* 191), 'Gli orecchini' (*OV* 194), 'Il ventaglio' (*OV* 198).
17. Pellini ('L'ultimo Montale', 290–302) examines in detail the 'contamination' of the figure of Clizia.

18. For an example of Montale's impatience with such questions see Greco, *Montale commenta Montale*, 57.
19. These are confirmed ibid., 65–6.
20. See Rebay, 'Montale, Clizia e l'America', 304 n. 40.
21. 'Il mio cronometro' can be linked to the Clizian episode first described in 'Due prose veneziane'. In 'Luni e altro' Clizia is named among the variants (*OV* 1152). The other poems are unmistakably addressed to Clizia.
22. Named in 'Interno/esterno' (*OV* 698). See also *Eugenio Montale: immagini di una vita*, ed. Contorbia, 154.
23. A similar photograph, taken on the same occasion and supplied by Irma Brandeis herself, can be seen ibid., 177.
24. It is possible that the 'punto' here is again an allusion to *Paradiso* XVII (see Chap. 4 above, n. 15).
25. Pellini, 'L'ultimo Montale', 295–6.
26. Montale's intention is indicated by Bettarini in 'Dedicato a Montale', 21. '*Poiché la vita fugge ...*' is chronologically the last poem in *Altri versi*, so far as can be determined.
27. See De Rosa, 'Scansioni dell'ultimo Montale', 49, 67.
28. Guido Mazzoni, 'Il posto di Montale nella poesia moderna', *Montale e il canone poetico del Novecento*, ed. Grignani and Luperini, 382–416 at 382.
29. Romano Luperini, 'Montale e il canone poetico del Novecento italiano', ibid., 361–8 at 365–7.
30. Rebecca West, 'Montale profeta del postmoderno', ibid., 202–10.
31. Luperini, *Storia di Montale*, 238.
32. Luperini, *Montale o l'identità negata*, 115.
33. Cataldi, *Montale*, 60.
34. Croce, *Storia della poesia di Eugenio Montale* , 89.
35. Ibid., 95–8.
36. Grignani (*Prologhi ed epiloghi*, 190) observes that in the later work 'il ricordo [...] utilizza l'ironia come elemento mediatore o meglio medianico, risvolto stilistico del pudore che, mentre riconosce il "nullificante magistero" della vita, salva con tenacia l'individuo e la sua storia'.

APPENDIX

❖

Montale's Women

These notes aim to give a brief account of the *ispiratrici* behind the principal female figures in Montale's work. They are listed here broadly in the order in which they appear in the poetic works.

Arletta

Montale first met Anna degli Uberti (1904–59) in Monterosso in 1920, and her family went on holiday there for the last time in 1923. According to Zampa, Montale's first trip to Rome took place in the autumn of 1923. If so, this may well be the occasion of the difficult meeting with Anna and her family recalled in 1978 in 'Una visita' (*OV* 706; this piece is, however, subtitled 'Roma 1922'). See Zampa's 'Cronologia' in *TP* (pp. lx–lxi, lxxvii).

The woman behind the figure of Arletta lived until 1959, thus giving the lie to Montale's much-quoted declaration to Guarnieri: 'Morì giovane e non ci fu nulla tra noi' (Greco, *Montale commenta Montale*, 42, 97–100). However, it is abundantly clear that from an early stage Arletta takes on a poetic life (and indeed, death) of her own, as indicated for example in her 'transformation' into Daphne in 'Incontro'. This poem was first published in 1926 under the title 'Arletta', where line 46 read: 'Poi ristò solo. Oh Arletta!' (*OV* 891). With its introduction under the new title into the 1928 edition of *Ossi* this would become 'Poi più nulla. Oh sommersa!', thus leaving Arletta's name deliberately (and doubly) 'submerged'. One may speculate that Montale had this in mind when writing a much later 'Arlettian' text, 'Quella del faro': 'Suppongo che tu sia passata / senza lasciare tracce. Sono certo / che il tuo nome era scritto altrove, non so dove.' (*OV* 594). Arletta is the first of several female figures who acquire poetic meaning and vitality precisely because of their absence, as is the case later with Clizia and Mosca. It seems that for Montale she had to 'die' in order to live poetically.

See also: Forti's 'Cronologia' in *PR*, pp. xcviii–xcix; *Per conoscere Montale*, ed. Forti, 34, 56; Alfonso Leone, 'Ed io non so chi va e chi resta', *Lingua nostra* 38 (1977), 117–19; Nascimbeni, *Montale: biografia di un poeta*, 58; *Eugenio Montale: immagini di una vita*, ed. Contorbia, 66–7; *Una dolcezza inquieta*, ed. Marcenaro, 62–5; Giusi Baldissone, *Le muse di Montale: galleria di occasioni femminili nella poesia montaliana* (Novara: Interlinea Edizioni, 1996), 90–2.

Esterina

Montale met Esterina Rossi (1904–1990), the inspiration for 'Falsetto', in the early 1920s through Francesco and Bianca Messina, with whom he used to swim at Quarto dei mille, near Genoa. Esterina is mentioned repeatedly in letters dated 1923–4: *Lettere e poesie a Bianca e Francesco Messina*, ed. Barile.

See also: Nascimbeni, *Montale: biografia di un poeta*, 57; *Eugenio Montale: immagini di una vita*, ed. Contorbia, 80–1; *Una dolcezza inquieta*, ed. Marcenaro, 87–8; Giuseppe Marcenaro, *Una amica di Montale: vita di Lucia Rodocanachi* (Milan: Camunia, 1991), 41–5; Baldissone, *Le muse di Montale*, 26–8.

Paola Nicoli and the 'peruviana'

In reply to Guarnieri's questionnaire, Montale refers to two separate women who appear as secondary figures in *Ossi* and *Occasioni*: 'Donna n. 2' (in 'Mottetti' 1–3) was 'una peruviana che però era di origine genovese e abitava a Genova'; while 'donna n. 3' appears in 'In limine', 'Casa sul mare', 'Crisalide' in *Ossi* (Greco, *Montale commenta Montale*, 42). On no. 3 (Paola Nicoli), an actress who left for South America with her husband, see Baldissone, *Le muse di Montale*, 31, and Silvio Ramat, 'Due lettere di Montale a Silvio Ramat', *Poesia* 99 (Oct. 1996), 17–20 at 18. These two women appear to overlap to some extent in their associations, and various commentators have referred to them as one figure, naming her as Paola Nicoli. See Nascimbeni, *Montale: biografia di un poeta*, 57, 91–2; *Per conoscere Montale*, ed. Forti, 33–4; Gioanola, 'La donna', 288–9; *Le occasioni*, ed. Isella, 77.

It seems certain, however, that two separate figures are involved, not least in view of Montale's clear distinction between them. This distinction is further supported by Rebay ('Sull' "autobiografismo" di Montale', 75), who quotes Montale as saying that he met the 'peruviana' of 'Mottetti' 1–3 in Florence in 1929–30, whereas he certainly knew Paola Nicoli in the early 1920s (see *Lettere e poesie a Bianca e Francesco Messina*, ed. Barile, 65, 67; *TP*, p. lxi). Bonora (*Montale e altro novecento*, 23) writes that the 'peruviana' represents 'un accordo totale con la vita, raggiunto attraverso l'amore'. Like Esterina, these are ultimately figures of secondary importance, whose function as biographical presences tends to limit their potential for allegorical or other transfiguration.

Gerti and Dora Markus

A friend of Bobi Bazlen's, Gerti Tolazzi Frankl appears in 'Carnevale di Gerti' and in the second part of 'Dora Markus'. See Nascimbeni, *Montale: biografia di un poeta*, 89–91; *OV* 898; Greco, *Montale commenta Montale*, 41, 43; *Eugenio Montale: immagini di una vita*, ed. Contorbia, 115; Baldissone, *Le muse di Montale*, 34–6. Dora Markus enters Montale's poetic world in 1928 as no more than a name (accompanied by a photograph of a pair of legs) in a letter from Bobi Bazlen: 'Gerti e Carlo: Bene. A Trieste, loro ospite, un'amica di Gerti, con delle gambe meravigliose. Falle una poesia. Si chiama Dora Markus' (*OV* 901). The photograph is in *Eugenio Montale: immagini di una vita*, ed. Contorbia, 122. This letter suggests either that Montale's date of 1926 for 'Dora Markus I' is an error, or that the poem existed before Bazlen provided the name of Dora. See *Le occasioni*, ed. Isella, 53–6. The poet's note to 'A Liuba che parte' tells us that Dora too was Jewish (*OV* 899). What is clear is that Montale never met Dora, underlining the fact that the poem bearing her name is concerned as much with a projection of the poet's own concerns as with those of the ostensible protagonist.

See also: Bettarini et al., 'Dedicato a Montale', 19; *Per conoscere Montale*, ed. Forti, 34; Baldissone, *Le muse di Montale*, 46–9; Luciano Rebay, 'Un cestello di Montale: le gambe di Dora Markus e una lettera di Roberto Bazlen', *La poesia di Eugenio Montale: atti del Convegno ... novembre 1982*, 107–17. On Gerti and Arsenio (Montale's alter ego), see Silvio Ramat, 'Da Arsenio a Gerti', *La poesia di Eugenio Montale: atti del Convegno ... settembre 1982*, 189–200.

Liuba

Liuba Blumenthal, like Gerti and Dora, was a Jewish friend of Bazlen's. According to Nascimbeni (*Montale: biografia di un poeta*, 90),

Montale saw her leave Florence around the time of the introduction of the racial laws in 1938. She subsequently settled in London.

Montale's correspondence with Guarnieri and Avalle on Liuba exemplifies his intolerance of attempts to pin his poetry too mechanically to biographical events. When Avalle seeks clarification on Liuba's baggage, Montale replies ironically: 'Liuba è un'invenzione [...] Non l'ho vista partire, non so nulla del suo eventuale bagaglio. Quindi ciò che ho detto a Guarnieri non vale nulla'. See Avalle, *Tre saggi su Montale*, 94–5 n. 1; Greco, *Montale commenta Montale*, 76–8.

See also: *Per conoscere Montale*, ed. Forti, 34, 57; *Le occasioni*, ed. Isella, 49–50; Marcenaro, *Una amica di Montale*, 194–5; Manuela La Ferla, *Diritto al silenzio: vita e scritti di Roberto Bazlen* (Palermo: Sellerio, 1994), 39–40, 46; Daniele Del Giudice, *Lo stadio di Wimbledon* (Turin: Einaudi, 1983), 92–4.

Clizia

Montale met Irma Brandeis (1905–90) when the young American scholar of Italian literature sought him out in 1933 at the Gabinetto Vieusseux, having read his poetry (*TP*, p. lxviii; *PR*, p. ci). She is the principal muse of *Occasioni* (dedicated to I.B.) and *Bufera*, where (in 'La primavera hitleriana') she is given the name of Clizia, the nymph who loved Apollo and turned into a sunflower (as recalled in the pseudo-Dantesque sonnet to Giovanni Quirini that provides the epigraph for this poem).

Their relationship lasted intermittently from 1933 until 1939, when Montale's hopes of joining her in America (and getting an academic post there) finally came to an end. He was now living with Drusilla Tanzi (Mosca). On this difficult year, see Rebay, 'Montale, Clizia, e l'America'. More recently, Rebay has suggested that Montale's relationship with Clizia was never physically consummated because she was a lesbian. See Luciano Rebay, 'Ripensando Montale: del dire e del non dire', *Il secolo di Montale: Genova 1896–1996* (Bologna: Il Mulino, 1998), 33–69. Nevertheless, Clizia was to remain the dominant female figure in his poetry for at least another decade.

See also: *Per conoscere Montale*, ed. Forti 34, 57 n. 42; Nascimbeni, *Montale: biografia di un poeta*, 92; Baldissone, *Le muse di Montale*, 53–4; *Eugenio Montale: immagini di una vita*, ed. Contorbia, 153 (also Contini's introduction, p. xii); Bettarini et al., 'Dedicato a Montale', 16–17; Ramat, 'Due lettere di Montale a Silvio Ramat', 17–18;

Eusebio e Trabucco, ed. Isella, 32; Paolo De Caro, *Journey to Irma: un'approssimazione all'ispiratrice americana di Eugenio Montale*, i: *Irma, un 'romanzo'* (Foggia: Matteo De Meo, 1996); Tom O'Neill, 'Dante, Montale and Miss Brandeis: A (partial) revisitation of Montale's Dantism', *Montale: Words in Time*, ed. George Talbot and Doug Thompson (Market Harborough: Troubadour, 1998), 27–42. O'Neill cites, among others, James Merrill, *A Different Person: A Memoir* (New York: Alfred A. Knopf, 1993), in which the American poet recounts some interesting conversations with Brandeis about Montale (83–5, 177–81).

Volpe

Montale met the much younger Maria Luisa Spaziani in January 1949 in Turin (see Spaziani's account in *Una dolcezza inquieta*, ed. Marcenaro, 236). It was the start of an intense relationship characterized by Guarnieri as the one 'vero amore' of Montale's life: 'Si trattava, almeno per me, di un Montale nuovo [...] del tutto pacificato con se stesso e con la vita; [...] non solo innamorato ma interamente preso da quell'amore, fiducioso di esso, ad esso affidato; di un Montale che sorprendentemente avesse la certezza di aver incontrato la felicità.' Guarnieri also tells here of Montale's bitter political disillusionment of this period, and goes on to suggest that the reluctant abandonment of the relationship with Spaziani was a decisive factor in his subsequent poetic silence. See Silvio Guarnieri, *L'ultimo testimone* (Milano: Mondadori, 1989), 51–5.

Spaziani herself ('Un carteggio inedito di Montale', *La poesia di Eugenio Montale: atti de Convegno ... novembre 1982*, 321–4) describes the relationship as in part a 'sodalizio letterario', involving a large body of unpublished correspondence, including poems by both parties. Three letters were published in the supplement to *Corriere della sera* (27 June 1986), *Montale e il Corriere*, 47. On this *carteggio*, see also Grignani, *Dislocazioni: epifanie e metamorfosi in Montale* (Lecce: Piero Manni, 1998), chap. 3; *Catalogo delle lettere di Eugenio Montale a Maria Luisa Spaziani (1949–1964)*, ed. Giuseppe Polimeni (Pavia: Università degli studi di Pavia, 1999).

Volpe features in many poems in *Bufera* (especially 'Madrigali privati'). Though she functions poetically as the antagonist of Clizia (see Greco, *Montale commenta Montale*, 42, 57, 60), her real-life rival (who eventually triumphed) was Mosca (see below). See also:

Nascimbeni, *Montale: biografia di un poeta*, 122–3; *Eugenio Montale: immagini di una vita*, ed. Contorbia, 218–19; Baldissone, *Le muse di Montale*, 72–4; *Eusebio e Trabucco*, ed. Isella, 207–9, 212–14.

Mosca

In a letter to Svevo in 1927, Montale asked him to send a copy of *Senilità* to Drusilla Tanzi (1885–1963), whom he had just met in Florence (see *Eugenio Montale: immagini di una vita*, ed. Contorbia, 108–9). Drusilla, then married to Matteo Marangoni, was to become Montale's lifelong companion. Her affectionate nickname of Mosca referred, according to Guarnieri, to her thick spectacles, while Contini tells us that the name was given to her by Gerti Tolazzi (see Contini's introduction to ibid., p. x). Montale moved in to the Marangoni household as a lodger in 1929 (*TP*, p. lxvi). Guarnieri (*L'ultimo testimone*, 26–9) gives an account of the development of the relationship in the following years, including the eventual breakup of the Marangoni marriage. Guarnieri paints a picture of a sometimes difficult relationship, in which Mosca emerges as the dominant partner. Contini (in Bettarini et al., 'Dedicato a Montale', 14–15) describes her as Montale's 'protettrice' in those years.

The relationship with Mosca was fraught with tensions: Montale repeatedly uses the term 'orrore' in connection with her in his letters to Bazlen in 1938–9, when he was contemplating joining Irma Brandeis in America (see Rebay, 'Montale, Clizia e l'America', 283–6; La Ferla, *Diritto al silenzio*, 40 n. 111). It seems that she exercised a kind of emotional blackmail over him on that occasion, as also a decade later, when she threatened to commit suicide if he left her for Maria Luisa Spaziani (Guarnieri, *L'ultimo testimone*, 52–7). Mosca's health was fragile: she suffered from severe sight problems and in 1944 was gravely ill with a spinal disorder (see *TP*, p. lxxiii; Nascimbeni, *Montale: biografia di un poeta*, 103; *Eusebio e Trabucco*, ed. Isella, 95–6). The couple married in 1962, and Mosca died in 1963 (*TP*, p. lxxvii). Her posthumous presence looms large in the poetry of *Satura*.

See also: Forti, 'Montale: ritratto milanese'; Marcenaro, *Una amica di Montale*, 122–3; Baldissone, *Le muse di Montale*, 66–70. There are numerous references to Mosca (as well as correspondence written partly by her) in *Eusebio e Trabucco*, ed. Isella; see especially 66–7, 95–6, 100–4, 172–4, 177, 182, 184–5, 188–9, 210–11. (It should be noted, however, that the index of names in this volume is quite unreliable.)

Others

Various other female figures appear in the poems, including:

The mysterious 'G.B.H.' (see *PR*, p. civ), whom Montale met in London in 1948 (see 'Di un Natale metropolitano').

Laura Papi, who appears in 'Dopo una fuga' (*Satura*). See Baldissone, *Le muse di Montale*, 80–1; *Eugenio Montale: immagini di una vita*, ed. Contorbia, 264–5; Dominique Papi, *Montale a Forte dei Marmi* (Florence and Siena: Maschietto & Musolino, 1997), esp. 65–96.

Gina Tiossi, Montale's *governante*, who worked for him and Mosca for decades and cared for him in his final years. See Nascimbeni, *Montale: biografia di un poeta*, 101–2, 144–7, 158–9; Domenico Porzio, *Con Montale a Stoccolma: diario di Svezia* (Milan: Ferro, 1976), passim; Baldissone, *Le muse di Montale*, 76–7.

Annalisa Cima, muse of the controversial *Diario Postumo*, who was close to the poet in the late 1960s and 1970s (ibid., 98–100).

BIBLIOGRAPHY

Primary Texts

1. Poetic texts

All quotations from Montale's poetic texts are taken from the critical edition:

L'opera in versi, ed. Rosanna Bettarini and Gianfranco Contini (Turin: Einaudi, 1980) [*OV*]

There are occasional references to the other principal edition:

Tutte le poesie, ed. Giorgio Zampa, I Meridiani (Milan: Mondadori, 1984) [*TP*]

The above editions bring together the following individual collections of poems (along with critical apparatus and bibliographical and other materials):

Ossi di seppia (Turin: Gobetti, 1925)
Le occasioni (Turin: Einaudi, 1939)
La bufera e altro (Vicenza: Neri Pozza, 1956)
Satura (Milan: Mondadori, 1971)
Diario del '71 e del '72 (Milan: Mondadori, 1973)
Quaderno di quattro anni (Milan: Mondadori, 1978)
Altri versi (Milan: Mondadori, 1981)

Reference is also made to:

Le occasioni, ed. and annotated by Dante Isella (Turin: Einaudi, 1996)

Complete English versions of the first three collections are contained in:

Eugenio Montale, Collected Poems 1920–1954, bilingual edn., trans. and annotated by Jonathan Galassi (New York: Farrar, Straus and Giroux, 1998)

The complete editions cited above do not include:

Diario postumo: 66 poesie e altre, ed. Annalisa Cima (Milan: Mondadori, 1996)

2. *Prose texts*

The collected prose writings are contained in the following volumes:

Prose e racconti, ed. Marco Forti, I Meridiani (Milan: Mondadori, 1995) [PR]
Il secondo mestiere: prose 1920–1979, ed. Giorgio Zampa, 2 vols., I Meridiani (Milan: Mondadori, 1996) [SM]
Il secondo mestiere: arte, musica, società, ed. Giorgio Zampa, I Meridiani (Milan: Mondadori, 1996) [SMAMS]

Many of the more important prose writings (published initially in journals and newspapers) also appeared in the following volumes published during the author's lifetime:

Farfalla di Dinard (Vicenza: Neri Pozzi, 1956)
Auto da fé: cronache in due tempi (Milan: Il Saggiatore, 1966)
Fuori di casa (Milan and Naples: Ricciardi, 1969)
Nel nostro tempo (Milan: Rizzoli, 1973)

Secondary Sources

ALMANSI, GUIDO, and MERRY, BRUCE. *Eugenio Montale: The Private Language of Poetry* (Edinburgh: Edinburgh University Press, 1977).

ANTONIELLI, SERGIO. 'Clizia e Altro', *Letteratura* 79–81 (1966), 102–7.

AVALLE, D'ARCO SILVIO. *Tre saggi su Montale*, 3rd edn. (Turin: Einaudi, 1972).

AVERSANO, MARIO. *Montale e il libretto d'opera* (Naples: Editrice Ferraro, 1984).

BALDISSONE, GIUSI. *Le muse di Montale: galleria di occasioni femminili nella poesia montaliana* (Novara: Interlinea Edizioni, 1996) [with anthology].

BARANSKI, ZYGMUNT. 'Dante and Montale: The Threads of Influence', *Dante Comparisons*, ed. Eric Haywood and B. Jones (Dublin: Irish Academic Press, 1985), 11–48.

BÀRBERI SQUAROTTI, GIORGIO. 'La storia', *Letture Montaliane in occasione dell'80° compleanno del poeta* (Genoa: Bozzi, 1977), 283–96.

BARILE, LAURA. *Adorate mie larve: Montale e la poesia anglosassone* (Bologna: Il Mulino, 1990).

—— (ed.). *Eugenio Montale: Lettere e poesie a Bianca e Francesco Messina, 1923–1925* (Milan: Scheiwiller, 1995).

BECKER, JARED. *Eugenio Montale* (Boston: Twayne, 1986).

BETTARINI, ROSANNA. 'Appunti sul "Taccuino" del 1926 di Eugenio Montale', *Studi di filologia italiana* 36 (1978), 457–512.

BETTARINI, ROSANNA; CONTINI, GIANFRANCO; ISELLA, DANTE; and ZAMPA, GIORGIO. 'Dedicato a Montale', *Antologia Vieusseux* 64 (Oct.–Dec. 1981), 13–25.

BINNI, WALTER. 'Omaggio a Montale', *Rassegna della letteratura italiana* 70 (1966), 227–46.

BO, CARLO. 'Montale: un gioco a nascondino nel mare inquieto della poesia', *Corriere della sera* (12 Oct. 1996), 35.

BOBBIO, NORBERTO. *Profilo ideologico del Novecento italiano* (Turin: Einaudi, 1986).

BONORA, ETTORE. *Le metafore del vero* (Rome: Bonacci, 1981).

—— 'Un grande trittico al centro della *Bufera*', *La poesia di Eugenio Montale: atti del Convegno Internazionale, Milano 12/13/14 settembre, Genova 15 settembre 1982* (Milan: Librex, 1983), 95–114.

—— *Montale e altro Novecento* (Caltanisetta (Rome): Sciascia, 1989).

BRANCA, VITTORE. 'Montale nelle Stalle di Augía', *La poesia di Eugenio Montale: atti del Convegno Internazionale tenuto a Genova dal 25 al 28 novembre 1982* (Florence: Le Monnier, 1984), 465–72.

CAMBON, GLAUCO. *Montale e l'Altro* (Milan: Bompiani, 1963).

—— *Eugenio Montale's Poetry: A Dream in Reason's Presence* (Princeton: Princeton University Press, 1982).

—— 'Ancora su "Iride", frammento di Apocalisse', *La poesia di Eugenio Montale: atti del Convegno Internazionale, Milano 12/13/14 settembre, Genova 15 settembre 1982* (Milan: Librex, 1983), 227–44.

CAMPAILLA, SERGIO, and GOFFIS, CESARE F. (eds.). *La poesia di Eugenio Montale: atti del Convegno Internazionale tenuto a Genova dal 25 al 28 novembre 1982* (Florence: Le Monnier, 1984).

CARPI, UMBERTO. *Montale dopo il Fascismo, dalla 'Bufera' a 'Satura'* (Padua: Liviana, 1971).

—— *Il poeta e la politica* (Naples: Liguori, 1978).

CASTELLANA, RICCARDO. '"L'alluvione ha sommerso il pack dei mobili"', *Montale Readings*, ed. Éanna Ó Ceallacháin and Federica Pedriali, Italian Research Studies, 3 (Glasgow: University of Glasgow Press, 2000), 103–25.

CATALDI, PIETRO. *Montale* (Palermo: Palumbo, 1991).

CIMA, ANNALISA. 'Le reazioni di Montale', *Eugenio Montale: profilo di un autore*, ed. Annalisa Cima and Cesare Segre (Milan: Rizzoli, 1977), 192–201.

CIMA, ANNALISA, and SEGRE, CESARE (eds.). *Eugenio Montale: profilo di un autore* (Milan: Rizzoli, 1977).

CONTINI, GIANFRANCO. *Una lunga fedeltà: scritti su Eugenio Montale* (Turin: Einaudi, 1974).

—— Introduction to *Eugenio Montale: immagini di una vita*, ed. Franco Contorbia (Milan: Mondadori, 1996).

CONTORBIA, FRANCO (ed.). *Eugenio Montale: immagini di una vita* (Milan, Mondadori: 1996).

CORTI, MARIA. '*Satura* e il genere "diario poetico"', *Per conoscere Montale*, ed. Marco Forti, rev. edn. (Milan: Mondadori, 1986), 349–72.

CROCE, BENEDETTO. *Storia d'Italia dal 1871 al 1915*, 2nd edn. (Bari: Laterza, 1928).

—— *Storia di Europa nel secolo decimonono* (Bari: Laterza, 1932).

—— *Filosofia, poesia, storia*, La letteratura italiana: storia e testi, 75 (Milan: Ricciardi, 1951).

CROCE, FRANCO. 'Due nuove poesie di Montale', *Rassegna della letteratura italiana* 67 (1963), 493–506.

—— 'L'ultimo Montale II: gli *Xenia*', *Rassegna della letteratura italiana* 78 (1974), 378–401.

—— 'La primavera hitleriana', *Letture Montaliane in occasione dell'80° compleanno del poeta* (Genoa: Bozzi, 1977), 223–53.

—— 'Satura', *La poesia di Eugenio Montale: atti del Convegno Internazionale, Milano 12/13/14 settembre, Genova 15 settembre 1982* (Milan: Librex, 1983), 353–80 .

—— *Storia della poesia di Eugenio Montale* (Genoa: Costa & Nolan, 1991).

DE CARO, PAOLO. *Journey to Irma: un'approssimazione all'ispiratrice americana di Eugenio Montale*, i: *Irma, un 'romanzo'* (Foggia: Matteo De Meo, 1996).

DE ROGATIS, TIZIANA. 'Alle origini del dantismo di Montale', *Montale e il canone poetico del Novecento*, ed. Maria Antonietta Grignani and Romano Luperini (Rome: Laterza, 1998), 189–201.

DE ROSA, FRANCESCO. 'Scansioni dell'ultimo Montale', *Montale e il canone poetico del Novecento*, ed. Maria Antonietta Grignani and Romano Luperini (Rome: Laterza, 1998), 47–72.

FORTI, MARCO. *Eugenio Montale: la poesia, la prosa di fantasia e d'invenzione* (Milan: Mursia, 1973).

—— 'Per *Diario del '71*', *La poesia di Eugenio Montale: atti del Convegno Internazionale, Milano 12/13/14 settembre, Genova 15 settembre 1982* (Milan: Librex, 1983), 161–9.

—— *Nuovi saggi montaliani* (Milan: Mursia, 1990).

—— (ed.). *Per conoscere Montale*, rev. edn. (Milan: Mondadori, 1986).

FORTINI, FRANCO. *Ventiquattro voci per un dizionario di lettere* (Milan: Il Saggiatore, 1968).

—— 'I latrati di fedeltà', *Letture Montaliane in occasione dell'80° compleanno del Poeta* (Genoa, Bozzi, 1976), 379–85.

GIOANOLA, ELIO. 'La donna nella vita e nella poesia di Montale', *Studium* 86 (1990), 281–96.

—— Introduction to *La poesia di Eugenio Montale: atti del Convegno Internazionale, Milano 12/13/14 settembre, Genova 15 settembre 1982* (Milan: Librex, 1983), 15.

GRAMIGNA, GIULIANO. 'Il pâté degli iddii pestilenziali', *La poesia di Eugenio Montale: atti del Convegno Internazionale tenuto a Genova dal 25 al 28 novembre 1982* (Florence: Le Monnier, 1984), 511–18.

GRAZIOSI, ELISABETTA. *Il tempo in Montale: storia di un tema* (Florence: La nuova Italia, 1978).

GRECO, LORENZO. 'Tempo e "fuor del tempo" nell'ultimo Montale', *La poesia di Eugenio Montale: atti del Convegno Internazionale, Milano 12/13/14 settembre, Genova 15 settembre 1982* (Milan: Librex, 1983), 487–94.

—— *Montale commenta Montale*, 2nd edn. (Parma: Pratiche, 1990).

GRIGNANI, MARIA ANTONIETTA. *Prologhi ed epiloghi sulla poesia di Eugenio Montale* (Ravenna: Longo, 1987).

—— *Dislocazioni: epifanie e metamorfosi in Montale* (Lecce: Piero Manni, 1998).

—— '"Se t'hanno assomigliato" e altro', *Montale Readings*, ed. Éanna Ó Ceallacháin and Federica Pedriali, Italian Research Studies, 3 (Glasgow: University of Glasgow Press, 2000), 53–75.

GRIGNANI, MARIA ANTONIETTA, and LUPERINI, ROMANO (eds.). *Montale e il canone poetico del Novecento* (Rome and Bari: Laterza, 1998).

GRIMSHAW, MARK. 'Vertical and Horizontal Sightings on Montale's *Satura*', *Italian Studies* 29 (1974), 74–87.

GUARNIERI, SILVIO. *L'ultimo testimone* (Milan: Mondadori, 1989).

HUFFMAN, CLAIRE DE C. L. *Montale and the Occasions of Poetry* (Princeton: Princeton University Press, 1983).

Il secolo di Montale: Genova 1896–1996 (Bologna: Il Mulino, 1998).

ISELLA, DANTE. *Ancora sulla struttura di Satura* (Naples: Edizioni Scientifiche Italiane, 1990).

—— (ed.), *Eusebio e Trabucco: carteggio di Eugenio Montale e Gianfranco Contini* (Milan: Adelphi, 1997).

JACOMUZZI, ANGELO. *La poesia di Montale: dagli 'Ossi' ai 'Diari'* (Turin: Einaudi, 1978).

—— 'Incontro: per una costante della poesia montaliana', *La poesia di Eugenio Montale: atti del Convegno Internazionale, Milano 12/13/14 settembre, Genova 15 settembre 1982* (Milan: Librex, 1983), 149–60.

LA FERLA, MANUELA. *Diritto al silenzio: vita e scritti di Roberto Bazlen* (Palermo: Sellerio, 1994).

La poesia di Eugenio Montale: atti del Convegno Internazionale, Milano 12/13/14 settembre, Genova 15 settembre 1982 (Milan: Librex, 1983).

La poesia di Eugenio Montale: atti del Convegno Internazionale tenuto a Genova dal 25 al 28 novembre 1982 (Florence: Le Monnier, 1984).

LEONE, ALFONSO. 'Ed io non so chi va e chi resta', *Lingua nostra* 38 (1977), 117–19.

Letteratura 79–81 (1966) [special issue dedicated to Montale for his 70th birthday].

Letture Montaliane in occasione dell'80° compleanno del poeta (Genoa: Bozzi, 1977).

LONARDI, GILBERTO. *Il Vecchio e il Giovane* (Bologna: Zanichelli, 1980).

—— 'L'altra madre', *La poesia di Eugenio Montale: atti del Convegno*

Internazionale, Milano 12/13/14 settembre, Genova 15 settembre 1982 (Milan: Librex, 1983), 263–79.

LONATI, C. 'Montale e Clizia', *Cultura* 8 (1990), 17–24.

LOTMAN, JURIJ M., and USPENSKI, BORIS A. *Tipologia della cultura*, ed. Remo Faccani and Marzio Marzaduri, trans. Manila Barbato Faccani et al., 2nd edn. (Milan: Bompiani, 1995).

LUPERINI, ROMANO. *Montale o l'identità negata* (Naples: Liguori, 1984).

—— *Storia di Montale* (Rome: Laterza, 1986).

—— 'Note sull'allegorismo Novecentesco: il caso di Montale', *Paragone (Letteratura)* 39 (1988), 54–76.

—— 'Montale e il canone poetico del Novecento italiano', *Montale e il canone poetico del Novecento*, ed. Maria Antonietta Grignani and Romano Luperini (Rome: Laterza, 1998), 361–8.

MACCHIA, GIOVANNI. *Saggi italiani* (Milan: Mondadori, 1983).

MACRÌ, ORESTE. 'L'"angelo nero" e il demonismo nella poesia montaliana', *L'Albero* 23/54 (1975), 3–75.

—— 'Dante e la "Musa comica" dell'ultimo Montale', *La poesia di Eugenio Montale: atti del Convegno Internazionale tenuto a Genova dal 25 al 28 novembre 1982* (Florence: Le Monnier, 1984), 493–510.

MARCENARO, GIUSEPPE. *Una amica di Montale: vita di Lucia Rodocanachi* (Milan: Camunia, 1991).

MARCENARO, GIUSEPPE, and BORAGINA, PIERO (eds.). *Una dolcezza inquieta* (Milan: Electa, 1996) [exhibition catalogue marking the poet's centenary].

MARCHESE, ANGELO. *Visiting angel: interpretazione semiologica della poesia di Montale* (Turin: SEI, 1977).

—— *Amico dell'invisibile: la personalità e la poesia di Eugenio Montale* (Turin: SEI, 1996).

MARTELLI, MARIO. *Il rovescio della poesia: interpretazioni montaliane* (Milan: Longanesi, 1977).

—— *Eugenio Montale: introduzione e guida allo studio dell'opera montaliana* (Florence: Le Monnier, 1982).

—— 'L'autocitazione nel secondo Montale', *La poesia di Eugenio Montale: atti del Convegno Internazionale, Milano 12/13/14 settembre, Genova 15 settembre 1982* (Milan: Librex, 1983), 201–17.

MAZZONI, GUIDO. 'Il posto di Montale nella poesia moderna', *Montale e il canone poetico del Novecento*, ed. Maria Antonietta Grignani and Romano Luperini (Rome: Laterza, 1998), 382–416.

MENGALDO, PIER VINCENZO. 'Primi appunti su *Satura*', *La tradizione del Novecento*, ed. Pier Vincenzo Mengaldo (Milan: Feltrinelli, 1975), 335–58.

—— 'La "Lettera a Malvolio"', *Eugenio Montale: profilo di un autore*, ed. Annalisa Cima and Cesare Segre (Milan: Rizzoli, 1977), 134–67.

MERRILL, JAMES. *A Different Person: A Memoir* (New York: Alfred A. Knopf, 1993).

Montale e il Corriere, supplement to *Corriere della sera* (27 June 1986).

NASCIMBENI, GIULIO. *Montale: biografia di un poeta* (Milan: Longanesi, 1986).

—— 'Rubò dall'archivio del *Corriere* l'articolo scritto per la sua morte', in *Montale e il Corriere*, supplement to *Corriere della sera* (27 June 1986), 4–9.

—— 'Montale nello zaino di Strehler', *Corriere della sera* (10 Feb. 1996), 25.

Ó CEALLACHÁIN, ÉANNA, and PEDRIALI, FEDERICA (eds.). *Montale Readings*, Italian Research Studies, 3 (Glasgow: University of Glasgow Press, 2000).

O'NEILL, TOM. 'Dante, Montale and Miss Brandeis: A (Partial) Revisitation of Montale's Dantism', *Montale: Words in Time*, ed. George Talbot and Doug Thompson (Market Harborough: Troubadour, 1998), 27–42.

ORELLI, GIORGIO. *Accertamenti montaliani* (Bologna: Il Mulino, 1984).

PAMPALONI, GENO. 'Con "Le occasioni" dentro lo zaino', *La poesia di Eugenio Montale: atti del Convegno Internazionale tenuto a Genova dal 25 al 28 novembre 1982* (Florence: Le Monnier, 1984), 265–9.

PAPI, DOMINIQUE. *Montale a Forte dei Marmi* (Florence and Siena: Maschietto & Musolino, 1997).

PASOLINI, PIER PAOLO. 'Satura', *Nuovi argomenti* 21 (Jan.–Mar. 1971), 17–20.

—— 'Outis', *Nuovi argomenti* 27 (May–June 1972), 146–50.

PELLINI, PIERLUIGI. 'L'ultimo Montale: donne miracoli treni telefoni sciopero generale', *Nuova corrente* 39 (1992), 289–324.

PIPA, ARSHI. *Montale and Dante* (Minneapolis: University of Minnesota Press, 1968).

—— 'L'ultimo Montale', *La poesia di Eugenio Montale: atti del Convegno Internazionale tenuto a Genova dal 25 al 28 novembre 1982* (Florence: Le Monnier, 1984), 241–64.

POLIMENI, GIUSEPPE (ed.). *Catalogo delle lettere di Eugenio Montale a Maria Luisa Spaziani (1949–1964)* (Pavia: Università degli studi di Pavia, 1999).

PORZIO, DOMENICO. *Con Montale a Stoccolma: diario di Svezia, con un prologo a Milano e sedici fotografie dell'autore* (Milan: Ferro, 1976).

RAMAT, SILVIO. 'Da Arsenio a Gerti', *La poesia di Eugenio Montale: atti del Convegno Internazionale, Milano 12/13/14 settembre, Genova 15 settembre 1982* (Milan: Librex, 1983), 189–200.

—— *L'acacia ferita e altri studi su Montale* (Venice: Marsilio, 1986).

—— 'Due lettere di Montale a Silvio Ramat', *Poesia* 99 (Oct. 1996), 17–20.

—— (ed.). *Omaggio a Montale* (Milan: Mondadori, 1966).

Rassegna della letteratura italiana 70 (1966) [special issue dedicated to Montale for his 70th birthday].

REBAY, LUCIANO. 'Sull' "autobiografismo" di Montale', *Innovazioni tematiche espressive e linguistiche della letteratura italiana del Novecento: atti dell'VIII Congresso dell'AISLLI, New York, 25–28 Aprile 1973* (Florence: Olschki, 1976) 73–83.

—— 'Montale, Clizia e l'America', *La poesia di Eugenio Montale: atti del*

Convegno Internazionale, Milano 12/13/14 settembre, Genova 15 settembre 1982 (Milan: Librex, 1983), 218–308.

—— 'Un cestello di Montale: le gambe di Dora Markus e una lettera di Roberto Bazlen', *La poesia di Eugenio Montale: atti del Convegno Internazionale tenuto a Genova dal 25 al 28 novembre 1982* (Florence: Le Monnier, 1984), 107–17.

—— 'Ripensando Montale: del dire e del non dire', *Il secolo di Montale: Genova 1896–1996* (Bologna: Il Mulino, 1998), 33–69.

RENZI, LORENZO. 'Effetti di sordina nell'ultimo Montale', *Studi Novecenteschi* 19 (1980), 81–94.

SAVOCA, GIUSEPPE. *Concordanza di tutte le poesie di Eugenio Montale*, Strumenti di lessicografia letteraria italiana, 1 (Florence: Olschki, 1987).

SCARPATI, CLAUDIO. 'Sullo stilnovismo di Montale', *La poesia di Eugenio Montale: atti del Convegno Internazionale, Milano 12/13/14 settembre, Genova 15 settembre 1982* (Milan: Librex, 1983), 253–62.

SCRIVANO, RICCARDO. 'La storia', *Letture Montaliane in occasione dell'80° compleanno del poeta* (Genoa: Bozzi, 1977), 299–320.

—— 'Eugenio Montale: *Quaderno di quattro anni* o i modi della ragione', *Critica letteraria* 6 (1978), 466–94.

SERENI, VITTORIO. 'Il ritorno', *Letture Montaliane in occasione dell'80° compleanno del poeta* (Genoa: Bozzi, 1977), 191–5.

SICILIANO, ENZO. *Pasolini: A Biography*, trans. John Shepley (New York: Random House, 1982).

SINGH, GHANSHYAM. *Eugenio Montale: A Critical Study of his Poetry, Prose and Criticism* (New Haven and London: Yale University Press, 1973).

SPAZIANI, MARIA LUISA. 'Un carteggio inedito di Montale', *La poesia di Eugenio Montale: atti del Convegno Internazionale tenuto a Genova dal 25 al 28 novembre 1982* (Florence: Le Monnier, 1984), 321–4.

TALBOT, GEORGE. *Montale's 'Mestiere Vile': The Elective Translations from English of the 1930s and 1940s* (Dublin: Irish Academic Press, 1995).

TALBOT, GEORGE, and THOMPSON, DOUG (eds.). *Montale: Words in Time* (Market Harborough: Troubadour, 1998).

VIRGILLITO, RINA. *La luce di Montale: per una rilettura della poesia montaliana* (Milan: Edizioni Paoline, 1990).

WARD, DAVID. *Antifascisms: Cultural Politics in Italy, 1943–46* (London: Associated University Presses, 1996).

WEST, REBECCA. *Eugenio Montale: Poet on the Edge*, (Cambridge, MA: Harvard University Press, 1981).

—— 'Montale profeta del postmoderno', *Montale e il canone poetico del Novecento*, ed. Maria Antonietta Grignani and Romano Luperini (Rome: Laterza, 1998), 202–10.

ZAMPA, GIORGIO (ed.). *Italo Svevo — Eugenio Montale: carteggio con gli scritti di Montale su Svevo* (Milan: Mondadori, 1976).

ZANZOTTO, ANDREA. 'Sviluppo di una situazione montaliana', *Letteratura* 79–81 (1966), 97–101.

—— 'In margine a *Satura*', *Nuovi argomenti* 23–4 (1971), 215–20.

—— 'Da "Botta e risposta I" a *Satura*', *Eugenio Montale: profilo di un autore*, ed. Annalisa Cima and Cesare Segre (Milan: Rizzoli, 1977), 115–23.

—— 'La freccia dei diari', *La poesia di Eugenio Montale: atti del Convegno Internazionale, Milano 12/13/14 settembre, Genova 15 settembre 1982* (Milan: Librex, 1983), 49–53.

INDEX OF NAMES

INDEX OF MONTALE'S POEMS